Edward Burnett Tylor

Anahuac

© 2025, Edward Burnett Tylor (domaine public)
Édition : BoD · Books on Demand, 31 avenue Saint-Rémy, 57600 Forbach, bod@bod.fr
Impression : Libri Plureos GmbH, Friedensallee 273, 22763 Hamburg (Allemagne)
ISBN : 978-2-3225-1603-2
Dépôt légal : Mars 2025

Anahuac

Edward Burnett Tylor

CHAPTER I.
THE ISLE OF PINES.

In the spring of 1856, I met with Mr. Christy accidentally in an omnibus at Havana. He had been in Cuba for some months, leading an adventurous life, visiting sugar-plantations, copper-mines, and coffee-estates, descending into caves, and botanizing in tropical jungles, cruising for a fortnight in an open boat among the coral-reefs, hunting turtles and manatis, and visiting all sorts of people from whom information was to be had, from foreign consuls and Lazarist missionaries down to retired slave-dealers and assassins.

As for myself, I had been travelling for the best part of a year in the United States, and had but a short time since left the live-oak forests and sugar-plantations of Louisiana. We agreed to go to Mexico together; and the present notes are principally compiled from our memorandum-books, and from letters written home on our journey.

Before we left Cuba, however, we made one last excursion across the island, and to the *Isla de Pinos*—the Isle of Pines—off the southern coast. A volante took us to the railway-station. The volante is the vehicle which the Cubans specially affect; it is like a Hansom cab, but the wheels are much taller, six and a half feet high, and the black driver sits postillion-wise upon the horse. Our man had a laced jacket, black leather leggings, and a pair of silver spurs fastened upon his bare feet, which seemed at a little distance to have well polished boots on, they were so black and shiny.

The railway which took us from Havana to Batabano had some striking peculiarities. For a part of the way the track passed between two walls of tropical jungle. The Indian fig trees sent down from every branch suckers, like smooth strings, which rooted themselves in the ground to draw up more water. Acacias and mimosas, the seiba and the mahagua, with other hard-wood trees innumerable, crowded close to one another; while epiphytes perched on every branch, and creepers bound the whole forest into a compact mass of vegetation, through which no bird could fly. We could catch the strings of convolvulus with our walking-sticks, as the train passed through the jungle. Sometimes we came upon a swamp, where clusters of bamboos were growing, crowned with tufts of pointed leaves; or had a glimpse for a moment of a group of royal palms upon the rising ground.

We passed sugar-plantations with their wide cane-fields, the sugar-houses with tall chimneys, and the balconied house of the administrador, keeping a sharp look out over the village of negro-cabins, arranged in double lines.

In the houses near the stations where we stopped, cigar-making seemed to be the universal occupation. Men, women, and children were sitting round tables hard at work. It made us laugh to see the black men rolling up cigars upon the hollow of their thighs, which nature has fashioned into a curve exactly suited to this process.

At Batabano the steamer was waiting at the pier, and our passports and ourselves were carefully examined by the captain, for Cuba is the paradise of passport offices, and one cannot stir without a visa. For once everybody was *en règle*, and we had no such scene as my companion had witnessed a few days before.

If you are a married man resident in Cuba, you cannot get a passport to go to the next town without your wife's permission in writing. Now it so happened that a respectable brazier, who lived at Santiago de Cuba, wanted to go to Trinidad. His wife would not consent; so he either got her signature by stratagem, or, what is more likely, gave somebody something to get him a passport under false pretences.

At any rate he was safe on board the steamer, when a middle-aged female, well dressed, but evidently arrayed in haste, and with a face crimson with hard running, came panting down to the steamer, and rushed on board. Seizing upon the captain, she pointed out her husband, who had taken refuge behind the other passengers at a respectful distance; she declared that she had never consented to his going away, and demanded that his body should be instantly delivered up to her. The husband was appealed to, but preferred staying where he was. The captain produced the passport, perfectly *en règle*, and the lady made a rush at the document, which was torn in half in the scuffle. All other means failing, she made a sudden dash at her husband, probably intending to carry him off by main force. He ran for his life, and there was a steeplechase round the deck, among benches, bales, and coils of rope; while the passengers and the crew cheered first one and then the other, till they could not speak for laughing. The husband was all but caught once; but a benevolent passenger kicked a camp-stool in the lady's way, and he got a fresh start, which he utilized by climbing up the ladder to the paddle-box. His wife tried to follow him, but the shouts of laughter which the black men raised at seeing her performances were too much for her, and she came down again. Here the captain interposed, and put her ashore, where she stood like black-eyed Susan till the vessel was far from the wharf, not waving her lily hand, however, but shaking her clenched fist in the direction of the fugitive.

To return to our voyage to the Isle of Pines.—All the afternoon the steamer threaded her way cautiously among the coral-reefs which rose almost to the surface. Sometimes there seemed scarcely room to pass between them, and by night navigation would have been impossible. We were just in the place where Columbus and his companions arrived on their expedition along the Cuban coast, to find out what countries lay beyond. They sailed by day, and lay to at night, till their patience was worn out. Another day or two of sailing would have brought them to where the coast trends northwards; but they turned back, and Columbus died in the belief that Cuba was the eastern extremity of the continent of Asia.

The Spaniards call these reefs "cayos," and we have altered the name to "keys," such as *Key West* in Florida, and *Ambergris Key* off Belize.

It was after sunset, and the phosphorescent animals were making the sea glitter like molten metal, when we reached the Isle of Pines, and steamed slowly up the river, among the mangroves that fringe the banks, to the village of Nueva Gerona, the port of the island. It consisted of two rows of houses thatched with palm-leaves, and surrounded by wide verandahs; and between them a street of unmitigated mud.

As we walked through the place in the dusk, we could dimly discern the inhabitants sitting in their thatched verandahs, in the thinnest of white dresses, gossipping, smoking, and love-making, tinkling guitars, and singing seguidillas. It was quite a Spanish American scene out of a romance. There was no romance about the mosquitos, however. The air was alive with them. When I was new to Cuba, I used to go to bed in the European fashion; and as the beds were all six inches too short, my feet used to find their way out in the night, and the mosquitos came down and sat upon them. Experience taught us that it was better to lie down half-dressed, so that only our faces and hands were exposed to their attacks.

The Isle of Pines used to be the favourite resort of the pirates of the Spanish main; indeed there were no other inhabitants. The creeks and rivers being lined with the densest vegetation, a few yards up the winding course of such a creek, they were lost in the forest, and a cruiser might pass within a few yards of their lurking-place, and see no traces of them. Captain Kyd often came here, and stories of his buried treasures are still told among the inhabitants. Now the island serves a double purpose; it is a place of resort for the Cubans, who come to rusticate and bathe, and it serves as a settlement for those free black inhabitants of Florida who chose to leave that country when it was given up to the United States. One of these Floridanos accompanied us as our guide next day to the Baños de Santa Fé.

When we left the village we passed near the mangrove trees, which were growing not only near the water but in it, and like to spread their roots among the thick black slime which accumulates so fast in this country of rapid vegetable growth, and as rapid decomposition. In Cuba, the mangoe is the abomination of the planters, for they supply the runaway slaves with food, upon which they have been known to subsist for months, whilst the mangroves give them shelter. A little further inland we found the guava, a thick-spreading tree, with smooth green leaves. From its fruit is made guava-jelly, but as yet it was not ripe enough to eat.

In the middle of the island we came upon marble-quarries. They are hardly worked now; but when they were first established, a number of emancipados were employed there. What emancipados are, it is worth while to explain. They are Africans taken from captured slavers, and are set to work under government inspection for a limited number of years, on a footing something like that of the apprentices in Jamaica, in the interregnum between slavery and emancipation. In Cuba it is remarked that the mortality among the emancipados is frightful. They seldom outlive their years of probation. The explanation of this piece of statistics is curious. The fact is that every now and then, when an old man dies, they bury him as one of the emancipados, whose register is sent in to the Government as dead; while the negro himself goes to work as a slave in some out-of-the-way plantation where no tales are told.

We left the marble-quarries, and rode for miles over a wide savannah. The soil was loose and sandy and full of flakes of mica, and in the watercourses were fragments of granite, brought down from the hills. Here flourished palm trees and palmettos, acacias, mimosas, and cactuses, while the mangoe and the guava tree preferred the damper patches nearer to the coast. The hills were covered with the pine-trees from which the island has its name; and on the rising ground at their base we saw the strange spectacle of palms and fir trees growing side by side.

Where we came upon a stream, the change in the vegetation was astonishing. It was a sudden transition from an English, plantation of fir trees into the jungle of the tropics, full of Indian figs, palms, lancewood, and great mahagua trees, all knotted together by endless creepers and parasites; while the parrots kept up a continual chattering and screaming in the tree-tops. The moment we left the narrow strip of tropical forest that lined the stream we were in the pine wood. Here the first two or three feet of the trunks of the pine trees were scorched and blackened by the flames of the tall dry savannah-grass, which grows close round them, and catches fire several times every year. Through the pine forest the conflagration spreads unobstructed, as in an American prairie; but it only runs along the edge of the dense river-vegetation, which it cannot penetrate.

The Baños de Santa Fé are situated in a cleared space among the fir trees. The baths themselves are nothing but a cavity in the rock, into which a stream, at a temperature of about 80°, continually flows. A partition in the middle divides the ladies from the gentlemen, but allows them to continue their conversation while they sit and splash in their respective compartments.

The houses are even more quaint than the bathing-establishment. The whole settlement consists of a square field surrounded by little houses, each with its roof of palm leaves and indispensable verandah. Here the Cubans come to stay for months, bathing, smoking cigarettes, flirting, gossiping, playing cards, and strumming guitars; and they seemed to be all agreed on one point, that it was a delightful existence. We left them to their tranquil enjoyments, and rode back to Nueva Gerona.

Next morning we borrowed a gun from the engineer of the steamboat, and I bought some powder and shot at a shop where they kept two young alligators under the counter for the children to play with. The creeks and lagoons of the island are full of them, and the negroes told us that in a certain lake not far off there lived no less a personage than "the crocodile king"—"*el rey de los crocodilos;*" but we had no time to pay his majesty a visit. Two of the Floridan negroes rowed us up the river. Even at some distance from the mouth, sting-rays and jelly-fish were floating about. As we rowed upwards, the banks were overhung with the densest vegetation. There were mahogany trees with their curious lop-sided leaves, the copal-plant with its green egg-like fruit, from which copal oozes when it is cut, like opium from a poppy-head, palms with clusters of oily nuts, palmettos, and guavas. When a palm-tree on the river-bank would not grow freely for the crowding of other trees, it would strike out in a slanting direction till it reached the clear space above the river, and then shoot straight upwards with its crown of leaves.

We shot a hawk and a woodpecker, and took them home; but, not many minutes after we had laid them on the tiled floor of our room, we became aware that we were invaded. The ants were upon us. They were coming by thousands in a regular line of march up our window-sill and down again inside, straight towards the birds. When we looked out of the window, there was a black stripe lying across the court-yard on the flags, a whole army of them coming. We saw it was impossible to get the skins of the birds, so threw them out of the window, and the advanced guard faced about and followed them.

On the sand in front of the village the Castor-oil plant flourished, the *Palma Christi*; its little nuts were ripe, and tasted so innocent that, undeterred by the example of the boy in the Swiss Family Robinson, I ate several, and was handsomely punished for it. In the evening I recounted my ill-advised experiment to the white-jacketed loungers in the verandah of the inn, and was assured that I must have eaten an odd number! The second nut, they told me with much gravity, counteracts the first, the fourth neutralizes the third, and so on ad infinitum.

We made two clerical acquaintances in the Isle of Pines. One was the Cura of New Gerona, and his parentage was the only thing remarkable about him. He was not merely the son of a priest, but his grandfather was a priest also.

The other was a middle-aged ecclesiastic, with a pleasant face and an unfailing supply of good-humoured fun. Everybody seemed to get acquainted with him directly, and to become quite confidential after the first half-hour; and a drove of young men followed him about everywhere. His reverence kept up the ball of conversation continually, and showed considerable skill in amusing his auditors and drawing them out in their turn. It is true the jokes which passed seemed to us mild, but they appeared to suit the public exactly; and indeed, the Padre was quite capable of providing better ones when there was a market for them.

We found that though a Spaniard by birth, he had been brought up at the Lazarist College in Paris, which we know as the training-school of the French missionaries in China; and we soon made friends with him, as everyone else did. A day or two afterwards we went to see him in Havana, and found him hard at his work, which was the superintendence of several of the charitable institutions of the city—the Foundling Hospital, the Lunatic Asylum, and others. His life was one of incessant labour, and indeed people said he was killing himself with over-work, but he seemed always in the same state of chronic hilarity; and when he took us to see the hospitals, the children and patients received him with demonstrations of great delight.

I should not have said so much of our friend the Padre, were it not that I think there is a moral to be got out of him. I believe he may be taken as a type, not indeed of Roman Catholic missionaries in general, but of a certain class among them, who are of considerable importance in the missionary world, though there are not many of them. Taking the Padre as a sample of his class, as I think we may—judging from the accounts of them we meet with in books, it is curious to notice, how the point in which their system is strongest is just that in which the Protestant system is weakest, that is, in social training and deportment. What a number of men go to India with the best intentions, and set to work at once, flinging their doctrines at the natives before they have learnt in the least to understand what the said natives' minds are like, or how they work,—dropping at once upon their pet prejudices, mortally offending them as a preliminary step towards arguing with them; and in short, stroking the cat of society backwards in the most conscientious manner. By the time they have accomplished this satisfactory result, a man like our Cuban Padre, though he may have argued but little and preached even less, would have a hundred natives bound to him by strong personal attachment, and ready to accept anything from him in the way of teaching.

We paid a regular round of visits to the Floridan settlers, and were delighted with their pleasant simple ways. It is not much more than thirty years since they left Florida, and many of the children born since have learnt to speak English. The patches of cultivated land round their cottages produce, with but little labour, enough vegetables for their subsistence, and to sell, procuring clothing and such luxuries as they care for. They seemed to live happily among themselves, and to govern their little colony after the manner of the Patriarchs.

Whether any social condition can be better for the black inhabitants of the West Indies, than that of these settlers, I very much doubt. They are not a hard-working people, it is true; but hard work in the climate of the tropics is unnatural, and can only be brought about by unnatural means. That they are not sunk in utter laziness one can see by their neat cottages and trim gardens. Their state does not correspond with the idea of prosperity of the political economist, who would have them work hard to produce sugar, rum, and tobacco, that they might earn money to spend in crockery and Manchester goods; but it is suited to the race and to the climate. If we measure prosperity by the enjoyment of life, their condition is an enviable one.

I think no unprejudiced observer can visit the West Indies without seeing the absurdity of expecting the free blacks to work like slaves, as though any inducement but the strongest necessity would ever bring it about. There are only two causes which can possibly make the blacks industrious, in our sense of the word,—slavery, or a population so crowded as to make labour necessary to supply their wants.

In one house in the Floridan colony we found a *ménage* which was surprising to me, after my experience of the United States. The father of the family was a white man, a Spaniard, and his wife a black woman. They received us with the greatest hospitality, and we sat in the porch for a long time, talking to the family. One or two of the mulatto daughters were very handsome; and there were some visitors, young white men from the neighbouring village, who were apparently come to pay their devoirs to the young ladies. Such marriages are not uncommon in Cuba; and the climate of the island is not unfavourable for the mixed negro and European race, while to the pure whites it is deadly. The Creoles of the country are a poor degenerate race, and die out in the fourth generation. It is only by intermarriage with Europeans, and continual supplies of emigrants from Europe, that the white population is kept up.

On the morning of our departure we climbed a high lull of limestone, covered in places with patches of a limestone-breccia, cemented with sandstone, and filling the cavities in the rock. All over the hill we found doubly refracting Iceland-spar in quantities. Euphorbias, in Europe mere shrubs, were here smooth-limbed trees, with large flowers. From the top of the hill, the character of the savannahs was well displayed. Every water-course could be traced by its narrow line of deep green forest, contrasting with the scantier vegetation of the rest of the plain.

As we steamed out of the river, rows of brilliant red flamingos were standing in the shallow water, fishing, and here and there a pelican with his ungainly beak. Our Chinese crew were having their meal of rice when we walked forward, and the national chopsticks were hard at work. We talked to several of them. They could all speak a little Spanish, and were very intelligent.

The history of these Chinese emigrants is a curious one. Agents in China persuade them to come out, and they sign a contract to work for eight years, receiving from three to five dollars a month, with their food and clothing. The sum seems a fortune to them; but, when they come to Cuba, they find to their cost that the value of money must be estimated by what it will buy. They find that the value of a black labourer is thirty dollars a month, and they have practically sold themselves for slaves; for there is no one to prevent the masters who have bought the contract for their work from treating them in all respects as slaves. The value of such a contract—that is, of the Chinaman himself, was from £30 to £40 when we were in the island. Fortunately for them, they cannot bear the severe plantation-work. Some die after a few days of such labour and exposure, and many more kill themselves; and the utter indifference with which they commit suicide, as soon as life seems not worth having, contributes to moderate the exactions of their masters. A friend of ours in Cuba had a Chinese servant who was impertinent one day, and his master turned him out of the room, dismissing him with a kick. The other servants woke their master early next morning, with the intelligence that the Chinese had killed himself in the night, to expiate the insult he had received.

Of African slaves brought into the island, the yearly number is about 15,000. All the details of the trade are matter of general notoriety, even to the exact sum paid to each official as hush-money. It costs a hundred dollars for each negro, they say, of which a gold ounce (about £3 16s.) is the share of the Captain-general. To this must be added the cost of the slave in Africa, and the expense of the voyage; but when the slave is once fairly on a plantation he is worth eight hundred dollars; so it may be understood how profitable the trade still is, if only one slaver out of three gets through.

The island itself with its creeks and mangrove-trees is most favourable for their landing, if they can once make the shore; and the Spanish cruisers will not catch them if they can help it. If a British cruiser captures them, the negroes are made emancipados in the way I have already explained.

Hardly any country in the world is so thoroughly in a false position as England in her endeavours to keep down the Cuban slave-trade, with the nominal concurrence of the Spanish government, and the real vigorous opposition of every Spaniard on the island, from the Captain-General downwards. Even the most superficial observer who lands for an hour or two in Havana, while his steamer is taking in coals, can have evidence of the slave-trade brought before his eyes in the tattooed faces of native Africans, young and middle-aged, in the streets and markets; just as he can guess, from the scored backs of the negroes, what sort of discipline is kept up among them.

We slept on board the steamboat off the pier of Batabano, and the railway took us back to Havana next morning.

CHAPTER II.
HAVANA TO VERA CRUZ—VERA CRUZ TO MEXICO.

On the 8th of March, we went on board the "Méjico" steamer, American-built, and retaining her American engineers, but in other respects converted into a Spanish vessel, and now lying in the harbour of Havana bound for Vera Cruz, touching at Sisal in Yucatan. At eight o'clock we weighed anchor, and were piloted through the narrow passage which leads out of the harbour past the castle of El Morro and the fort of Cabañas, the view of whose ramparts and batteries caused quite a flourish of trumpets among our Spanish fellow-passengers, who firmly believe in their impregnability.

Among our fellow-passengers were a company of fifth-rate comedians, going to Merida by way of Sisal. There was nothing interesting to us about them. Theatrical people and green-room slang vary but little over the whole civilized world. There were two or three Spanish and French tradesmen going back to Mexico. They talked of nothing but the dangers of the road, and not without reason as it proved, for they were all robbed before they got home. Several of the rest were gamblers or political adventurers, or both, for the same person very often unites the two professions out here. Spain and the Spanish American Republics produce great numbers of these people, just as Missouri breeds border-ruffians and sympathizers. But the ruffian is a good fellow in comparison with these well-dressed, polite scoundrels, who could have given Fielding a hint or two he would have been glad of for the characters of Mr. Jonathan Wild and his friend the Count.

On the morning of the third day of our voyage we reached Sisal, and as soon as the captain would let us we went ashore, in a canoe that was like a flat wooden box. This said captain was a Catalan, and a surly fellow, and did not take the trouble to disguise the utter contempt he felt for our inquisitive ways, which he seemed quite to take pleasure in thwarting. It was the only place we were to see in Yucatan, a country whose name is associated with ideas of tropical fruits, where you must cut your forest-path with a machete, and of vast ruins of deserted temples and cities, covered up with a mass of dense vegetation. But here there was nothing of this kind. Sisal is a miserable little town, standing on the shore, with a great salt-marsh behind it. It has a sort of little jetty, which constitutes its claim to the title of *port*; and two or three small merchant-vessels were lying there, taking in cargoes of logwood (the staple product of the district), mahogany, hides, and deerskins. The sight of these latter surprised us; but we found on enquiry that numbers of deer as well as horned cattle inhabit the thinly-peopled districts round the shores of the Mexican Gulf, and flourish in spite of the burning climate, except when a year of drought comes, which kills them off by thousands.

One possible article of export we examined as closely as opportunity would allow, namely, the Indian inhabitants. There they are, in every respect the right article for trade:—brown-skinned, incapable of defending themselves, strong, healthy, and industrious; and the creeks and mangrove-swamps of Cuba only three days' sail off. The plantations and mines that want one hundred thousand men to bring them into full work, and swallow aborigines, Chinese, and negroes indifferently—anything that has a dark skin, and can be made to work—would take these Yucatecos in any quantity, and pay well for them. And once on a sugar-estate or down a mine, when their sham registers are regularly made out, and the Governor has had his ounce of gold apiece for passing them, and his subordinates their respective rights, who shall get them out again, or even find them?

This idea struck us as we sat looking at the Indians hard at work, loading and unloading; and finding an intelligent Spaniard, we fell to talking with him. Indians had been carried off to Cuba, he said, but very few, none since 1854, when two Englishmen came to the coast with a schooner on pretence of trading, and succeeded in getting clear off with a cargo of seventy-two natives on board. But being caught in a heavy gale of wind, they put in for safety—of all places in the world—into the British part of Belize. There some one found out what their cargo consisted of, the vessel was seized, the Indians sent back, and the two adventurers condemned to hard labour, one for four years, the other for two and a half. In a place where the fatigue and exposure of drill and mounting guard is death to a European soldier, this was most likely a way of inflicting capital punishment, slow, but pretty sure.

When the Spaniards came to these countries, as soon as they had leisure to ask themselves what could be the origin of the people they found there, the answer came at once, "the lost tribes of Israel," of course. And as we looked at these grave taciturn men, with their brown complexions, bright eyes, and strikingly aquiline noses, it did not seem strange that this belief should have been generally held, considering the state of knowledge on such matters in those days. We English found the ten tribes in the Red men of the north; Jews have written books in Hebrew for their own people, to make known to them that the rest of their race had been found in the mountains of Chili, retaining unmistakable traces of their origin and conversing fluently in Hebrew; and but lately they turned up, collected together and converted to Christianity, on the shores of the Caspian. The last two theories have their supporters at the present day. Crude as most of these ideas are, one feels a good deal of interest in the first inquiry that set men thinking seriously about the origin of races, and laid the foundation of the science of ethnology.

Our return on board was a long affair, for there was a stiff breeze, almost in our teeth; and our unwieldy craft was obliged to make tack after tack before we could reach the steamer. Great Portuguese men-of-war were floating about, waiting for prey; and we passed through patches of stringy gulf-weed, trailing out into long ropes. The water was hot, the thermometer standing at 84° when we dipped it over the side.

On the morning of the 12th, when we went on deck, there was a grand sight displayed before us. No shore visible, but a heavy bank of clouds on the horizon; and, high above them, towering up into the sky, the snowy summit of Orizaba, a hundred and fifty miles off.

Before noon, we are entering the harbour of Vera Cruz. The little island and fort of San Juan de Ulúa just opposite the wharfs, the island of Sacrificios a little farther to the left. A level line of city-wall along the water's edge; and, visible above it, the flat roofs of the houses, and the towers and cupolas of many churches. All grey stone, only relieved by the colored Spanish tiles on the church-roofs, and a flag or two in the harbour. Not a scrap of vegetation to be seen, and the rays of a tropical sun pouring down upon us.

Established in the Casa de Diligencias, we deliberated as to our journey to Mexico. The diligences to the capital, having been stopped for some months on account of the disturbed state of the country, had just begun to run again, avoiding Puebla, which was being besieged. We were anxious to be off at once; but Mr. Christy sagaciously remarking that the robbers would know of the arrival of the steamer, and would probably take the first diligence that came afterwards, we booked our places for the day after.

We were very kindly received by the English merchants to whom my companion had letters, and we set ourselves to learn what was the real state of things in Mexico.

On an average, the Presidency of the Republic of Mexico had changed hands once every eight months for the last ten years; and Don Ignacio Comonfort had stepped into the office in the previous December, on the nomination of his predecessor the mulatto general Alvarez, who had retired to the southern provinces with his army.

President Comonfort, with empty coffers, and scarcely any real political power, had felt it necessary to make some great effort to get popularity for himself and his government. He had therefore adopted the policy of attacking the *fueros*, the extraordinary privileges of the two classes of priests and soldiers, which had become part of the constitution under the first viceroys, and which not even the war of independence, and the adoption of republican forms, ever did away with. Neither class is amenable to the civil tribunals for debt or for any offences. The clergy have immense revenues, and much spiritual influence among the lower classes; and as soon as they discovered the disposition of the new President, they took one Don Antonio Haro y Tamirez, set him up as a counter-President, and installed him at Puebla, the second city of the Republic, where priests swarm, and priestly influence is unbounded. At the same time, they tried a pronunciamiento in the capital; but the President got the better of them after a slight struggle, and marched all his regular soldiers on Puebla. At the moment of our arrival in the country, the siege of this city was going on quite briskly, ten thousand men being engaged, commanded by forty-three general officers.

Whenever anything disagreeable is happening in the country, Vera Cruz is sure to get its full share. A month before our arrival, one Salcedo, who was a prisoner in the castle of San Juan de Ulúa, talked matters over with the garrison, and persuaded them to make a pronunciamento in favour of the insurgents. They then summoned the town to join their cause, which it declined doing for the present; and the castle opened fire upon it, knocking about some of the principal buildings, and doing a good deal of damage. A 30-pound shot went through the wall of our hotel, taking off the leg of an unfortunate waiter who was cleaning knives, and falling into the patio, or inner court. A daub of fresh plaster just outside our bedroom door indicated the spot; and the British Consul's office had a similar decoration. The Governor of the city could offer no active resistance, but he cut off the supplies from the island, and in three or four days Salcedo—finding himself out of ammunition, and short of water—surrendered in a neat speech, and the revolution ended.

We have but a short time to stay in Vera Cruz, so had better make our observations quickly; for when we come back again there will be a sun nearly in the zenith, and yellow fever—at the present moment hardly showing itself—will have come for the summer; under those circumstances, the unseasoned foreigner had better lie on his back in a cool room, with a cigar in his mouth, and read novels, than go about hunting for useful information.

There are streets of good Spanish houses in Vera Cruz, built of white coral-rock from the reefs near the shore, but they are mildewed and dismal-looking. Outside the walls is the Alameda; and close by is a line of houses, uninhabited, mouldy, and in ruins. We asked who built them. "Los Españoles," they said.

Even now, when the "nortes" are blowing, and the city is comparatively healthy, Vera Cruz is a melancholy place, with a plague-stricken look about it; but it is from June to October that its name, "the city of the dead"—la ciudad de los muertos—is really deserved. In that season comes an accumulation of evils. The sun is at its height; there is no north wind to clear the air; and the heavy tropical rains—more than three times as much in quantity as falls in England in the whole year—come down in a short rainy season of four months. The water filters through the sand-hills, and forms great stagnant lagoons; a rank tropical vegetation springs up, and the air is soon filled with pestilential vapours. Add to this that the water is unwholesome; the city too is placed in a sand-bath which keeps up a regular temperature, by accumulating heat by day and giving it out into the air by night, so that night gives no relief from the stifling closeness of the day. No wonder that Mr. Bullock, the Mexican traveller, as he sat in his room here in the hot season, heard the church-bells tolling for the dead from morning to night without intermission; for weeks and weeks, one can hardly even look into the street without seeing a funeral.

We turned back through the city, and walked along watching the Zopilotes—great turkey-buzzards—with their bald heads and foul dingy-black plumage.

They were sitting in compact rows on parapets of houses and churches, and seemed specially to affect the cross of the cathedral, where they perched, two on each arm, and some on the top. When some offal was thrown into the streets, they came down leisurely upon it, one after another; their appearance and deportment reminding us of the undertaker's men in England coming down from the hearse at the public-house door, when the funeral is over. In all tropical America these birds are the general scavengers, and there is a heavy fine for killing them.

Scarcely any one is about in the streets this afternoon, except a gang or two of convicts dragging their heavy chains along, sweeping and mending the streets. This is a punishment much approved of by the Mexican authorities, as combining terror to evil-doers with advantage to the community. That it puts all criminals on a level, from murderers down to vagrants, does not seem to be considered as a matter of much consequence.

At the city-gate stands a sentry—the strangest thing I ever saw in the guise of a soldier—a brown Indian of the coast, dressed in some rags that were a uniform once, shoeless, filthy in the extreme, and armed with an amazing old flint-lock. He is bad enough to look at, in all conscience, and really worse than he looks, for—no doubt—he has been pressed into the service against his will, and hates white men and their ways with all his heart. Of course he will run away when he gets a chance; and, though he will be no great loss to the service, he will add his mite to the feeling of hatred that has been growing up for these so many years among the brown Indians against the whites and the half-cast Mexicans. But more of this hereafter.

One step outside the gate, and we are among the sand-hills that stretch for miles and miles round Vera Cruz. They are mere shifting sand-mounds; and, though some of them are fifty feet high, the fierce north wind moves them about bodily. The Texans know these winds well, and call them "northers." They come from Hudson's Bay to the Gulf of Mexico, right down the Continent of North America, over a level plain with hardly a hill to obstruct their course, the Rocky Mountains and the Alleghanies forming a sort of trough for them. When the "norte" blows fiercely you can hardly keep your feet in the streets of Vera Cruz, and vessels drag their anchors or break from their moorings in the ill-protected harbour, and are blown out to sea—lucky if they escape the ugly coral-reefs and sand-banks that fringe the coast. There are a few bushes growing outside the walls, and there we found the Nopal bush, the great prickly pear—the same that has established itself all round the shores of the Mediterranean—growing in crevices of rocks, and cracks in lava-beds, and barren places where nothing else will live. But what made us notice these Nopals was, that they were covered with what looked like little white cocoons, out of which, when they were pressed, came a drop of deep crimson fluid.

This is the cochineal insect, but only the wild variety; the fine kind, which is used for dye, and conies from the province of Oajaca, miles off, is covered only with a mealy powder. There the Indians cultivate great plantations of Nopals, and spread the insects over them with immense care, even removing them, and carrying them up into the mountains in baskets when the rainy season begins in the plains, and bringing them back when it is over.

On Friday, the 14th of March, at three o'clock in the morning, we took our places in a strong American-built diligence, holding nine inside, and began our journey by being dragged along the railroad—which was commenced with great energy some time ago, and got fifteen miles on its way to the capital, at which point it has stopped ever since. When day broke we had left the railroad, and were jolting along through a parched sandy plain, thinly covered with acacias, nopals, and other kinds of cactus, bignonias, and the great tree-euphorbia, with which we had been so familiar in Cuba, with its smooth limbs and huge white flowers. At last we reached the first hill, and began gently to ascend. The change was wonderful. Once out of the plain, we are in the midst of a tropical forest. The trees are crowded close together, and the convolvulus binds their branches into an impassable jungle, while ferns and creepers weave themselves into a dense mass below; and here and there a glimpse up some deep ravine shows great tree-ferns, thirty feet high, standing close to the brink of a mountain-stream, and flourishing in the damp shade.

Indian Ranchos become more frequent as we ascend; and the inhabitants—squatting on the ground, or leaning against the door-posts—just condescend to glance at us as we pass, and then return to their meditations, and their cigarettes, if they happen to have any. These ranches are the merest huts of canes, thatched with palm-leaves; and close by each a little patch of ground is enclosed by a fence of prickly cactus, within which are growing plantains, with their large smooth leaves and heavy ropes of fruit, the great staple of the "tierra caliente."

Our road winds along valleys and through pass after pass; and now and then a long zig-zag brings us out of a valley, up to a higher level. The air grows cooler, we are rapidly changing our climate, and afternoon finds us in the region of the sugar-cane and the coffee-plant. We pass immense green cane-fields, protected from the visits of passing muleteers and peasants by a thick hedge of thorny coffee-bushes. The cane is but young yet; but the coffee-plant, with its brilliant white flowers, like little stars, is a beautiful feature in the landscape.

At sunset we are rattling through the streets of the little town of Cordova. There is such a thoroughly Spanish air about the place, that it might be a suburb of the real Cordova, were it not for the crowds of brown Indians in their scanty cotton dresses and great flat-brimmed hats, and the Mexican costumes of the whiter folks. Low whitewashed houses, with large windows to the street, protected by the heavy iron-gratings, like cages, that are so familiar to travellers in Southern Europe. Inside the grating are the ladies of the family, outside stand their male acquaintance, and energetic gossiping is going on. The smoky little lamp inside gives us a full view of the interior. Four whitewashed walls; a table; a few stiff-backed chairs; a virgin or saint resplendent in paint and tinsel; and, perhaps, two or three coloured engravings, red, blue, and yellow.

A few hours in the dark, and we reach Orizaba. We have changed our climate for the last time to-day, and have reached that district where tobacco flourishes at an altitude of 4,000 feet above the sea. But of this we see nothing, for we are off again long before daylight; and by the time that external objects can be made out we find ourselves in a new region. A valley floored with rich alluvial soil from the hills that rise steeply on both sides, their tops shrouded in clouds. Signs of wonderful fertility in the fields of maize and barley along the roadside. The air warm, but full of mist, which has already penetrated our clothes and made them feel damp and sticky. "Splendid country, this, Señores," said an old Mexican, when he had twisted himself round on his seat to get a good stare at us. "It seems so," said I, "judging by the look of the fields, but it is very unpleasantly damp just now." "Just now," said the old gentleman, echoing my words, "it is always damp here. You see that drizzling mist; that is the chipi-chipi. Never heard of the chipi-chipi! Why it is the riches and blessing of the country. Sometimes we never see the sun here for weeks at a time, and it rains a little every day nearly; but look at the fields, we get three crops a year from them where you have but one on the fields just above. And it is healthy, too; look at those fellows at work there. When we get up to the Llanos you will see the difference."

The valley grew narrower as we drove on; and at last, when it seemed to end in a great ravine, we began to climb the steep hill by a zig-zag road. Soon the air grows clearer again, the sunshine appears and gets brighter and brighter, we have left the mist behind, and are among ranges of grand steep hills, covered with the peculiar vegetation of the plateau,—Cactus, Opuntia, and the Agave Americana. In the trough of the valley lies a regular opaque layer of white clouds, hiding the fields and cottages from our view. We have already passed the zone of perpetual moisture, whose incessant clouds and showers are caused by the stratum of hot air—charged with water evaporated from the gulf —striking upon the mountains, and there depositing part of the aqueous vapour it contains.

You may see the same thing happening in almost every mountainous district; but seldom on so grand a scale as here, or with so little disturbance from other agents. Yesterday was passed in the "tierra caliente," the hot country; our journey of to-day and to-morrow is through the "tierra templada" and the "tierra fría," the temperate and the cold country. Here a change of a few hundred feet in altitude above the sea, brings with it a change of climate as great as many degrees of latitude will cause, and in one day's travel it is possible to descend from the region of eternal snow to the utmost heat of the tropics. Our ascent is more gradual; but, though we are three days on the road, we have sometimes scarcely time to notice the different zones of vegetation we pass through, before we change again.

To make the account of the journey from the coast to Mexico somewhat clearer, a few words must be said about the formation of the country, as shown in a profile-map or section. The interior of Mexico consists of a mass of volcanic rocks, thrust up to a great height above the sea-level. The plateau of Mexico is 8,000 feet high, and that of Puebla 9,000 feet. This central mass consists principally of a greyish trachytic porphyry, in some places rich in veins of silver-ore. The tops of the hills are often crowned with basaltic columns, and a soft porous amygdaloid abounds on the outskirts of the Mexican valley. Besides this, traces of more recent volcanic action abound, in the shape of numerous extinct craters in the high plateaus, and immense "pedrigals" or fields of lava not yet old enough for their surface to have been disintegrated into soil. Though sedimentary rocks occur in Mexico, they are not the predominant feature of the country. Ridges of limestone hills lie on the slopes of the great volcanic mass toward the coast; and at a still lower level, just in the rise from the flat coast-region, there are strata of sandstone. On our road from Vera Cruz we came upon sandstone immediately after leaving the sandy plains; and a few miles further on we reached the limestone, very much as it is represented in Burkart's profile of the country from Tampico upwards towards San Luis Potosi. The mountain-plateaus, such as the plains of Mexico and Puebla, are hollows filled up and floored with horizontal strata of tertiary deposits, which again are covered by the constantly accumulating layers of alluvium.

Our heavy pull up the mountain-side has brought us into a new scene. Every one knows how the snow lies in the valleys of the Alps, forming a plain which slopes gradually downward towards the outlet Imagine such a valley ten miles across, with just such a sloping plain, not of snow but of earth. There has been no rain for months, and the surface of the ground is parched and cracked all over. There is hardly a tree to be seen except clumps of wood on the mountain-sides miles off,—no vegetation but tufts of coarse grass, among which herds of disconsolate-looking cattle are roaming; the vaqueros, (herdsmen) are cantering about after them on their lean horses, with their lazos hanging in coils on their left arms, and now and then calling to order some refractory beast who tries to get away from the herd, by sending the loop over his horns or letting it fall before him as he runs, and hitching it up with a jerk round his hind legs as he steps within it. But the poor creatures are too thirsty and dispirited just now to give any sport, and the first touch of the cord is enough to bring them back to their allegiance.

From the decomposed porphyry of the mountains carbonate of soda comes down in solution to the valleys. Much of this is converted into natron by the organic matter in the soil, and forms a white crust on the earth. More of the carbonate of soda, mixed in various proportions with common salt, drains continually out in the streams, or filters into the ground and crystallizes there. This is why there is not a field to be seen, and the land is fit for nothing but pasture. But when the rains come on in a few months, say our friends in the diligence, this dismal waste will be a luxuriant prairie, and the cattle will be here by thousands, for most of them are dispersed now in the lower regions of the tierra templada where grass and water are to be had.

My companion and I climb upon the top of the diligence to spy out the land. The grand volcano of Orizaba had been hidden from us ever since that morning when we saw it from far out at sea, but now it rises on our left, its upper half covered with snow of dazzling whiteness,—a regular cone, for from this side the crater cannot be seen. It looks as though one could walk half a mile or so across the valley and then go straight up to the summit, but it is full thirty miles off. The air is heated as by a furnace, and as we jolt along the road the clouds of dust are suffocating. We go full gallop along such road as there is, banging into holes, and across the trenches left by last year's watercourses, until we begin to think that it must end in a general smash. We came to understand Mexican roads and Mexican drivers better, even before we got to the capital.

Before us and behind lay wide lakes, stretching from side to side of the valley; but the lake behind followed us as steadily as the one before us receded. It was only the mirage that tantalizes travellers in these scorched valleys, all the long eight months of the rainless season. It seemed beautiful at first, then monotonous; and long before the day was out we hated it with a most cordial and unaffected hatred.

Soon a new appearance attracted our attention. First, clouds of dust, which gradually took a well-defined shape, and formed themselves into immense pillars, rapidly spinning round upon themselves, and travelling slowly about the plain. At one place, where several smaller valleys opened upon us, these sand-pillars, some small, some large, were promenading about by dozens, looking much like the genie when the fisherman had just let him out of the bottle, and saw him with astonishment beginning to shape himself into a giant of monstrous size. Indeed I doubt not that the story-teller was thinking of such sand-pillars when he wrote that wonderful description. You may see them in the East by thousands. As they moved along, they sucked up small stones, dust, and leaves; and our driver declared that they had been known to take the roofs off houses, and carry flocks of sheep into the air; "but these that you see now," said he, "are no great matter." We estimated the size of the largest at about four hundred feet in height, and thirty in diameter; and this very pillar, walking by chance against a house, most decidedly got the worst of it, and had its lower limbs knocked all to pieces.

When the sun grows hot, the bare earth heats the air that lies upon it so much that an upward current rises from the whole face of the valley; and to supply its place the little valleys and ravines that open into it pour in each its stream of cooler air; and wherever two of these streams, flowing in different directions, strike one another, a little whirlwind ensues, and makes itself manifest as a sand-pillar. The coachman's "molino de viento," as he called it, may very well have happened, but it must have been a whirlwind on a large scale, caused by the meeting of great atmospheric currents, not by the little apparatus we saw at work.

There seems to be hardly a village in the plain; and the only buildings we see for miles are the herdsmen's houses of stone, flat-roofed, dark inside, and uninviting in their appearance, and the great cattle-pens, the corrals, which seem absurdly too large for the herds that we have yet seen; but in two or three months there will be rain, the ground will be covered with rank grass, the corrals will be crowded with cattle every evening; the mirage will depart when real water comes, dust and sand-pillars will be no longer to be seen, and all the nine horses and mules of the diligence-team, floundering, splashing, and kicking, will hardly keep the heavy coach from settling down inextricably in the mire. And so on until October, and then the season of water, "la estación de las aguas," will cease, and things will be again as they are now.

In the usual course of travel to the capital, the second night would have been passed at Puebla. This is the second city of the Republic, and numbers some 70,000 inhabitants. As it was then in revolt, and besieged by the President and his army, we made a detour to the north when about 20 miles from it, in order to sleep for a few hours at Huamantla, a place with a most evil reputation for thieves and vermin; and about ten at night we drove into the court-yard of a dismal-looking inn. Three or four dirty fellows stood round as we alighted, wrapped in their serapes—great woollen blankets, the universal wear of the Mexicans of the plateaus. One end of the serape was thrown across from shoulder to shoulder, and hid the lower part of their faces; and the broad-brimmed Mexican sombrero was slouched over their eyes; we particularly disliked the look of them as they stood watching us and our baggage going into the inn. A few minutes after, we returned to the court-yard to complete our observation of them, but they were all gone.

A party of Spaniards and Mexicans were at the other table in the sala when we marched in, and as soon as we had taken off the edge of our fierce hunger, we began to compare notes with them. "Had a pleasant journey from Mexico?" They all answered at once, delighted to find an audience to whom to tell their sorrows, as men always are under such circumstances. It appeared that they had reached Huamantla an hour or two before us, and to their surprise and delight no robbers had appeared. But between the outskirts of the town and the inn, the cords behind the diligence were cut, and every particle of luggage had disappeared. At the inn-gate they got out and discovered their loss. They set upon the Administrador of the diligence-company, who sympathized deeply with them, but had no more substantial comfort to offer. They declared the driver must have been an accomplice, and the driver was sent for, for them to wreak their fury upon. He appeared with his mouth full of beans, and told them, as soon as he could speak, that they ought to be very thankful they had come off so easily, and, looking at them with an expression of infinite disgust, returned to his supper; they followed his example, and seemed to have at last found consolation in hot dishes and Catalan wine. It was wonderful to hear of the fine things that were in the lost portmanteaus,—the rings, the gold watches, the rouleaux of dollars, the "papers of the utmost importance."

I am afraid the Spanish American has not always a very strict regard for truth.

These gentlemen had indeed got off easily, as the driver said; for the last diligence from Vera Cruz, with our steamboat acquaintances in it, had been stopped just outside this very town of Huamantla as they left it before daylight in the morning. The robbers were but three, but they had plundered the unfortunate travellers as effectually as thirty could have done. Now, all this was very pretty to hear as a tale, but not satisfactory to travellers who were going by the same road the next morning; and in the disagreeable barrack-room where our beds stood in long lines, we, the nine passengers of the "up" diligence, held a council, standing, like Mr. Macaulay's senators, and there decided on a most Christian line of conduct—that when the three bore down upon us, and the muzzle of the inevitable escopeta was poked in at our window, we would descend meekly, and at the command of "boca abajo," ("mouth downwards,") we would humiliate ourselves with our noses in the dirt, and be robbed quietly. Having thus decided beforehand, according to the etiquette of the road, whether we were to fight or submit, and being tired with a long day's journey, we all turned in, and were fast asleep in a moment.

It seemed that almost directly afterwards the dirtiest man possible came round, and shook us till we were conscious; and we washed in the customary saucers, by the light of a real, flaring, smoking, Spanish lamp with a beak, exactly what the Romans used in Pompeii, except that this is of brass, not bronze.

With our eyes still half-shut we crawled into the kitchen for our morning chocolate, and demanded our bill. Such a bill! One of us, a stout Spaniard, sent for the landlord and abused him in a set speech. The "patron" divested his countenance of every trace of expression, scratched his head through his greasy nightcap, and stood listening patiently. The stout man grew fiercer and fiercer, and wound up with a climax. "If we meet with the robbers," said he, rolling himself up in his great cloak, "we must tell them that we have passed through your worship's hands, and there is none left for them." The landlord bowed gravely, saw us into the diligence, and hoped we should have a fortunate journey, and meet with no novelty on the road. A "novelty" in Spanish countries means a misfortune.

We met with no "novelty," though, when we looked out of the window in the early dawn and spied three men with muskets, following us at a short distance, we thought our time had come, and watches and valuables were plunged into boots and under seats, and through slits into the padding of the diligence; but the three men came no nearer, and we supposed them to be an escort of soldiers. When it was light the difficulty was to recover the valuables—no easy matter, so securely had they been hidden.

We heard afterwards of a little peculiarity which distinguished the robbers of Huamantla. It seems that no less a personage than the parish priest was accustomed to lead his parishioners into action, like the Cornish parson in old times when a ship went ashore on the coast. What has become of his reverence since, I do not know. He is very likely still in his parish, carrying on his double profession, unless somebody has shot him. I wonder whether it is sacrilege to shoot a priest who is also a highwayman, as it used to be to kill a bishop on the field of battle.

We are at last on the high lands of Mexico, the districts which at least three different races have chosen to settle in, neglecting the fertile country below. A sharp turn in the road brings its fairly out into the plain; and then on our left are the two snowy mountains that lie at the edge of the valley of Mexico, Popocatepetl and Iztaccihuatl, famous in all Mexican books. Like Orizaba of yesterday, they seem to rise from the plain close to us; and from the valley between them there pours down upon us such a flood of icy wind, that, though windows are pulled up and great-coats buttoned round our throats, we shiver piteously, and our teeth fairly chatter till we get out of the river of cold air; and then comes hot sunshine and dust again.

Anxious to make sure that we have really got into the land of Aztec civilization, Mr. Christy gets down from the diligence, and hunting about for a few minutes by the road-side, returns in triumph with a broken arrowhead of obsidian. A deep channel cut by a water-course gives us our first idea of the depth of the soil; for these plateaus were once nothing but deep hollows among the mountains, which rain and melted snow, bringing down fragments of porphyry and basalt—partly in their original state and partly decomposed—have filled up and formed into plains. Signs of volcanic action are abundant. To say nothing of the two great mountains we have just left behind, there is a hill of red volcanic tufa just beyond us; and still further on, though this is anticipating, our road passes over the lava-field at the foot of the little volcano of Santa Barbara.

There is a population here at any rate, village after village; and between them are great plantations of maize and aloes; for this is the district where the best pulque in Mexico is made, the "llanos de Apam." It is the *Agave Americana*, the same aloe that is so common in southern Europe, where indeed it flowers, and that grows in our gardens and used to have the reputation of flowering once in a hundred years. I do not exaggerate when I say that we saw hundreds of thousands of them that day, planted in long regular lines. Among them were walking the Indian "tlachiqueros," each with his pigskin on his back, and his long calabash in his hand, milking such plants as were in season.

The fine buildings of the haciendas, and more especially the churches, contrast strongly with the generality of houses, all of one story, built of adobes (mud-bricks dried in the sun), with flat roofs of sand and lime resting on wooden rafters, and the naked ground for a floor, all dark, dirty, and comfortless. There are even many huts built entirely of the universal aloe. The stems of wild aloes which have been allowed to flower are stuck into the ground, side by side, and pieces of leaves tied on outside them with aloe-fibre. These cut leaves are set like tiles to form a roof, and pegged down with the thorns which grow at their extremities. Picturesque and cheap, though hardly comfortable, for we are in the "tierra fría" now, and the mornings and evenings in winter are often bitterly cold.

But the churches! Is it possible that they can belong to these wretched filthy little cottages. As black Sam, our driver, a runaway Texan slave, suggested, it looked as though the villagers might pull down their houses and locate themselves and their families in their churches. We thought of Mr. Ruskin, who has somewhere expressed an earnest desire that all the money and energy that England has wasted in making railroads, had been spent in building churches; and we wished he had been here to see his principles carried out.

I have travelled on rough roads in my time, but on such a road as this never. My companion refused for a time to award the premium of badness to our thoroughfare; but, just while we were discussing the question and recounting our experience of bone-smashing highways, we reached a pass where the road consisted of a series of steps, nearly a foot in depth, down which steps we went at a swinging trot, holding on for our lives, in terror lest the next jerk should fairly wrench our arms out of their sockets, while we could plainly hear the inside passengers howling for mercy, as they were shot up against the roof which knocked them back into their seats. Aching all over, we reached level ground again, and Mr. Christy withdrew his claims, and agreed that no road anywhere else could possibly be so bad as a Mexican road; a decision which later experiences only served to confirm.

Our start, every time we changed horses, was a sight to see. Nine half-broken horses and mules, in a furious state of excitement, were harnessed to our unwieldy machine; the helpers let go, and off they went, kicking, plunging, rearing, biting, and screaming, into ruts and watercourses that were like the trenches they make for gas-pipes in London streets, with our wheels on one side on a stone wall, and in a pit on the other, and Black Sam leaning back with his feet on the board, waiting with perfect tranquillity until the animals had got rid of their superfluous energy and he could hold them in. We were always just going to have some frightful accident, and always just missed it. The last stage before we reached Otumba, a small dusky urchin ran across the road just before us. How Black Sam contrived to pull up I cannot tell, though, indeed, his arms were about the size of an ordinary man's thighs; but he did, and they got the child out from the horses' feet quite unhurt.

It was at the inn where we stopped to breakfast that we made our first acquaintance with the great Mexican institutions—tortillas and pulque. The pulque was being brewed on a large scale in an adjoining building. The vats were made of cow-skins (with the hair inside), supported by a frame of sticks; and in them was pulque in every stage, beginning with the sweet aguamiel—honeywater—the fresh juice of the aloe, and then the same in different degrees of fermentation till we come to the *madre pulque*, the mother pulque, a little of which is used like yeast, to start the fermentation, and which has a combined odour of gas-works and drains. Pulque, as you drink it, looks like milk and water, and has a mild smell and taste of rotten eggs. Tortillas are like oat-cakes, but made of Indian corn meal, not crisp, but soft and leathery. We thought both dreadfully nasty for a day or two; then we could just endure them; then we came to like them; and before we left the country we wondered how we should do without them.

CHAPTER III.
CITY OF MEXICO.

Some thirty years ago, Don Agustín Yturbide, the first and last Emperor of Mexico, found that he wanted a palace wherein to house his newly-fledged dignity; and began to build one accordingly, in the high street of Mexico, close to the great convent of San Francisco. It could not have been nearly finished when its founder was shot: and it became the *Hotel d'Yturbide*. We are now settled in it, in very comfortable quarters. There is a restaurant down below, where the son of the late Yturbide dines daily, and everybody points him out to us, and moralises over him.

Mr. Christy's drawer-roll of letters of introduction has produced an immediate crop of pleasant acquaintances, whose hospitality is boundless. We are not idle, far from it; and a long day's work is generally followed by a social dinner, and an evening spent in noting down the results of our investigations.

Prescott's *Conquest of Mexico* has been more read in England than most historical works; and the Mexico of Montezuma has a well-defined idea attached to it. The amphitheatre of dark hills surrounding the level plain, the two snowy mountain-peaks, the five lakes covering nearly half the valley, the city rising out of the midst of the waters, miles from the shore, with which it was connected by its four causeways, the straight streets of low flat-roofed houses, the numbers of canals crowded with canoes of Indians going to and from the market, the floating gardens moved from place to place, on which vegetables and flowers were cultivated, the great pyramid up which the Spanish army saw their captured companions led in solemn procession, and sacrificed on the top—all these are details in the mental picture.

Much of this has changed since the Spaniards first saw it. Cortes tried all ordinary means to overcome the desperate obstinacy with which the Aztecs defended their capital. The Spaniards conquered wherever they went; but, as they moved forward, the Mexicans closed in again behind, and from every house-top showers of darts, arrows, and stones were poured down upon them. Cortes resolved upon the utter demolition of the city. He was grieved to destroy it, he said, for it was the most beautiful thing in the whole world; but there was no alternative. He moved slowly towards the great teocalli, his fifty thousand Tlascalan allies following him, throwing down every house, and filling the canals with the ruins. When the conquest was finished, but one district of the city was left standing, and in it were crowded a quarter of the population, miserable famished wretches, who had surrendered when their king was taken. All that was left besides was a patch of swampy ground strewed with fragments of walls, a few pyramids too large for present destruction, and such great heaps of dead bodies that it was impossible to get from place to place without walking over them.

Cortes had resolved that a new city should be built, but it was not so easy to decide where it was to be. The Aztecs, it seemed, had not originally established themselves on the spot where Mexico was built. When they came down from the north country, and across the hills into the valley of Mexico, they were but an insignificant tribe, and as yet mere savages. They settled down in one place after another, and were always driven out by the persecutions of the neighbouring tribes. At last they took possession of a little group of swampy islands in the lake of Tezcuco; and then at last, safe from their enemies, they increased and multiplied, and became a great and powerful nation.

The first beginnings of Mexico, a cluster of huts built on wooden piles, must have borne some likeness to those curious settlements of early tribes in the shallow part of the lakes of Switzerland and the British Isles, of which numerous remains are still to be found. As the nation increased in numbers, Tenochtitlán, as the inhabitants called their city (they called themselves *Tenochques*), came to be a great city of houses built on piles, with canals running through the straight streets, along which the natives poled their flat-bottomed canoes. The name which the Spaniards gave to the city, the "Venice of the New World," was appropriate, not only to its situation in the midst of the water, with canals for thoroughfares, but also to the history of the causes which led to its being built in such a situation.

The habit of building houses upon piles, which was first forced upon the people by the position they had chosen, was afterwards followed as a matter of taste, just as it is in Holland. Even after the Aztecs became masters of the surrounding country, they built towns round the lake, partly on the shore, and partly on piles in the water. The Spanish chroniclers mention Iztapalapán, and many other towns, as built in this way. Like the Swiss tribes, the early inhabitants of Mexico depended much upon their fishing, for which their position gave them great facilities.

If you look at the arms of the Mexican Republic, on a passport or a silver dollar, you will see a representation of a rock surrounded by water. On the rock grows a cactus, and on the cactus sits an eagle with a serpent in his beak. The story is that the wandering tribe preserved a tradition of an oracle which said that when they should find an eagle, holding a serpent, and perched on a cactus growing out of a rock, then they should cease their wanderings. On an island in the lake of Tezcuco, they found eagle, serpent, cactus, and rock, as described, and they settled there in due course. What fragment of truth is hidden in this myth it is hard to say. Tenochtitlán means "The Stone-cactus place;" and the Aztec picture-writings express its name by a hieroglyph of a prickly pear growing on a rock. Putting this history out of the question, the Aztecs had excellent reasons for choosing this peculiar site for their city; but these reasons were not equally valid in the case of the new invaders. For them the surrounding salt-water was not needed as a protection, and was merely a nuisance. Every year, when the lake rose, the place was flooded, with enormous damage to the property of the inhabitants; and sometimes an inundation of greater depth than usual threatened as complete a destruction as Cortes and the Tlascalans had made. At the best of times, the site was a salt-swamp, an ugly place to build upon. And, lastly, all the fresh water must be brought from the hills by aqueducts, which an enemy would cut off without difficulty, as the Spaniards themselves had done during the siege. Now Cortes was certainly not ignorant of all this, and he knew of many places on the rising ground close by, where he could found his new city under more favourable circumstances. He deliberated four or five months on the matter, and at last decided in favour of the old site, giving as his reason that "the city of Tenochtitlán had become celebrated, its position was wonderful, and in all times it had been considered as the capital and mistress of all these provinces."

The invaders were old hands at slave-driving, and so hard did they drive the conquered Mexicans, that in four years there had arisen a fine Spanish city, with massive stone houses of several storeys, having the indispensable inner courts, flat roofs, and grated windows,—every man's house literally his castle, when once the great iron entrance-gates were closed. The Indians had, of course, been converted en masse, and churches were being built in all directions. The great pyramid where Huitzilopochtli, the God of war, was worshipped, had been razed to the ground, and its great sculptured blocks of basalt were sunk in the earth as a foundation for a cathedral. The old lines of the streets, running toward the four points of the compass, were kept to; and to this it is that the present Mexico is indebted for much of its beauty. Most of the smaller canals were filled up, and the thoroughfares widened for carriages, things of course unknown to the Mexicans, who had no beasts of burden. In the suburbs the natives settled themselves after their own fashion, baking adobes, large mud bricks, in the sun, and building with them one-storey houses with flat roofs, much as they do at the present day. And thus a new Mexico, nearly the same as that we are now exploring, came to be planted in the midst of the waters. Three centimes have elapsed since; the city has grown larger, churches, convents, and public buildings have increased, but the architectural character of the place has scarcely altered. It is the situation that has changed. The lake of Tezcuco is four miles off, though the causeways which once connected the city with the dry land still exist, and have even been enlarged. They look like railway-embankments crossing the low ground, and serve as dykes when there is a flood, a casualty which still often happens.

This change is interesting to the student of physical geography; and Humboldt's account of the causes which have brought it about is full and explicit. When Mexico had been built a few years, the frightful inundations which threatened its very existence at length awoke the Spaniards to a sense of the mistake that had been made in placing themselves but a few feet above the lowest level of the valley, in such a way that, from whatever point the flood might come, they were sure to get the benefit of it. The Spanish authorities at home, with their usual sagacity, sent over peremptory orders that the city should be abandoned, and a new capital built at Tacubaya—a proposal something like intimating to the inhabitants of Naples that their position, at the foot of Mount Vesuvius, was most dangerous, and that they must leave it and settle somewhere else. In those days the valley was a complete basin, with no outlet—at least not one worth mentioning; and the heavy tropical rains and the melted snow from the mountains, poured vast quantities of water into it. Had the valley been at the level of the sea, it would simply have become a great lake, surrounded by hills; but at three thousand feet higher, the atmosphere is rarefied, and evaporation goes on with such rapidity as to keep the accumulation of water in check. So the affair had adjusted itself in this wise, that the land and the five lakes should divide the valley about equally between them. It became necessary to alter this state of things, and a passage was cut at a place where the hills were but little above the level of the highest lake. The history of this passage, the famous "Desague de Huehuetoca," is instructive enough, but it has been written so threadbare that I cannot touch it. Suffice it to say, that by this means a constant outlet was made for the lake of Zumpango, the highest of the five, and for the Rio de Guatitlán, a stream which formerly ran into it.

So much for one cause of the change in the present appearance of the city. Then the Spaniards were great cutters down of forests. They rather liked to make their new country bear a resemblance to the arid plains of Castile, where, when you arrive in Madrid, people ask you whether you noticed *the tree* on the road; and moreover, as they wanted wood, they cut it, without troubling themselves to plant for the benefit of future generations. Now, when the trees were cut down, the small plants which grew in their shade died too, and left the bare earth to serve as a kind of natural evaporating apparatus. And, between these two causes, it has come to pass that the extent of the lakes has been so much reduced, and that Mexico stands on the dry land—if, indeed, that may be called dry land, where you cannot dig a foot without coming to water.

During the Tertiary period the whole valley of Mexico was one great lake. Whether the proportion of water to land had adjusted itself before the country was inhabited, or whether during historical times the lakes were still gradually diminishing by the excess of evaporation over the quantity of water supplied by rain and snow, is an open question. At any rate the two causes I have mentioned will account for the changes which have taken place since the conquest.

Taking it as a whole, Mexico is a grand city, and, as Cortes truly said, its situation is marvellous. But as for the buildings, I should be sorry to inflict upon any one who may read these sketches, a detailed description of any one of them. It is a thousand pities that, just at the time when the Italians and Spaniards were most zealous in church-building, so very questionable an architectural taste should have been prevalent.

The churches and convents in Mexico belong to that kind of renaissance style that began to flourish in southern Europe in the sixteenth century, and has held its ground there ever since. High façades abound, with pilasters crowned by elaborate Corinthian capitals, forming a curious contrast with the mean little buildings crouched behind the tall front. In the doors of the churches outside, and the chapels within, one is constantly coming upon that peculiar construction which consists of what would be an arch, resting on two pillars, were not the keystone wanting. Columns with shafts elaborately sculptured, and twisted marble pillars of the bed-post pattern, are to be seen by hundreds, very expensive in material and workmanship, but unfortunately very ugly; while the numbers of puffy cherubs, inside and out, remind the Englishman of the monuments of St. Paul's.

As to the interior decoration of the churches, the richer ones are crowded with incongruous ornaments to a wonderful degree. Gold, silver, costly marbles, jewels, stucco, paint, tinsel, and frippery are all mixed up together in the wildest manner. We found the inside of the churches to be generally the worst part of them. The Cathedral, for instance, is really a very grand building when seen from a little distance, with its two high towers and its cupola behind. I was greatly edified by finding it described in the last book of Mexican travels I have read, as built in the purest Doric style.

The Minería, or School of Mines, is a fine building, something after the manner of Somerset House on a small scale. As for the famous Plaza Mayor, the great square, it is a very great square indeed, large enough to review an army in, and large enough to damage by its size the effect of the cathedral, and to dwarf the other buildings that surround it into mere insignificance. However, one thing is certain, that we have not come all this way to see Spanish architecture and great squares, but must look for something more characteristic.

I have said we arrived in Mexico on the eve of Palm Sunday, and next morning we proceeded to consult with one of our newly-made acquaintances as to our prospects for the ensuing Holy Week. This gentleman, a man who took a practical view of things, mentioned a circumstance which led him to expect that the affair would go off with éclat. The Mexicans, both the nearly white Mestizos and the Indians of pure race, delight in pulque. The brown people are grave and silent in their sober state, but pulque stirs up their sluggish blood, and they get into a condition of positive enjoyment. But very soon after this comes a state of furious intoxication, and a general scuffle is a common termination to a drinking-bout. Fortunately, the Indians are not a bloodthirsty people; and, though every man carries a knife or machete, or—if he can get nothing better—a bit of hoop-iron tempered, sharpened, and fixed into a handle, yet nothing more serious than cuffs and scratches generally ensues. Even if severe wounds are given, the Indian has many chances in his favor, for his organization is somewhat different from that of white men, and he recovers easily from wounds that would kill any European outright.

The lower orders of the half-breed population are also given to pulque-drinking, but with far more serious consequences. Unlike the pure Indians, they are a hot-blooded and excitable race, and drunkenness with them is utter madness while it lasts. Knives are drawn at the very beginning of a squabble, and scarcely an evening passes without one or two bodies of men killed in these drunken mêlées being carried to the Police Cuartel in the great square. On Sundays and holidays the number increases; but on this Palm Sunday there were fourteen, not killed in one great battle, but brought in by ones and twos, from different parts of the city. It was this little piece of statistics that induced our friend to conclude that the citizens of Mexico had made up their minds to enjoy themselves thoroughly, and that Holy Week would be a grand affair. Monday, Tuesday, and Wednesday of the Semana Santa have only this to distinguish them from ordinary days, that the churches are crowded with men and women waiting their turn at the confessional; and that in the afternoons the old promenade of Las Vigas, down in the Indian quarter by the canal of Chalco, is patronized by fashionable Mexico, which, except on some four or five special days, frequents the new Alameda. The sight of these confessionals, so constantly filled, prompts one to ask—why just before Easter? Just after would be more appropriate; for as we find the Glasgow people much worse on Sundays than on week-days, so the Mexican population, not very virtuous at the best of times, are specially and particularly wicked when the great Church-festivals come round. The name of Shrove Tuesday survives in our Calendar, to remind us of the time when we also used to go to be shriven before Easter.

On Thursday at noon mass is over, the bells cease to ring, the organs in the churches are silent, and all carriages disappear from the streets, except the dusty Diligence which, like French law, "est athée," and cares nothing for fasts or festivals. Now we come to understand the wonderful wooden machine like a water-wheel, which was put up yesterday on one tower of the Cathedral. We had asked people in the great square, just below, what it was, but could get no answer except that it was *la Matraca*, the rattle, for to-morrow. And now we found that, the church bells being incapacitated, this rattle does duty instead, striking the hours, and occasionally going off into furious fits of clattering, without apparent reason, for ten minutes at a time, till the two men who worked it, who were either convicts or soldiers in fatigue-dress, were tired out. It was not this one rattle only that was disturbing the public peace that day and the next. Everybody was walking about with a rattle, and working it like mad, and all over the city there was a noise like the sound of the back-scratchers at Greenwich Fair, or of an American forest when the woodpeckers are busy. These little rattles stand for Judas's bones, and all good Catholics express in this odd way their desire to break them. They do the same thing in Italy, but it is not so prominent a part of the celebration as in Mexico, where old and young, rich and poor, all do their part in it. As soon as we found out what it all meant, we bought matracas for ourselves, and joined the rest of the world in their noisy occupation. The breaking of his bones is but a preliminary measure. In the square a fair is being held, in the booths of which the great articles of trade now are Judas's bones, of many patterns, at all prices, and Judas himself in pasteboard, who is to be carried about and insulted till Saturday morning, and then, hanging up by a string, is to burst asunder by means of a packet of powder and a slow match in his inside, and finally to perish in a bonfire.

The first sight of these pasteboard Judases convinced us of one thing, that we had unexpectedly come upon the old custom, of which our processions and burning of Guy Fawkes in England are merely an adaptation. After giving up the old custom as a Popish rite, what a blight idea to revive it in this new shape, and to give the boys something to carry about, bang, blow up, and make a final bonfire of, and all in the Protestant interest! There was another thing to be noticed about the Judases. The makers had evidently tried to vary them as much as they could; and, by that very means, had shown how impossible it was to them to strike out anything new. There were two types; one was the Neapolitan *Polichinello*, whom we have naturalised as *Punch*; and the other the God *Pan*, with his horns, and hoofs, and tail, whom the whole Christian world has recognised as the devil, for these many ages. Well, some took one type and some the other; and a few tried to combine the two, of course spoiling both. But, beyond this, their power of invention could not go. They were always trying to conceal the old idea, and could do no more than to distort it. We could see through their flimsy pretensions to originality much as a schoolmaster recognises the extracts from the encyclopaedia in his boys' essays.

As with this Judas trade, so it is with other more important arts and sciences in this country. The old types descend, almost unchanged, from generation to generation. Everything that is really Mexican is either Aztec or Spanish. Among the Spanish types we may separate the Moorish. Our knowledge of Mexico is not sufficient to enable us to analyse the Aztec civilization, so we must be content with these three classes. I will not go further into the question here, for occasions will continually occur to show how—for three centuries at least—the inhabitants of Mexico, both white and brown, have taken their ideas at second-hand, always copying but never developing anything.

All this time my companion and I have been walking about the streets; in evening-dress, as the etiquette of the place demands, on these three days, from the "better classes." The Mexican ladies may be advantageously studied just now in their church-going black silk dress and mantilla, one of the most graceful costumes in the world. It is not often that one has the chance of seeing them out of doors, except hurrying to and from Mass in the morning, or in carriages on the Alameda; but on these festival days one meets them by hundreds. They do not contrast favorably with the ladies of Cadiz and Seville. The mixture of Aztec blood seems to have detracted from the beauty of the Spanish race; the dryness of the atmosphere spoils their complexions; and the monstrous quantity of capsicums that are consumed at every meal cannot possibly leave the Mexican digestion in its proper state.

We dined that day with Don José de A., who, though Spanish-American by birth, was English by education and feeling, and had known my companion's family well. Our dinner was half English, half Mexican; and the favourite dishes of the country were there, to aid in our initiation into Mexican manners and customs. The cooks at the inns, mindful of our foreign origin, had dealt out the red pepper with a sparing hand; but to-day the dish of "mole" was the genuine article, and the first mouthful set as coughing and gasping for breath, while the tears streamed down our faces, and Don Pepe and Don Pancho gravely continued their dinner, assuring us that we should get quite to like it in time. *Pepe* and *Pancho*, by the way, are short for José and Francisco. Dinner over, it was time to visit the churches, to which people crowd by thousands, this evening and to-morrow, to see the monuments, as they are called. Pancho departed, being on duty as escort to his sisters; and we having, by Pepe's advice, left our watches and valuables in his room, and put our handkerchiefs in our breast-pockets, started with him. Mr. Christy, always on the look-out for a new seed or plant, had taken possession of the seeds of two *mameis*, which are fleshy fruits—as big as cocoa-nuts—each containing a hard smooth seed as large as a hen's egg. These not being of great value, he put one in each tail-pocket of his coat. When we got out, we found the streets full of people, hurrying from one church to another, anxious to get as many as possible visited in the evening. We went first to the monastery of San Francisco, close to our hotel, the largest, and perhaps the richest convent in the country. Entering through a great gate, we find ourselves in a large courtyard, full of people, who are visiting—one after another—the four churches which the establishment contains, going in at one door and out at the other. At the door of the largest church, stands a tall monk, soliciting customers for the rosaries of olive-wood, crosses, and medals from Jerusalem, which are displayed on a stall close by—shouting in a stentorian voice, every two or three minutes, "He who gives alms to Holy Church, shall receive plenary indulgence, and deliver one soul from purgatory." We bought some, but there did not seem to be many other purchasers. Indeed, we found, when we had been longer in the country, that a few pence would buy all sorts of church indulgences, from the permission to eat meat on fast-days up to plenary absolution in the hour of death; and the trade, once so flourishing here, is almost used up. The churches were hung with black, and lighted up; and in each was a "monument," a kind of bower of green branches decorated with flowers, mirror's, and gold and silver church-plate, and supposed to stand for the Garden of Gethsemane. Inside was reclining a wax figure of our Saviour, gaudily dressed in silk and velvet; and there were also representations of the Last Supper, with wax-work figures as large as life. To visit and criticise these "monuments" was the object of the sort of pilgrimage people were making from church to church, and they seemed thoroughly to enjoy it. It was not a superfluous precaution that we had taken, in leaving our valuables in a place of safety, for, on our exit from the first church, we found that Pepe had lost his handkerchief and a cigar-case, which he had stowed away in an inner pocket, and Mr. Christy had been relieved of one of his mamei seeds by some "lepero" who probably took it for a snuff-box. His feelings must have been like those of the English pickpocket in Paris, when he robbed the Frenchman of the article he had pocketed with so much care, and found it was a lump of sugar. And so relieved of further care for our worldly goods, we went through with the work of seeing monuments, till we were tired and disgusted with the whole affair, and at last went home to bed.

Next day, appropriate sermons in the churches, processions in the afternoon, in which wax figures of Christ and the Virgin Mary were carried by men got up in fancy dresses as soldiers and centurions, and so called penitents, walking covered with black shrouds and veils, with small round holes to look through, or in the yellow dress and extinguisher cap, both with flames and devils painted on them. These are exactly the costumes worn in old times, the first by the familiars of the Inquisition, and the second by the criminals it condemned; and the sight of them set us thinking of the processions they used to figure in, when the Holy Office was flourishing at Santo Domingo, a little way down the street where we are standing.

In the evening the Crucifixion is represented in wax in the churches, and the visiting goes on as the night before; and the next morning is the Sábado de Gloria, the Saturday which ends Lent. We go to the Jesuits' church in the morning to hear the last sermon. Since Thursday at noon, as the organs have been silenced, harps and violins have taken their places. The sermon is long and prosy, and we rejoice that it is the last. Then the service of the day goes on until they come to the "Gloria in excelsis." The organ peals out again, the black curtain—which has hidden the high altar—parts in the middle, and displays a perfect blaze of gold and jewels: all the bells in the city begin to ring: the carriages, which have been waiting ready harnessed in court yards, pour out into the streets: the lumbering hackney coaches go racing to the great square, striving to get the first fare for luck: the Judases, which have been hanging all the morning out of windows and across streets, are set light to as the first bell begins to ring, and fizzing and popping burst all to pieces, and then are thrown into a heap in the street, where a bonfire is made of them, and the children join hands and dance round it. So Holy Week ends.

The arrangement of the day in Mexico is this. Early in the morning your servant knocks at your door, and brings in a little cup of coffee or chocolate and a small roll, which *desayuno*—literally breakfast—you discuss while dressing. Going down into the courtyard, you find your horse waiting for you, and off you go for an hour or two's ride, and back to a dejeuner-à-la-fourchette somewhere between ten and one o'clock. Then you have seven or eight hours before dinner, so that a good deal of work may be got into a day so divided. Things are managed very differently in country places, but this is the fashion in the capital among the higher class, that is, of course, the class of people who put on dress-coats in the evening.

When we had been a day or two in Mexico, we took our first ride to Tacubaya and Chapultepec. Mexican saddles and bridles were a novelty to us, but when we come to describe our Mexican and his appurtenances it will be time enough to speak of them.

The barricades in the streets constructed during the last revolution of two or three weeks back had not yet been removed, but an opening at one side allowed men and horses to get past. Carriages had to go round, an easy matter in a city built as this is in squares like a chess-board. The barricades mount two guns each, and as the streets are quite straight they can sweep them in both directions, to the whole length of their range. As in Turin, you can look backward and forward along the straight streets from every part of the city, and see mountains at each end. The suburbs of the city are quite as repulsive as our first glimpse of them led us to expect; and, as far as one could judge by the appearance of the half-caste inhabitants, it is not good to go there alone after dark. Here is the end of the aqueduct of Chapultepec, the Salto del Agua;

and—crowded round it—a thoroughly characteristic group of women and water-carriers, filling their great earthen jars with water, which they carry about from house to house. The women are simply and cheaply dressed, and though not generally pretty, are very graceful in their movements. Their dress consists of a white cotton under-dress, a coloured cotton skirt, generally blue, brown, or grey, with some small pattern upon it, but never brilliant in colour, and a rebozo, which is a small sober-coloured cotton shawl, long and narrow. This rebozo passes over the back of the head, where it is somehow fixed to a back hair-comb, and the two ends hang down over the shoulders in front; or, more often, one end is thrown over the opposite shoulder, so that the young lady's face is set in it, like a picture in a frame. Add to this a springy step, the peculiarly unconstrained movement in walking which comes of living in the open air and wearing a loose dress, a pleasant pale face, small features, bright eyes, small hands and feet, little slippers and no stockings, and you have as good a picture of a Mexican half-caste girl as I can give. A book of Mexican engravings, however, will give a much better idea of her. Then we went past the great prison, the Acordada, and out at the gate (we had purposely gone out of our way to see more of the city), and so into the great promenade, the Pased or Alameda. The latter is the Spanish name for this necessary appendage to every town. It comes from *álamo*, which means a poplar. Imagine a long wide level road, a mile or so long, generally so chosen as to have a fine view, with footpaths on each side, lines of poplar trees, a fountain at each end and a statue in the middle, and this description will stand pretty nearly for almost every promenade of the kind I have seen in Spain or Spanish America.

Tacubaya is a pleasant place on the ride of the first hills that begin to rise towards the mountain-wall of the valley. Here rich Mexicans have country-houses in large gardens, which are interesting from the immense variety of plants which grow there, though badly kept up, and systematically stripped by the gardeners of the fruit as it gets ripe—for their own benefit, of course. From Tacubaya we go to Chapultepec (Grasshopper Mountain), which is a volcanic hill of porphyry rising from the plain. On the top is the palace on which the viceroy Galvez expended great sums of money some seventy years ago, making it into a building which would serve either as a palace or as a fortress in cases of emergency. Though the Americans charged up the hill and carried it easily in '47, it would be a very strong place in proper hands. It is a military school now. On the hill is the famous grove of cypresses—ahuehuetes—as they are called, grand trees with their branches hung with fringes of the long grey Spanish moss—barba Española—Spanish beard. I do not know what painters think of the effect of this moss, trailing in long festoons from the branches of the trees, but to me it is beautiful; and I shall never forget where I first saw it, on a bayou of the Mississippi, winding through the depths of a great forest in the swamps of Louisiana. In this grove of Chapultepec, there were sculptured on the side of the hill, in the solid porphyry, likenesses of the two Montezumas, colossal in size. For some reason or other, I forget now what, one of the last Spanish viceroys thought it desirable to destroy them, and tried to blow them up with gunpowder. He only partially succeeded, for the two great bas-reliefs were still very distinguishable as we rode past, though noseless and considerably knocked about.

We went home to breakfast with our friends, and looked at the title-deeds of their house in crabbed Spanish of the sixteenth century, and the great Chinese treasure-chest, still used as the strong-box of the firm, with an immense lock, and a key like the key of Dover castle. Fine old Chinese jars, and other curiosities, are often to be found in Mexico; and they date from the time when the great galleon from Manila, which was called "el nao"—the ship—to distinguish it from all other ships, came once a year to Acapulco.

After breakfast, business hours begin; so we took ourselves off to visit the canal of Chalco, and the famous floating gardens—as they are called. On our way we had a chance of studying the conveyances our ancestors used to ride in, and availed ourselves of it. In books on Spanish America, written at the beginning of this century, there are wonderful descriptions of the gilt coaches, with six or eight mules, in which the great folks used to drive in state on the promenades. They are exactly the carriages that it was the height of a lady's ambition to ride in, in the days of Sir Charles Grandison, and Mr. Tom Jones. Here, in Mexico, they were still to be found, after they had disappeared from the rest of the habitable globe; and even now, though the private carriages are all of a more modern type, there are still left a few of these amazing vehicles, now degraded to the cab-stand; and we got into one that was embellished with sculptured Cupids—their faces as much mutilated as the two Montezumas—and with the remains of the painting and gilding, which once covered the whole affair, just visible in corners, like the colouring of the ceilings of the Alhambra. We had to climb up three high steps, and haul ourselves into the body of the coach, which hung on strong leather straps; springs belong to a later period. By the time we had got to the Paseo de las Vigas we were glad enough to get out, wondering at the sacrifice of comfort to dignity those highly respectable grandees must have made, and not surprised at the fate of some inquisitive travellers who have done as we did, and have been obliged to stop by the qualms of sea-sickness. At the bridge we chartered a canoe to Santa Anita. This Santa Anita is a little Indian village on the canal of Chalco, and to-day there is to be a festival there. For this, however, we shall be too early, as we have to be back in time to see Mexico turn out for a promenade on the Paseo de las Vigas, and then to go out to dinner. So we must just take the opportunity of looking at the Indian population as they go up and down the canal in canoes, and see their gardens and their houses. However, as the Indian notion of a festival consists in going to mass in the morning, and getting drunk and fighting in the afternoon, we are perhaps as well out of it. We took our passage to Santa Anita and back in a canoe—a mere flat-bottomed box with sloping sides, made of boards put together with wooden pegs. There was a mat at the stern for us to squat upon, and an awning over our heads. An old Indian and his son were the crew; and they had long poles, which they set against the banks or the bottom of the shallow canal, and so pushed us along. Besides these two, an old woman with two little girls got in, as we were starting—without asking our leave, by the way—and sat down at the other end of the canoe. Of course, the old woman began to busy herself with the two little girls, in the usual occupation of old women here, during their idle moments; and though she left off at our earnest request, she evidently thought us very crotchety people for objecting.

The scene on the canal was a curious one. There were numbers of boats going up and down; and the Indians, as soon as they caught sight of an acquaintance, began to shout out a long string of complimentary phrases, sometimes in Spanish and sometimes in Mexican: "How is your worship this morning?" "I trust that I have the happiness of seeing your worship in good health." "If there is anything I can have the honour of doing for your worship, pray dispose of me," and so forth; till they are out of hearing. All this is accompanied by a taking-off of hats, and a series of low bows and complimentary grimaces. As far as we could ascertain, it is all mere matter of ceremony. It may be an exaggeration of the formal, complimentary talk of the Spaniards, but its origin probably dates further back.

The Indians here no longer appeared the same dull, melancholy men whom we had seen in the richer quarter of the town. There they were under a strong feeling of constraint, for their language is not understood by the whites and mestizos; and they, for their part, know but little Spanish; and besides, there is very little sympathy between the two classes. One thing will shew this clearly enough. By a distinct line of demarcation, the Indians are separated from the rest of the population, who are at least partly white. These latter call themselves "gente de razón"—people of reason,—to distinguish themselves from the Indians, who are people without reason. In common parlance the distinction is made thus: the whites and mixed breed are "gente"—*people,*—the brown men being merely "Indios"—Indians—and not people at all.

Here, in their own quarter, and among their own people, they seem talkative enough. We can only tell what they are chattering about when they happen to speak Spanish, either for our benefit, or to show off their proficiency in that tongue. People who can speak the Aztec language say that their way of forming compound words gives constant occasion for puns and quibbles, and that the talk of the Indians is full of such small jokes. In this respect they differ exceedingly from the Spaniards, whose jests are generally about *things*, and seldom about their *names*, as one sees by their almost always bearing translation into other languages.

Most of the canoes were tastefully decorated with flowers, for the Aztecs have not lost their old taste for ornamenting themselves, and everything about them, with garlands and nosegays. The fruits and vegetables they were carrying to market were very English in their appearance. Mexico is supplied with all kinds of tropical fruits, which come from a distance; but the district we are now in only produces plants which might grow in our own country—barley, potatoes, cabbages, parsnips, apples, pears, plums, peaches, and so forth, but scarcely anything tropical in its character. One thing surprises us, that the Indians, in a climate where the mornings and evenings are often very chilly, should dress so scantily. The men have a general appearance of having outgrown their clothes; for the sleeves of the kind of cotton-shirt they wear only reach to their elbows, and their trousers, of the same material, only fall to their knees. To these two garments add a sort of blanket, thrown over the shoulders, a pair of sandals, and a palm-leaf hat, and the man is dressed. His skin is brown, his limbs muscular—especially his legs—his lips thick, his nose Jewish, his hair coarse, black, and hanging straight down. The woman's dress is as simple as the man's. She has on a kind of cotton sack, very short in the sleeves, and very open at the shoulders, and some sort of a skirt or petticoat besides. Sometimes she has a folded cotton cloth on her head, like a Roman contadina; but, generally, nothing covers her thick black hair, which hangs down behind in long twisted tails.

In old times, when Mexico was in the middle of a great lake, and the inhabitants were not strong enough to hold land on the shores, they were driven to strange shifts to get food. Among other expedients, they took to making little floating islands, which consisted of rafts of reeds and brushwood, on which they heaped mud from the shores of the lakes. On the banks of the lake of Tezcuco the mud was, at first, too full of salt and soda to be good for cultivation; but by pouring the water of the lake upon it, and letting it soak through, they dissolved out most of the salts, and the island was fit for cultivation, and bore splendid crops of vegetables. These islands were called *chinampas*, and they were often large enough for the proprietor to build a hut in the middle, and live in it with his family. In later times, when the Mexicans came to be no longer afraid of their neighbours, the chinampas were not of much use; and when the water was drained off, and the city stood on dry land, one would have supposed that such a troublesome and costly arrangement would have been abandoned. The Mexican, however, is hard to move from the customs of his ancestors; and we have Humboldt's word for it, that in his time there were some of these artificial islands still in the lake of

Chalco, which the owners towed about with a rope, or pushed with a long pole. They are all gone now, at any rate, though the name of *chinampa* is still applied to the gardens along the canal. These gardens very much resemble the floating islands in their construction of mud, heaped on a foundation of reeds and branches; and though they are not the real thing, and do not float, they are interesting, as the present representatives of the famous Mexican floating gardens. They are narrow strips of land, with a frontage of four or five yards to the canal, and a depth of one hundred, or a hundred and fifty yards. Between the strips are open ditches; and one principal occupation of the proprietor seems to be bringing up mud from the bottom of the ditch with a wooden shovel, and throwing it on the garden, in places where it has sunk. The reason of the narrowness of the strips is that he may be able to throw mud all over them from the ditches on either side.

While we are busy observing all these matters, and questioning our boatmen about them, we reach Santa Anita. Here there are swampy lanes and more swampy gardens, a little village of Indian houses, three or four pulque-shops, and a church. Outside the pulque-shops are fresco-paintings, representing Aztec warriors carousing, and draining great bowls of pulque. These were no specimens of Aztec art, however, but seemed to be copied (by some white or half-caste sign-painter, probably) from the French coloured engravings which represent the events of the Conquest. These extraordinary works of art are to be seen everywhere in this country, where, of all places in the world, one would have thought that people would have noticed that the artist had not the faintest idea of what an Aztec was like, but supposed that his limbs and face and hair were like an European's. Here, with the real Aztec standing underneath, the difference was striking enough. One ought not to be too critical about these things, however, when one remembers the pictures of shepherds and shepherdesses that adorn our English farmhouses. We drank pulque at the sign of *The Cacique,* and liked it, for we had now quite got over our aversion to its putrid taste and smell. I wonder that our new faculty of pulque-drinking did not make us able to relish the suspicious eggs that abound in Mexican inns, but it had no such effect, unfortunately.

Our canoe took us back to the Promenade of Las Vigas, which is a long drive, planted with rows of trees, and extends along the last mile or two of the canal. Indeed, its name comes from the beam (Viga) which swings across the canal at the place where the canoes pay toll. This was the great promenade, once upon a time; but the new Alameda has taken away all the promenaders to a more fashionable quarter, except on certain festival days, three or four times in the year, when it is the correct thing for society to make a display of itself—on horseback or in carriages—in this neglected Indian quarter. We had happened upon one of these festival days; so, as we crawled along the side-path, tired and dusty, we had a good opportunity of seeing the Mexican beau monde. The display of really good carriages was extraordinary; but it must be recollected that many families here are content to live miserably enough at home, if they can manage to appear in good style at the theatre and on the promenade. This is one reason why so many of the Mexicans who are so friendly with you out of doors, and in the cafés, are so very shy of letting you see the inside of their houses. They say, and very likely it is true, that among the richer classes, it is customary to put a stipulation in the marriage-contracts, that the husband shall keep a carriage and pair, and a box at the theatre, for his wife's benefit. The horsemen turned out in great style, and the foreigners were fully represented among them. It was noticeable that while these latter generally adopted the high-peaked saddle, and the jacket, and broad-brimmed felt hat of the country, and looked as though the new arrangements quite suited them, the native dandies, on the other hand, were prone to dressing in European fashion, and sitting upon English saddles—in which they looked neither secure nor comfortable.

We walked home past the old Bull-ring, now replaced by a new one near the new promenade, and found, to our surprise, that in this quarter of the town many of the streets were under water. We knew that the level of the lake of Tezcuco had been raised by a series of three very wet seasons, but had no idea that things had got so far as this. Of course the ground-floors had to be abandoned, and the people had made a raised pathway of planks along tho street, and adopted various contrivances for getting dryshod up to their first floors; and in some places canoes were floating in the street. The city looked like this some two hundred years ago, when Martinez the engineer tried an unfortunate experiment with his draining tunnel at Huehuetoca, and flooded the whole city for five years. It was by the interference, they tell us, of the patroness of the Indians, our Lady of Guadalupe, who was brought from her own temple on purpose, that the city was delivered from the impending destruction. A number of earthquakes took place, which caused the ground to split in large fissures, down which the superfluous water disappeared. For none of her many miracles has the Virgin of Guadalupe got so much credit as for this. To be sure, it is not generally mentioned in orthodox histories of the affair, that she was brought to the capital a year or two before the earthquakes happened.

Talking of earthquakes, it is to be remembered that we are in a district where they are of continual occurrence. If one looks carefully at a line of houses in a street, it is curious to see how some walls slope inwards, and some outwards, and some are cracked from top to bottom. There is hardly a church-tower in Mexico that is not visibly out of the perpendicular. Any one who has noticed how the walls of the Cathedral of Pisa have been thrown out of the perpendicular by the settling down of the foundations, will have an idea of the general appearance of the larger buildings of Mexico. On different occasions the destruction caused by earthquakes has been very great. By the way, the liability of Mexico to these shocks, explains the peculiarity of the building of the houses. A modern English town with two-or-three-storied houses, with their thin brick walls, would be laid in ruins by a shock which would hardly affect Mexico. Here, the houses of several storeys have stone walls of such thickness that they resist by sheer strength; and the one-storey mud houses, in the suburbs, are too low to suffer much by being shaken about. A few days before we arrived here, our friends Pepe and Pancho were playing at billiards in the Lonja, the Merchants' Exchange; and Pepe described to us the feeling of utter astonishment with which he saw his ball, after striking the other, go suddenly off at an absurd angle into a pocket. The shock of an earthquake had tilted the table up on one side. While we were in Mexico there was a slight shock, which set the chandeliers swinging, but we did not even notice it. In April, a solemn procession goes from the Cathedral, on a day marked in the Calendar as the "Patrocinio de Señor San Jose", to implore the "Santissimo Patriarca" to protect the city from earthquakes (temblores). In connection with this subject there is an opinion, so generally received in Mexico that it is worth notice. Everybody there, even the most educated people, will tell you that there is an earthquake-season, which occurs in January or February; and that the shocks are far more frequent than at any other time of the year. My impression is that this is all nonsense; but I should like to test it with a list of the shocks that have been felt, if such a thing were to be had. It does not follow that, because the Mexicans have such frequent opportunities of trying the question, they should therefore have done so. In fact, experience as to popular beliefs in similar matters rather points the other way. I recollect that in the earthquake districts of southern Italy, when shocks were of almost daily occurrence, people believed that they were more frequent in the middle four hours of the night, from ten to two, than at other times. Of course, this proved on examination to be quite without foundation. To take one more case in point. How many of our almanack-books, even the better class of them, contain prophecies of wet and fine weather, deduced from the moon's quarters! How long will it be before we get rid of this queer old astrological superstition?

We made a few rough observations of the thermometer and barometer during our stay in Mexico. The barometer stands at about 22-1/2 inches, and our thermometer gave the boiling point of water at 199 degrees. We could never get eggs well boiled in the high lands, and attributed this, whether rightly or not I cannot say, to the low temperature of boiling water.

CHAPTER IV.
TACUBAYA. PACHUCA. REAL DEL MONTE.

We went one morning to the house of our friend Don Pepe, and were informed by the servant as we entered the courtyard that the niño, the child, was up stairs waiting for us. "The Child" seemed an odd term to apply to a young man of five and twenty. The young ladies, in the same way are called the nias, and keep the appellation until they marry.

We went off with the niño to his uncle's house at Tacubaya, on the rising ground above Mexico. In the garden there we found a vegetation such as one would find in southern Europe—figs, olives, peaches, roses, and many other European trees and flowers—growing luxuriantly, but among them the passion-flower, which produces one of the most delicious of fruits, the granadita, and other semi-tropical plants. The live creatures in the garden, however, were anything but European in their character. There were numbers of immense butterflies of the most brilliant colours; and the garden was full of hummingbirds, darting backwards and forwards with wonderful swiftness, and dipping their long beaks into the flowers. They call them chupa-mirtos—myrtle-suckers, and the Indians take them by blowing water upon them from a cane, and catching them before they have recovered from the shock. One day we bought a cage full of them, and tried to keep them alive in our room by feeding them with sugar and water, but the poor little things pined away. In old times the Mexicans were famous for their ornaments of humming-bird's feathers. The taste with which they arranged feathers of many shades of colour, excited the admiration of the conquerors; and the specimens we may still see in museums are beautiful things, and their great age has hardly impaired the brilliancy of their tints. This curious art was practised by the highest nobility, and held in great esteem, just as working tapestry used to be in Europe, only that the feather-work was mostly done by men. It is a lost art, for one cannot take much account of such poor things as are done now, in which, moreover, the designs are European. In this garden at Tacubaya we saw for the first time the praying Mantis, and caught him as he sat in his usual devotional attitude. His Spanish name is "el predicador," the preacher.

We got back to Mexico in time for the Corrida de Toros. The bull-ring was a large one, and there were many thousands of people there; but as to the spectacle itself, whether one took it upon its merits, or merely compared it with the bull-fights of Old Spain, it was disgusting. The bulls were cautious and cowardly, and could hardly be got to fight; and the matadors almost always failed in killing them; partly through want of skill, partly because it is really harder to kill a quiet bull than a fierce one who runs straight at his assailant. To fill up the measure of the whole iniquitous proceeding, they brought in a wretch in a white jacket with a dagger, to finish the unfortunate beasts which the matador could not kill in the legitimate way. It was evidently quite the regular thing, for the spectators expressed no surprise at it.

After the bull-fight proper was finished, there came two or three supplementary performances, which were genuinely Mexican, and very well worth seeing. A very wild bull was turned into the ring, where two lazadores, on beautiful little horses, were waiting for him. The bull set off at full speed after one of the riders, who cantered easily ahead of him; and the other, leisurely untying his lazo, hung it over his left arm, and then, taking the end in his light hand, let the cord fall through the loop into a running noose, which he whirled two or three times round his head, and threw it so neatly that it settled gently down over the bull's neck. In a moment the other end of the cord was wound several times round the pummel of the saddle, and the little horse set off at full speed to get ahead of the bull. But the first rider had wheeled round, thrown his lazo upon the ground, and just as the bull stepped within the noose, whipped it up round his hind leg, and galloped off in a contrary direction. Just as the first lazo tightened round his neck, the second jerked him by the leg, and the beast rolled helplessly over in the sand. Then they got the lazos off, no easy matter when one isn't accustomed to it, and set him off again, catching him by hind legs or fore legs just as they pleased, and inevitably bringing him down, till the bull was tired out and no longer resisted. Then they both lazo'd him over the horns, and galloped him out, amid the cheers of the spectators. The amusements finished with the "colear." This is quite peculiar to Mexico, and is done on this wise. The coleador rides after the bull, who has an idea that something is going to happen, and gallops off as fast as he can go, throwing out his hind legs in his awkward bullish fashion. Now, suppose you are the coleador, sitting in your peaked Mexican saddle, that rises behind and before, and keeps you in your seat without an effort on your part. You gallop after the bull, and when you come up with him, you pull as hard as you can to keep your horse back; for, if he is used to the sport, as almost all Mexican horses are, he is wild to get past, not noticing that his rider has got no hold of the toro. Well, you are just behind the bull, a little to the left of him, and out of the way of his hind legs, which will trip your horse up if you don't take care; you take your right foot out of the stirrup, catch hold of the end of the bull's tail (which is very long), throw your leg over it, and so twist the end of the tail round your leg below the knee. You have either got the bridle between your teeth or have let it go altogether, and with your left hand you give your horse a crack with the whip; he goes forward with a bound, and the bull, losing his balance by the sudden jerk behind, rolls over on the ground, and gets up, looking very uncomfortable. The faster the bull gallops, the easier it is to throw him over; and two boys of twelve or fourteen years of age coleered a couple of young bulls in the arena, in great style, pitching them over in all directions. The farmers and landed proprietors are immensely fond of both these sports, which the bulls—by the way—seem to dislike most thoroughly; but this exhibition in the bull-ring was better than what one generally sees, and the leperos were loud in their expressions of delight.

When we had been a week or two in the city of Mexico, we decided upon making an excursion to the great silver mining district of the Real del Monte. Some of our English friends were leaving for England, and had engaged the whole of the Diligence to Pachuca, going from thence up to the Real, and thence to Tampico, with all the pomp and circumstance of a train of carriages and an armed escort. We were invited to go with them as far as Pachuca; and accordingly we rose very early on the 28th of March, got some chocolate under difficulties, and started in the Diligence, seven grown-up people, and a baby, who was very good, and was spoken of and to as "leoncito." On the high plateaus of Mexico, the children of European parents grow up as healthy and strong as at home; it is only in the districts at a lower elevation above the sea, on the coasts for instance, that they do not thrive. Mr. G., who was leaving Mexico, was the head of a great merchant-house, and it was as a compliment to him and Mrs. G. that we were accompanied by a party of English horsemen for the first two or three leagues. Englishmen take much more easily to Mexican ways about horses than the Mexicans do to ours, and a finer turn-out of horses and riders than our amateur escort could hardly have been found in Mexico. There was our friend Don Guillermo, who rode a beautiful horse that had once belonged to the captain of a band of robbers, and had not its equal in the city for swiftness; and Don Juan on his splendid little brown horse Pancho, lazoing stray mules as he went, and every now and then galloping into a meadow by the roadside after a bull, who was off like a shot the moment he heard the sound of hoofs. I wonder whether I shall ever see them again, those jovial open-hearted countrymen of ours. At last our companions said good-bye, and loaded pistols were carefully arranged on the centre cushion in case of an attack, much to the edification of my companion and myself, as it rather implied that, if fighting were to be done, we two should have to sit inside to be shot at without a chance of hitting anybody in return.

The hedges of the Organ Cactus are a feature in the landscape of the plains, and we first saw them to perfection on the road between Mexico and Pachuca. This plant, the Cereus hexagonus, grows in Italy in the open air, but seems not to be turned to account anywhere except in Mexico for the purpose to which it is particularly suited. In its wild state it grows like a candelabrum, with a thick trunk a few feet high, from the top of which it sends out shoots, which, as soon as they have room, rise straight upwards in fluted pillars fifteen or twenty feet in height. Such a plant, with pillars rising side by side and almost touching one another, has a curious resemblance to an organ with its pipes, and thence its name "órgano."

To make a fence, they break off the straight lateral shoots, of the height required, and plant them closely side by side, in a trench, sufficiently deep to ensure their standing firmly; and it is a curious sight to see a labourer bearing on his shoulder one of these vegetable pillars, as high as himself, and carefully guarding himself against its spines. A hedge perfectly impassable is obtained at once; the cactus rooting so readily, that it is rare to see a gap where one has died. The villagers surround their gardens with these fences of cactus, which often line the road for miles together. Foreigners used to point out such villages to us, and remark that they seemed "well organized," a small joke which unfortunately bears translation into all ordinary European languages, and was inflicted without mercy upon us as new comers.

We reached Pachuca early in the afternoon, and took up our quarters in the inn there, and our friends went on to Real del Monte.

This little town of Pachuca has long been a place of some importance in the world, as regards mining-operations. The Aztecs worked silver-mines here, as well as at Tasco, long before the Spaniards came, and they knew how to smelt the ore. It is true that, if no better process than smelting were known now, most of the mines would scarcely be worth working; but still, to know how to extract silver at all was a great step; and indeed at that time, and for long after the Conquest, there was no better method known in Europe. It was in this very place that a Spaniard, Medina by name, discovered the process of amalgamation with mercury, in the year 1557, some forty years after the invasion. We went to see the place where he first worked his new process, and found it still used as a "hacienda de beneficio" (establishment for extracting silver from the ore.) So few discoveries in the arts have come out of Mexico, or indeed out of any Spanish colony, that we must make the most of this really very important method, which is more extensively used than any other, both in North and South America. As for the rest of the world, it produces, comparatively, so little silver, that it is scarcely worth taking into account.

We had forgotten, when we went to bed, that we were nearly seven hundred feet higher than Mexico; but had the fact brought to our remembrance by waking in the middle of the night, feeling very cold, and finding our thermometer marking 40 degrees Fahr.; whereupon we covered ourselves with cloaks, and the cloaks with the strips of carpet at our bedsides, and went to sleep again.

We had hired, of the French landlord, two horses and a mozo to guide us, and sorry hacks they were when we saw them in the morning. It was delightful to get a little circulation into our veins by going at the best gallop our horses would agree to; for we were fresh from hot countries, and not at all prepared for having our hands and feet numbed with cold, and being as hoarse as ravens —for the sore throat which is the nuisance of the district, and is very severe upon new comers, had not spared us. Evaporation is so rapid at this high altitude that if you wet the back of your hand it dries almost instantly, leaving a smart sensation of cold. One may easily suppose, that when people have been accustomed to live under the ordinary pressure of the air, their throats and lungs do not like being dried up at this rate; besides their having, on account of the rarity of the air, to work harder in breathing, in order to get in the necessary quantity of oxygen.

Coughs seem very common here, especially among the children, though people look strong and healthy, but in the absence of proper statistics one cannot undertake to say whether the district is a healthy one or not.

For a wonder we have a good road, and this simply because the Real del Monte Company wanted one, and made it for themselves. How unfortunate all Spanish countries are in roads, one of the most important first steps towards civilization! When one has travelled in Old Spain, one can imagine that the colonists did not bring over very enlightened ideas on the subject; and as the Mexicans were not allowed to hold intercourse with any other country, it is easy to explain why Mexico is all but impassable for carriages. But if the money—or half of it—that has been spent in building and endowing churches and convents had been devoted to road-making, this might have been a great and prosperous country.

For some three hours we rode along among porphyritic mountains, getting higher at every turn, and enjoying the clear bright air. Now and then we met or passed a long recua (train) of loaded mules, taking care to keep the safe side of the road till we were rid of them. It is not pleasant to meet a great drove of horned cattle in an Alpine pass, but I really think a recua of loaded mules among the Andes is worse. A knowing old beast goes first, and the rest come tumbling after him anyhow, with their loads often projecting a foot or two on either side, and banging against anybody or anything. Then, wherever the road is particularly narrow, and there is a precipice of two or three hundred feet to fall over, one or two of them will fall down, or get their packs loose, and so block up the road, and there is a general scrimmage of kicking and shoving behind, till the arrieros can get things straight again. At last we reach the top of a ridge, and see the little settlement of Real del Monte below us. It is more like a Cornish mining village than anything else; but of course the engine-houses, chimneys, and mine-sheds, built by Cornishmen in true Cornish fashion, go a long way towards making up the resemblance. The village is built on the awkwardest bit of ground possible, up and down on the side of a steep ravine, one house apparently standing on the roof of another; and it takes half a mile of real hard climbing to get from the bottom of the town to the top.

We put up our horses at a neat little inn kept by an old Englishwoman, and walked or climbed up to the Company's house. We made several new acquaintances at the Real, though we left within a few hours, intending to see the place thoroughly on our return.

One peculiarity of the Casa Grande—the great house of the Company—was the warlike appearance of everybody in it. The clerks were posting up the ledgers with loaded revolvers on the desk before them; the manager's room was a small arsenal, and the gentlemen rode out for exercise, morning and evening, armed to the teeth. Not that there is anything to be apprehended from robbers—indeed I should like to see any of the Mexican ladrones interfering with the Cornish miners, who would soon teach them better manners. I am inclined to think there is a positive pleasure in possessing and handling guns and pistols, whether they are likely to be of any use or not. Indeed, while travelling through the western and southern States of America, where such things are very generally carried, I was the possessor of a five-barrelled revolver, and admit that I derived an amount of mild satisfaction from carrying it about, and shooting at a mark with it, that amply compensated for the loss of two dollars I incurred by selling it to a Jew at New Orleans.

We rode on to Regla, soon finding that our guide had never been there before; so, next morning, we kept the two horses and dismissed him with ignominy. A fine road leads from the Real to Regla, for all the silver-ore from the mines is conveyed there to have the silver separated from it. My notes of our ride mention a great water-wheel: sections of porphyritic rocks, with enormous masses of alluvial soil lying upon them: steep ravines: arroyos, cut by mountain-streams, and forests of pine-trees—a thoroughly Alpine district altogether. At Regla it became evident that our letter of introduction was not a mere complimentary affair. There is not even a village there; it is only a great hacienda, belonging to the Company, with the huts of the workmen built near it. The Company, represented by Mr. Bell, received us with the greatest hospitality. Almost before the letter was opened our horses and mozo were off to the stables, our room was ready, and our dinner being prepared as fast as might be. What a pleasant evening we had, after our long day's work! We had a great wood-fire, and sat by it, talking and looking at Mr. Bell's photographs and minerals, which serve as an amusement in his leisure-hours. The Company's Administrador leads rather a peculiar life here. There is no want of work or responsibility; he has two or three hundred Indians to manage, almost all of whom will steal and cheat without the slightest scruple, if they can but get a chance; he has to assay the ores, superintend a variety of processes which require the greatest skill and judgment, and he is in charge of property to the value of several hundred thousand pounds. Then a man must have a constitution of iron to live in a place where the air is so rarefied, and where the temperature varies thirty and forty degrees between morning and noon. As for society, he must find it in his own family; for even the better class of Mexicans are on so different a level, intellectually, from an educated Englishman, that their society bores him utterly, and he had rather be left in solitude than have to talk to them. Well, it is a great advantage to travellers that circumstances fix pleasant people in such out-of-the-way places.

One necessary part of a hacienda is a church. The proprietors are compelled by law to build one, and pay the priest's fees for mass on Sundays and feast-days. Now, almost all the English one meets with engaged in business, or managing mines and plantations, are Scotch, and one may well suppose that there is not much love lost between them and the priests. The father confessor plays an important part in the great system of dishonesty that prevails to so monstrous an extent throughout the country. He hears the particulars of the thefts and cheatings that have been practised on the proprietor who builds his church and pays for his services, and he complacently absolves his penitents in consideration of a small penance. Not a word about restitution; and just a formal injunction to go and sin no more, which neither priest nor penitent is very sincere about. The various evils of the Roman Catholic system have been reiterated till the subject has become tiresome, but this particular practice is so contrary to the simplest notions of morality, and has produced such fearful effects on the character of this nation, that one cannot pass it by without notice. If the Superintendent should roast the parish priest in front of the oxidising furnace, till he confessed all he knew about the thefts of his parishioners from the Company, he would tell strange stories,—how Juan Fernandez carried off sixpennyworth of silver in each car every day for a month; and how Pedro Alvarado (the Indian names have almost disappeared except in a few families, and Spanish names have been substituted) had a hammer with a hollow handle, like the stick that Sancho Panza delivered his famous judgment about, and carried away silver in it every day when he left work; and how Vasco Nuñez stole the iron key from the gate (which cost two dollars to replace), walking twenty miles and losing a day's work in order to sell it, and eventually getting but twopence for it; and plenty more stories of the same kind. The Padre at Regla, we heard, was not given to preaching sermons, but had lately favoured his congregation with a very striking one, to the effect that the Company paid him only three dollars a time for saying mass, and that he ought to have four.

Almost every traveller who visits Mexico enlarges on the dishonesty which is rooted in the character of the people. That they are worse now in this respect than they were before the Conquest is highly probable. Their position as a conquered and enslaved people, tended, as it always does, to foster the slavish vices of dissimulation and dishonesty. The religion brought into the country by the Spanish missionaries concerned itself with their belief, and left their morals to shift for themselves, as it does still.

In the mining-districts stealing is universal. Public feeling among the Indians does not condemn it in the least, quite the contrary. To steal successfully is considered a triumph, and to be found out is no disgrace. Theft is not even punishable. In old times a thief might be put in the stocks; but Burkart, who was a mining-inspector for many years, says that in his time, some twenty years ago, tins was abolished, and I believe the law has not been altered since. It is a miserable sight to see the Indian labourers searched as they come out of the mines. They are almost naked, but rich ore packs in such a small compass, and they are so ingenious in stowing it away, that the doorkeepers examine their mouths and ears, and their hair, and constantly find pieces that have been secreted, while a far greater quantity escapes. It is this system of thieving that accounts for the existence of certain little smelting-sheds, close to the works of the Company, who look at them with such feelings as may be imagined. These places profess to smelt ore from one or two little mines in the neighbourhood, but their real object is no secret. They buy the stolen bits of rich ore from the Indian labourers, giving exactly half the value for it.

Of course, we must not judge these Mexican labourers as though we had a very high standard of honesty at home. That we should see workmen searched habitually in England, at the doors of our national dock-yards, is a much greater disgrace to us. And not merely a disgrace, but a serious moral evil, for to expose an honest man to such a degradation is to make him half a thief already.

People who know the Indian population best assure us that their lives are a perpetual course of intrigue and dissimulation. Always trying to practise some small fraud upon their masters, and even upon their own people, they are in constant fear that every one is trying to overreach them. They are afraid to answer the simplest question, lest it should be a trap laid to catch them. They ponder over every word and action of their European employers, to find out what hidden intrigue lies beneath, and to devise some counter-plot. Sartorius says that when he has met an Indian and asked his name, the brown man always gave a false one, lest the enquirer should want to do him some harm.

Never did any people show more clearly the effects of ages of servitude and oppression; but, hopeless as the moral condition of this mining population seems, there is one favourable circumstance to be put on record. The Cornish miners, who have been living among them for years, have worked quite perceptibly upon the Indian character by the example of their persevering industry, their love of saving, and their utter contempt for thieves and liars.

Instead of squandering their wages, or burying them in the ground, many of the Indian miners take their savings to the Banks; and the opinions of the foreigners are gradually—though very slowly—altering the popular standard of honesty, the first step towards the moral improvement of the Mexican population.

In the morning we went off for an excursion, having got a lively young fellow from the hacienda in exchange for our stupid mozo. There was hoar frost on the ground, and the feeling of cold was intense at first; but the sun began to warm the ground about eight o'clock, and we were soon glad to fasten our great coats and shawls to our saddles. Three leagues took us to the town of Atotonilco el Grande, which gives its name to the plateau we were crossing. Here we are no longer in the valley of Mexico, which is separated from this plain by the mountains of the Real del Monte. We rode on two leagues more to the village of Soquital where, it being Sunday, we found the inhabitants—mostly Indians—amusing themselves by standing in the sun, doing nothing. I can hardly say "doing nothing," though, for we went into the tienda, or shop, and found a brisk trade going on in raw spirits. *Tienda*, in Spanish, means a tent or booth. The first shops were tents or booths at fairs or in market-places; and thence "tienda" came to mean a shop in general; a derivation which corresponds with that of the word "shop" itself. Such of the population as had money seemed to drop in at regular intervals for a dram, which consisted of a small wine-glassful of white-corn-brandy, called *chinguerito*. We tasted some, while the people at the shop were frying eggs and boiling beans for our breakfast; and found it so strong that a small sip brought tears into our eyes, to the amusement of the bystanders. It seemed that everybody was drinking who could afford it; from the old men and women to the babies in their mothers' arms; everybody had a share, except those who were hard up, and they stood about the door looking stolidly at the drinkers. There was nothing like gaiety in the whole affair; only a sort of satisfaction appeared in the face of each as he took his dose. It is the drinkers of pulque who get furiously drunk, and fight; here it is different. These drinkers of spirits are not much given to that enormous excess that kills off the Red Indians; indeed, they are seldom drunk enough to lose their wits, and they never have delirium tremens, which would come upon a European, with much less provocation. They get into a habit of daily—almost hourly—dram-drinking, and go on, year after year, in this way; seeming, as far as we could judge, to live a long while, such a life as it is. As we mounted our horses and rode on, we agreed that we had seldom seen a more melancholy and depressing sight.

We met some arrieros, who had brought up salt from the coast; and they, seeing that we were English, judged we had something to do with mines, and proposed to sell us their goods. The price of salt here is actually three-pence per lb., in a district where its consumption is immense, as it is used in refining the silver ore. It must be said, however, that this is an unusual price; for the muleteers have been so victimised by their mules being seized, either by the government or the rebels (one seems about as bad as the other in this respect), that they must have a high price to pay them for the risk. Generally seven reals, or 3s. 6d. per arroba of 25 lbs. is the price. This salt is evaporated in the salinas of Campeche, taken by water to Tuzpan, and then brought up the country on mules' backs—each beast carrying 300 lbs. Of course, this salt is very coarse and very watery; all salt made in this way is. It suits the New Orleans people better to import salt from England, than to make it in this way in the Gulf of Mexico, though the water there is very salt, and the sun very hot. The fact, that it pays to carry salt on mules' backs, tells volumes about the state of the country. At the lowest computation, the mules would do four or five times as much work if they were set to draw any kind of cart—however rough—on a carriageable road. It is true that there is some sort of road from here to Tampico, but an English waggoner would not acknowledge it by that name at all; and the muleteers are still in possession of most of the traffic in this district, as indeed they are over almost all the country.

It was mid-day by this time; and, as we could not get to the Rio Grande without taking our chance for the night in some Indian rancho, we turned back. The heat had become so oppressive that we took off our coats; and Mr. Christy, riding in his shirt-sleeves and holding a white umbrella over his head, which he had further protected with a turban, declared that even in the East he had not had so fatiguing a ride. We passed through Soquital, and there the natives were idling and drinking spirits as before, and seemed hardly to have moved since we left. This plateau of Atotonilco el Grande, called for shortness Grande, is, like most of the high plains of Mexico, composed mostly of porphyry and obsidian, a valley filled up with débris from the surrounding mountains, which are all volcanic, embedded in reddish earth. The mountain-torrents—in which the water, so to speak, comes down all at once, not flowing in a steady stream all the year round as in England—have left evidences of their immense power in the ravines with which the sides of the hills, from their very tops downward, are fluted.

These fluted mountain-ridges resemble the "Kamms" (combs) of the Swiss Alps, called so from their toothed appearance.

We had met numbers of Indians, bringing their wares to the Sunday market in the great square of Atotonilco el Grande; and when we reached the town on our way home, business was still going on briskly; so we put up our horses, and spent an hour or two in studying the people and the commodities they dealt in. It was a real old-fashioned Indian market, very much such as the Spaniards found when they first penetrated into the country. A large proportion of the people could speak no Spanish, or only a few words. The unglazed pottery, palm-leaf mats, ropes and bags of aloe-fibre, dressed skins, &c., were just the same wares that were made three centuries ago; and there is no improvement in their manufacture. This people, who rose in three centuries from the condition of wandering savages to a height of civilization that has no equal in history—considering the shortness of the time in which it grew up—have remained, since the Conquest, without making one step in advance. They hardly understand any reason for what they do, except that their ancestors did things so—they therefore must be right. They make their unglazed pottery, and carry it five and twenty miles to market on their heads, just as they used to do when there were no beasts of burden in the country. The same with their fruits and vegetables, which they have brought great distances, up the most difficult mountain-paths, at a ruinous sacrifice of time and trouble, considering what a miserable sum they will get for them after all, and how much even of this will be spent in brandy. By working on a hacienda they would get double what their labour produces in this way, but they do not understand this kind of reasoning. They cultivate their little patches of maize, by putting a sharp stick into the ground, and dropping the seed into the hole. They carry pots of water to irrigate their ground with, instead of digging trenches. This is the more curious, as at the time of the Conquest irrigation was much practised by the Aztecs in the plains, and remains of water-canals still exist, showing that they had carried the art to great perfection. They bring logs of wood over the mountains by harnessing horses or mules to them, and dragging them with immense labour over the rough ground. The idea of wheels or rollers has either not occurred to them, or is considered as a pernicious novelty.

It is very striking to see how, while Europeans are bringing the newest machinery and the most advanced arts into the country, there is scarcely any symptom of improvement among the people, who still hold firmly to the wisdom of their ancestors. An American author, Mayer, quotes a story of a certain people in Italy, as an illustration of the feeling of the Indians in Mexico respecting improvements. In this district, he says that the peasants loaded their panniers with vegetables on one side, and balanced the opposite pannier by filling it with stones; and when a traveller pointed out the advantage to be gained by loading both panniers with vegetables, he was answered that their forefathers from time immemorial had so carried their produce to market, that they were wise and good men, and that a stranger showed very little understanding or decency who interfered in the established customs of a country. I need hardly say that the Indians are utterly ignorant; and this of course accounts to a great extent for their obstinate conservatism.

There were several shops round the market-place at Grande, and the brandy-drinking was going on much as at Soquital. The shops in these small towns are general stores, like "the shop" in coal- and iron-districts in England. It is only in large towns that the different retail-trades are separated. One thing is very noticeable in these country stores, the certainty of finding a great stock of sardines in bright tin boxes. The idea of finding *Sardines à l'huile* in Indian villages seemed odd enough; but the fact is, that the difficulty of getting fish up from the coast is so great that these sardines are not much dearer than anything else, and they go a long way. Montezuma's method of supplying his table with fresh fish from the gulf, by having relays of Indian porters to run up with it, is too expensive for general use, and there is no efficient substitute. It is in consequence of this scarcity of fish, that Church-fasts have never been very strictly kept in Mexico.

The method of keeping accounts in the shops—which, it is to be remembered, are almost always kept by white or half-white people, hardly ever by Indians—is primitive enough. Here is a score which I copied, the hieroglyphics standing for dollars, half-dollars, medios or half-reals, cuartillos or quarter-reals, and tlacos—or clacos—which are eighths of a real, or about 3/4d. While account-keeping among the comparatively educated trades-people is in this condition, one can easily understand how very limited the Indian notions of calculation are. They cannot realize any number much over ten; and twenty—cempoalli—is with them the symbol of a great number, as a hundred was with the Greeks. There is in Mexico a mountain called in this indefinite way "Cempoatepetl"—the twenty-mountain. Sartorius mentions the Indian name of the many-petaled marigold—"cempoaxochitl"—the twenty-flower. We traded for some trifles of aloe-fibre, but soon had to count up the reckoning with beans.

I have delayed long enough for the present over the Indians and their market; so, though there is much more to be said about them, I will only add a few words respecting the commodities for sale, and then leave them for awhile.

There seemed to be a large business doing in costales (bags) made of aloe-fibre, for carrying ore about in the mines. True to the traditions of his ancestors, the Indian much prefers putting his load in a bag on his back, to the far easier method of wheeling it about. Lazos sold at one to four reals, (6d. to 2s.) according to quality. There are two kinds of aloe-fibre; one coarse, *ichtli*, the other much finer, *pito*; the first made from the great aloe that produces pulque, the other from a much smaller species of the same genus. The stones with which the boiled maize is ground into the paste of which the universal tortillas are made were to be had here; indeed, they are made in the neighbourhood, of the basalt and lava which abound in the district. The metate is a sort of little table, hewn out of the basalt, with four little feet, and its surface is curved from the ends to the middle. The metalpile is of the same material, and like a rolling-pin. The old-fashioned Mexican pottery I have mentioned already. It is beautifully made, and very cheap. They only asked us nine-pence for a great olla, or boiling-pot, that held four or five gallons, and no doubt this was double the market-price. I never so thoroughly realized before how climate is altered by altitude above the sea as in noticing the fruits and vegetables that were being sold at this little market, within fifteen or twenty miles of which they were all grown. There were wheat and barley, and the piñones (the fruit of the stone-pine, which grows in Italy, and is largely used instead of almonds); and from these representatives of temperate climates the list extended to bananas and zapotes, grown at the bottom of the great barrancas, 3,000 or 4,000 feet lower in level than the plateau, though in distance but a few miles off. Three or four thousand miles of latitude would not give a greater difference.

It would never do to be late, and break our necks in one of the awkward water-courses that cut the plateau about in all directions; so we started homewards, soon having to unfasten great-coats and shawls from our saddles, to keep out the cold of the approaching sunset; and so we got back to the hospitable hacienda, and were glad to warm ourselves at the fire.

Next morning, we went off to get a view of the great barranca of Regla. A ride over the hills brought us to a wood of oaks, with their branches fringed with the long grey Spanish moss, and a profusion of epiphytes clinging to their bark, some splendidly in flower, showing the fantastic shapes and brilliant colours one sees in English orchid-houses. Cactuses of many species complete the picture of the vegetation in this beautiful spot. This is at the top of the barranca. Then imagine a valley a mile or two in width, with sides almost perpendicular and capped with basaltic pillars, and at the bottom a strip of land where the vegetation is of the deepest green of the tropics, with a river winding along among palm-trees and bananas. This great barranca is between two and three thousand feet deep, and the view is wonderful. We went down a considerable way by a zig-zag road, my companion collecting armfuls of plants by the way, but unfortunately losing his thermometer, which could not be found, though a long hunt for it produced a great many more plants, and so the trouble was not wasted. The prickly pear was covered with ripe purple fruit a little way down, and we refreshed ourselves with them, I managing—in my clumsiness—to get into my fingers two or three of the little sheaves of needles which are planted on the outside of the fruit, and thus providing myself with occupation for leisure moments for three or four days after in taking them out.

Many species of cactus, and the nopal, or prickly pear, especially, are full of watery sap, which trickles out in a stream when they are pierced. In these thirsty regions, when springs and brooks are dry, the cattle bite them to get at the moisture, regardless of the thorns. On the north coast of Africa the camels delight in crunching the juicy leaves of the same plant. I have often been amused in watching the camel-drivers' efforts to get their trains of laden beasts along the narrow sandy lanes of Tangier, between hedges of prickly pears, where the camels with their long necks could reach the tempting lobes on both sides of the way.

In this thirsty season, while the cattle in the Mexican plains derive moisture from the cactus, the aloe provides for man a substitute for water. It frequently happened to us to go from rancho to rancho asking for water in vain, though pulque was to be had in abundance.

To attempt any description of the varied forms of cactus in Mexico would be out of the question. In the northern provinces alone, botanists have described above eight hundred species. The most striking we met with were the prickly pear (cactus opuntia), the órgano, the night-blowing cereus, the various mamillarias—dome-shaped mounds covered with thorns, varying in diameter from an inch to six or eight feet—and the greybeard, *el viejo*, "the old man," as our guide called them, upright pillars like street-posts, and covered with grey wool-like filaments.

Getting to the top of the ravine again, we found an old Indian milking an aloe, which flourishes here, though a little further down the climate is too hot for it to produce pulque. This old gentleman had a long gourd, of the shape and size of a great club, but hollow inside, and very light. The small end of this gourd was pushed in among the aloe-leaves into the hollow made by scooping out the inside of the plant, and in which the sweet juice, the aguamiel, collects. By having a little hole at each end of the gourd, and sucking at the large end, the hollow of the plant emptied itself into the Acocote, (in proper Mexican,*Acocotl*, Water-throat), as this queer implement is called. Then the Indian stopped the hole at the end he had been sucking at, with his finger, and dexterously emptied the contents of the gourd into a pig-skin which he carried at his back. We went up with the old man to his rancho, and tested his pulque, which was very good, though we could not say the same of his domestic arrangements. It puzzled us not a little to see people living up at this height in houses built of sticks, such as are used in the hot lands, and hardly affording any protection from the weather, severe as it is here. The pulque is taken to market in pig-skins, which, though the pig himself is taken out of them, still retain his shape very accurately; and when nearly full of liquor, they roll about on their backs, and kick up the little dumpy legs that are left them, in the most comical and life-like way. When we went away we bought the old man's acocote, and carried it home in triumph, and is it not in the Museum at Kew Gardens to this day? *(See the illustration at page 36.)*

At the hacienda of Regla are to be seen on a large scale most of the processes which are employed in the extraction of silver from the ore—the *beneficio*, or making good, as it is called.

In the great yard, numbers of men and horses were walking round and round upon the "tortas," tarts or pies, as they are called, consisting of powdered ore mixed with water, so as to form a circular bed of mud a foot deep. To this mud, sulphate of copper, salt, and quicksilver are added, and the men and mules walk round and round in it, mixing it thoroughly together, a process which is kept up, with occasional intervals of rest, for nearly two months. By that time the whole of the silver has formed an amalgam with the mercury, and this amalgam is afterwards separated from the earth by being trampled under water in troughs. We were surprised to find that men and horses could pass their lives in wading through mud containing mercury in a state of fine division without absorbing it into their bodies, but neither men nor horses suffer from it.

We happened to visit the melting-house one evening, while silver and lead were being separated by oxidizing the lead in a reverberatory furnace. Here we noticed a curious effect. The melted litharge ran from the mouth of the furnace upon a floor of damp sand, and spread over it in a sheet. Presently, as the heat of the mass vaporized the water in the sand below, the sheet of litharge, still slightly fluid, began to heave and swell, and a number of small cones rose from its surface. Some of these cones reached the height of four inches, and then burst at the top, sending out a shower of red-hot fragments. I removed one of these cones when the litharge was cool. It had a regular funnel-shaped crater, like that which Vesuvius had until three or four years ago.

The analogy is complete between these little cones and those on the lava-field at the foot of the volcano of Jorullo, the celebrated "hornitos;" the concentric structure of which, as described by Burkart, proves that they were formed in precisely the same manner. Until lately, the formation of the great cone of Jorullo was attributed to the same kind of action as the hornitos, but later travellers have established the fact that this is incorrect. One of the De Saussure family, who was in Mexico a few years back, describes Jorullo as consisting of three terraces of basaltic lava, which have flowed one above another from a central orifice, the whole being surmounted by a cone of lapilli thrown up from the same opening, from which also later streams of lava have issued.

The celebrated cascade of Regla is just behind the hacienda. There is a sort of basin, enclosed on three sides by a perpendicular wall of basaltic columns, some eighty feet high. On the side opposite the opening, a mountain stream has cut a deep notch in this wall, and pours down in a cascade. The basaltic pillars rest upon an undisturbed layer of basaltic conglomerate five feet thick, and that upon a bed of clay. The place is very picturesque; and two great

Yuccas which project over the waterfall, crowned with their star-like tufts of pointed leaves, have a strange effect. These basalt-columns are very regular, with from five to eight sides; and are almost black in colour. They have a curiously well-defined circular core in the middle, five or six inches in diameter. This core is light grey, almost white. The Indians bring down numbers of short lengths or joints of the columns, and they are used at the hacienda in making a primitive kind of ore-crushing mill, in which they are dragged round and round by mule-power, on a floor also of basalt.

When we had visited the falls we took leave of our hospitable friend, and set off to return to the Real. We stopped at San Miguel, another of the haciendas of the Company, where the German barrel-process is worked. Just behind the hacienda is the Ojo de Agua—the Eye of Water—a beautiful basin, surrounded by a green sward and a wood of oaks and fir-trees. A little stream takes its rise from the spring which bubbles up into this basin, and the name "Ojo de Agua," is a general term applied to such fountain-heads. When one looks down from a high hill upon one of these Eyes of Water, one sees how the name came to be given, and indeed, the idiom is thousands of years older than the Spanish tongue, and belongs as well to the Hebrew and Arabic. A Mexican calls a lake *atezcatl*, Water-Mirror, an expressive word, which reminds one of the German *Wasserspiegel*.

Soon after nightfall we got back to the English inn, and went to bed without any further event happening, except the burning of some outhouses, which we went out to see. The custom of roofing houses with pine-shingles ("tacumeniles"), and the general use of wood for building all the best houses, make fires very common here. During the few days we spent in the Real district, I find in my notebook mention of three fires which we saw. We spent the next day in resting, and in visiting the mine-works near at hand. The day after, an Englishman who had lived many years at the Real offered to take us out for a day's ride; and the Company's Administrador lent us two of his own horses, for the poor beasts from Pachuca could hardly have gone so far. The first place we visited was Peñas Cargadas, the "loaded rocks." Riding through a thick wood of oaks and pines, we came suddenly in view of several sugar-loaf peaks, some three hundred feet high, tapering almost to a point at the top, and each one crowned with a mass of rocks which seem to have been balanced in unstable equilibrium on its point,—looking as though the first puff of wind would bring them down. The pillars were of porphyritic conglomerate, which had been disintegrated and worn away by wind and rain; while the great masses resting on them, probably of solid porphyry, had been less affected by these influences. It was the most curious example of the weathering of rocks that we had ever seen. From Peñas Cargadas we rode on to the farm of Guajalote, where the Company has forests, and cuts wood and burns charcoal for the mines and the refining works. Don Alejandro, the tenant of the farm, was a Scotchman, and a good fellow. He could not go on with us, for he had invited a party of neighbours to eat up a kid that had been cooked in a hole in the ground, with embers upon it, after Sandwich Island fashion. This is called a *barbacoa*—a barbecue. We should have liked to be at the feast, but time was short, so we rode on to the top of Mount Jacal, 12,000 feet above the sea, where there was a view of mountains and valleys, and heat that was positively melting. Thence down to the Cerro de Navajas, the "hill of knives." It is on the sides of this hill that obsidian is found in enormous quantities. Before the conquerors introduced the use of iron, these deposits were regularly mined, and this place was the Sheffield of Mexico.

We were curious to see all that was to be seen; for Mr. Christy's Mexican collection, already large before our visit, and destined to become much larger, contained numbers of implements and weapons of this very peculiar material. Any one who does not know obsidian may imagine great masses of bottle-glass, such as our orthodox ugly wine-bottles are made of, very hard, very brittle, and—if one breaks it with any ordinary implement—going, as glass does, in every direction but the right one. We saw its resemblance to this portwine-bottle-glass in an odd way at the Ojo de Agua, where the wall of the hacienda was armed at the top, after our English fashion, apparently with bits of old bottles, but which turned out to be chips of obsidian. Out of this rather unpromising stuff the Mexicans made knives, razors, arrow- and spear-heads, and other things, some of great beauty. I say nothing of the polished obsidian mirrors and ornaments, nor even of the curious masks of the human face that are to be seen in collections, for these were only laboriously cut and polished with jewellers' sand, to us a common-place process.

Cortes found the barbers at the great market of Tlatelolco busy shaving the natives with such razors, and he and his men had experience of other uses of the same material in the flights of obsidian-headed arrows which "darkened the sky," as they said, and the more deadly wooden maces stuck all over with obsidian points, and of the priests' sacrificial knives too, not long after. These things were not cut and polished, but made by chipping or cracking off pieces from a lump. This one can see by the traces of conchoidal fracture which they all show.

The art is not wholly understood, for it perished soon after the Conquest, when iron came in; but, as far as the theory is concerned, I think I can give a tolerably satisfactory account of the process of manufacture. In the first place, the workman who makes gun-flints could probably make some of the simpler obsidian implements, which were no doubt chipped off in the same way. The section of a gun-flint, with its one side flat for sharpness and the other side ribbed for strength, is one of the characteristics of obsidian knives. That the flint knives of Scandinavia were made by chipping off strips from a mass is proved by the many-sided prisms occasionally found there, and particularly by that one which was discovered just where it had been worked, with the knives chipped off it lying close by, and fitting accurately into their places upon it.

Now to make the case complete, we ought to find such prisms in Mexico; and, accordingly, some months ago, when I examined the splendid Mexican collection of Mr. Uhde at Heidelberg, I found one or two. No one seemed to have suspected their real nature, and they had been classed as maces, or the handles of some kind of weapon.

I should say from memory that they were seven or eight inches long, and as large as one could conveniently grasp; and one or both of them, as if to remove all doubt as to what they were, had the stripping off of ribbons not carried quite round them, but leaving an intermediate strip rough. There is another point about the obsidian knives which requires confirmation. One can often see, on the ends of the Scandinavian flint knives, the bruise made by the blow of the hard stone with which they were knocked off. I did not think of looking to this point when at Mr. Uhde's museum, but the only obsidian knife I have seen since seems to be thus bruised at the end.

Once able to break his obsidian straight, the workman has got on a long way in his trade, for a large proportion of the articles he has to make are formed by planes intersecting one another in various directions. But the Mexican knives are generally not pointed, but turned up at the end, as one may bend up a druggist's spatula. This peculiar shape is not given to answer a purpose, but results from the natural fracture of the stone.

Even then, the way of making several implements or weapons is not entirely clear. We got several obsidian maces or lance-heads—one about ten inches long—which were taper from base to point, and covered with taper flutings; and there are other things which present great difficulties. I have heard on good authority, that somewhere in Peru, the Indians still have a way of working obsidian by laying a bone wedge on the surface of a piece, and tapping it till the stone cracks. Such a process may have been used in Mexico.

We may see in museums beautiful little articles made in this intractable material, such as the mirrors and masks I have mentioned, and even rings and cups. But, as I have said, these are mere lapidaries' work.

The situation of the mines was picturesque; grand hills of porphyritic rock, and pine-forest everywhere. Not far off is the broad track of a hurricane, which had walked through it for miles, knocking the great trees down like ninepins, and leaving them to rot there. The vegetation gave evident proof of a severe climate; and yet the heat and glare of the sun were more intolerable than we had ever felt it in the region of sugar-canes and bananas. About here, some of the trachytic porphyry which forms the substance of the hills had happened to have cooled, under suitable conditions, from the molten state into a sort of slag or volcanic glass, which is the obsidian in question; and, in places, this vitreous lava—from one layer having flowed over another which was already cool—was regularly stratified.

The mines were mere wells, not very deep; with horizontal workings into the obsidian where it was very good and in thick layers. Round about were heaps of fragments, hundreds of tons of them; and it was clear, from the shape of these, that some of the manufacturing was done on the spot. There had been great numbers of pits worked; and it was from these "minillas," little mines, as they are called, that we first got an idea how important an element this obsidian was in the old Aztec civilization. In excursions made since, we travelled over whole districts in the plains, where fragments of these arrows and knives were to be found, literally at every step, mixed with morsels of pottery, and here and there a little clay idol. Among the heaps of fragments were many that had become weathered on the upper side, and had a remarkable lustre, like silver. Obsidian is called *bizcli* by the Indians, and the silvery sort is known as *bizcli platera*. They often find bits of it in the fields; and go with great secrecy and mystery to Mr. Bell, or some other authority in mining matters, and confide to him their discovery of a silver-mine. They go away angry and unconvinced when told what their silver really is; and generally come to the conclusion that he is deceiving them, with a view of throwing them off the scent, that he may find the place for himself, and cheat them of their share of the profits—just what their own miserable morbid cunning would lead them to do under such circumstances.

The family-likeness that exists among the stone tools and weapons found in so many parts of the world is very remarkable. The flint-arrows of North America, such as Mr. Longfellow's arrow-maker used to work at in the land of the Dacotahs, and which, in the wild northern states of Mexico, the Apaches and Comanches use to this day, might be easily mistaken for the weapons of our British ancestors, dug up on the banks of the Thames. It is true that the finish of the Mexican obsidian implements far exceeds that of the chipped flint and agate weapons of Scandinavia, and still more those of England, Switzerland, and Italy, where they are dug up in such quantities, in deposits of alluvial soil, and in bone-caves in the limestone rocks. But this higher finish we may attribute partly to the superiority of the material; for the Mexicans also used flint to some extent, and their flint weapons are as hard to distinguish by inspection as those from other parts of the world. We may reasonably suppose, moreover, that the skill of the Mexican artificer increased when he found a better material than flint to work upon. Be this as it may, an inspection of any good collection of such articles shows the much higher finish of the obsidian implements than of those of flint, agate, and rock-crystal. They say there is an ingenious artist who makes flint arrow-heads and stone axes for the benefit of English antiquarians, and earns good profits by it: I should like to give him an order for ribbed obsidian razors and spear-heads; I don't think he would make much of them.

The wonderful similarity of character among the stone weapons found in different parts of the world has often been used by ethnologists as a means of supporting the theory that this and other arts were carried over the world by tribes migrating from one common centre of creation of the human species. The argument has not much weight, and a larger view of the subject quite supersedes it.

We may put the question in this way. In Asia and in Europe the use of stone tools and weapons has always characterized a very low state of civilization; and such implements are only found among savage tribes living by the chase, or just beginning to cultivate the ground and to emerge from the condition of mere barbarians. Now, if the Mexicans got their civilization from Europe, it must have been from some people unacquainted with the use of iron, if not of bronze. Iron abounds in Mexico, not only in the state of ore, but occurring nearly pure in aerolites of great size, as at Cholula, and at Zacatecas, not far from the great ruins there; so that the only reason for their not using it must have been ignorance of its qualities.

The Arabian Nights' story of the mountain which consisted of a single loadstone finds its literal fulfilment in Mexico. Not far from Huetamo, on the road towards the Pacific, there is a conical hill composed entirely of magnetic iron-ore. The blacksmiths in the neighbourhood, with no other apparatus than their common forges, make it directly into wrought iron, which they use for all ordinary purposes.

Now, in supposing civilization to be transmitted from one country to another, we must measure it by the height of its lowest point, as we measure the strength of a chain by the strength of the weakest link. The only civilization that the Mexicans can have received from the Old World must have been from some people whose cutting implements were of sharp stone, consequently, as we must conclude by analogy, some very barbarous and ignorant tribe.

From this point we must admit that the inhabitants of Mexico raised themselves, independently, to the extraordinary degree of culture which distinguished them when Europeans first became aware of their existence. The curious distribution of their knowledge shows plainly that they found it for themselves, and did not receive it by transmission. We find a wonderful acquaintance with astronomy, even to such details as the real cause of eclipses,

—and the length of the year given by intercalations of surprising accuracy; and, at the same time, no knowledge whatever of the art of writing alphabetically, for their hieroglyphics are nothing but suggestive pictures. They had earned the art of gardening to a high degree of perfection; but, though there were two kinds of ox, and the buffalo at no great distance from them, in the countries they had already passed through in their migration from the north, they had no idea of the employment of beasts of burden, nor of the use of milk. They were a great trading people, and had money of several kinds in general use, but the art of weighing was utterly unknown to them; while, on the other hand, the Peruvians habitually used scales and weights, but had no idea of the use of money.

To return to the stone knives; the Mexicans may very well have invented the art themselves, as they did so many others; or they may have received it from the Old World. The things themselves prove nothing either way.

The real proof of their having, at some early period, communicated with inhabitants of Europe or Asia rests upon the traditions current among them, which are recorded by the early historians, and confirmed by the Aztec picture-writings; and upon several extraordinary coincidences in the signs used by them in reckoning astronomical cycles. Further on I shall allude to these traditions.

On the whole, the most probable view of the origin of the Mexican tribes seems to be the one ordinarily held, that they really came from the Old World, bringing with them several legends, evidently the same as the histories recorded in the book of Genesis. This must have been, however, at a time, when they were quite a barbarous, nomadic tribe; and we must regard their civilization as of independent and far later growth.

We rode back through the woods to Guajalote, where the Mexican cook had made us a feast after the manner of the country, and from her experience of foreigners had learnt to temper the chile to our susceptible throats. Decidedly the Mexicans are not without ideas in the matter of cookery. We stayed talking with the hospitable Don Alejandro and his sister till it was all but dark, and then rode back to the Real, admiring the fire-flies that were darting about by thousands, and listening to our companion's stories, which turned on robberies and murders——as stories are apt to do in wild places after dark. But, save an escape from being robbed some twenty years back, and the history of an Indian who was murdered just here by some of his own people, for a few shillings he was taking home, our friend had not much reason to give for the two huge horse-pistols ho carried, ready for action. His story of the death of a German engineer in these parts is worth recording here. He was riding home one dark night, with a companion; and, trusting to his knowledge of the country, tried a short cut through the woods, among the old open mines near the Regla road. They had quite passed all the dangerous places, he thought, so he gave his horse the spur, and plunged sheer down a shaft, hundreds of feet deep. His friend pulled up in time, and got home safely.

We had one more day among the mines, and then went back to Pachuca, and next day to Mexico in the Diligence. Everywhere the same hospitality and good-natured interest in us and our doings, often shown by people with whom we had hardly the slightest acquaintance. Travelling here is very different from what it is in a country on which the shadow of Murray's Handbook has fallen.

Almost all the interest Europe takes in Mexico, politically and commercially, turns upon the exportation of silver. The gold, cochineal, and vanilla are of small account. It is the silver dollars that pay for the Manchester goods, woollens, hardware, and many other things—those ubiquitous boxes of sardines à l'huile, for instance. The Mexicans send to Europe some five millions sterling in silver every year, that is, about twelve shillings apiece for all the population. It is just about what their government spends annually in promoting the maladministration of the country (and, looking at the matter in that point of view, they don't do their work badly for the money). The income of the Mexican church is not quite so much, but not far off.

Baron Humboldt has expressed a hope that, at some future day, the Mexicans will turn their attention to producing articles of real intrinsic value, and not those which are merely a sign to represent it. He tells us, quite feelingly, how the Peace of Amiens stopped the working of the iron-mines that had been opened when they could get no iron from abroad; for, when trade was reopened, people preferred buying in Europe probably a better article at one-third the price. He even hopes an enlightened government will encourage (that is, protect) more useful industries. This was written fifty years ago, though. If an enlightened government will give people some security for life and property, and make reasonable laws, and execute them,—leaving men of business to find out for themselves how it suits them to employ their capital, it seems probable that the balance between articles of real value and articles of imaginary value will adjust itself, perhaps better than an enlightened government could do it. The Mexican government has, unfortunately, followed Humboldt's advice in some respects. Cotton goods, woollens, and hardware are thus protected. We may sum up the statistics of the Mexican cotton-manufacture in a rough way thus,—taking merely into question the coarse cotton cloth called *manta*, and used principally by the Indians. We may reckon roughly that for this article alone the Mexicans have to pay a million sterling annually more than they could get it for if there were no protection-duty. The only advantage anybody gets by this is that a certain part of the population is employed in a manufacture unsuited to the country, and is thus taken away from work that may be done profitably. The actual amount of money paid in wages to the class of operatives thus forced into existence is much *less* than the amount which the country forfeits for the sake of making its manta at home. Thus a sum actually amounting to a third of the annual taxation of the country is thrown away upon this one article; and more goes the same way, to encourage similar unprofitable manufactures.

With respect to the silver-mines, it is stated, on competent authority, that the northern States of Mexico are very rich in silver; but there is scarcely any population, and that consisting mostly of Red Indians who will not work. When this district becomes a territory of the United States—as seems almost certain, this silver will, no doubt, be worked. We may make three periods in the history of Mexican silver-mining. Before the Conquest, the Aztecs worked the silver-ore at Tasco and other places; and were very familiar with silver, though they did not value it much. Under the Spaniards, the working of silver became the prominent industry of the country; and, until the Mexican Independence, the production steadily increased. The Spaniards invented amalgamation by the *patio*-process, a most, important improvement. Then came above twenty years of confusion, when little was done. But when the Republic had fairly got under way, and the country was in some measure open to foreigners, Europe, especially England, in hot haste to take advantage of the opportunity, sent over engineers and machinery, and great sums of money, much of which was quite wasted, to the hopeless ruin of a great part of the adventurers.

The improvements and the machinery remained, however; and the mines passed into other hands. Of late years the companies have been doing very well, and now export nearly as much silver as during the latter years of the Spanish government—nearly, but not quite. The financial history of the Real del Monte Company is worth putting down. The original English company spent nearly one million sterling on it, without getting any dividend. They sold it to two or three Mexicans for about twenty-seven thousand pounds, and the Mexicans spent eighty thousand more on it, and then began to make profits. The annual profit is now some £200,000.

I have said that the modern Mexican Indian has but little idea of arithmetic. This was not the case with his ancestors, who had a curious notation, serving for the highest numbers. The Indians of the present day use the old Aztec numerals, and from these there is something to be learnt.

Baron Humboldt, speaking of the Muysca Indians of South America, says that their word for eleven is *quihicha ata*, that is, "foot one;" meaning that they have counted all their fingers, and are beginning their toes. He proceeds to compare the Persian words, *pentcha*, hand, and *pendj*, five, as being connected with one another, and gives various other curious instances of finger-numeration. We may carry the theory further. The Zulu language reckons from one up to five, and then goes on with *tatisitupe* ("take the thumb"), meaning *six*; *tatukomba* ("take the pointer," or forefinger), meaning *seven*, and so on. The Vei language counts from one up to nineteen, and for twenty says *mo bande*—"a person is finished"—that is, both fingers and toes. I venture to add another suggestion. Eichhoff gives a Sanskrit word for finger, "daiçini" (taken apparently from *pra-deçinî*, forefinger), and which corresponds curiously with "daçan," ten; and we have the same resemblance running through many of the Indo-European languages, as and , *decem* and *digitus*; German, *Zehn* and *Zehe*, and so on.

Here the Mexican numerals will afford us a new illustration. Of the meaning of the first four of them—*çe, ome, yei, nahui*—I can give no idea, any more than I can of the meaning of the words one, two, three, four, which correspond to them; but the Mexican for *five* is *macuilli*, "hand-depicting." Then we go on in the dark as far as *ten*, which is *matlactli*, "hand-half," as I think it means, (from *tlactli*, half); and this would mean, not the halving of a hand, but the half of the whole person, which you get by counting his hands only. The syllable *ma*, which means "hand," makes its appearance in the words five and ten, and no where else; just as it should do. When we come to twenty, we have *cempoalli*, "one counting;" that is, one whole man, fingers and toes—corresponding to the Vei word for twenty, "a person is finished."

I think we need no more examples to show that people—in almost all countries—reckon by fives, tens, or twenties, merely because they began to count upon their fingers and toes. If the strong man who had six fingers on each hand, and six toes on each foot, had invented a system of numeration, it would have gone in twelves, nearly like the duodecimals which our carpenters use; unless, indeed, he had been stupid after the manner of very strong men, and not gone beyond sixes. We see how the Romans, though they inherited from their Eastern ancestors a numeration by tens up to *decem*, and then beginning again *undecim*, &c., yet when they began to write a notation could get no farther than five—I., II., III., IV., V.; and then on again, VI., VII., up to ten, from ten to fifteen, and so on.

There is a very curious vulgar error which prevails, even among people who have a good practical acquaintance with arithmetic. It is that the number *ten* has some special virtue which fits it for counting up to. The fact is that ten is not the best number for the purpose; you can halve it, it is true, but that is about all you can do with it, for its being divisible by five is of hardly any use for practical purposes. *Eight*would be a much better number, for you can halve it three times in succession; and *twelve* is perhaps the most convenient number possible, as it will divide by two, three, and four. It is this convenient property that leads tradesmen to sell by dozens, and grosses, rather than by tens and hundreds. If we used eights or twelves instead of tens for numeration, we might of course preserve all the advantages of the Indian or Arabic numerals; in the first case, we should discard the ciphers 8 and 9, and reckon 5, 6, 7, 10; and in the second case, we should want two new ciphers for ten and eleven; and 10 would stand for twelve, and 11 for thirteen. Our happening to have ten fingers has really led us into a rather inconvenient numerical system.

CHAPTER V.
MEXICO. GUADALUPE.

While we were away at the Real del Monte, the news had reached Mexico that Puebla had capitulated, and that the rebel leader had fled. The victory was celebrated in the capital with the most triumphal entries, harangues, bull-fights, and illuminations done to order. If you had a house in one of the principal streets, the police would make you illuminate it, whether you liked or not. The newspapers loudly proclaimed the triumph of the constitutional principle, and the inauguration of a reign of law and order that was never to cease.

As for the newspapers, indeed, one looked in vain in them for any free expression of public opinion. They were all either suppressed, or converted into the merest mouthpieces of the government. The telegraph was under the strictest surveillance, and no messages were allowed to be sent which the government did not consider favourable to their interests; a precaution which rather defeated itself, as the people soon ceased to believe any public news at all. In all these mean little shifts, which we in England consider as the special property of despotic governments, the authorities of the Mexican Republic showed themselves great proficients.

We were left, therefore, to form what idea we could of the real state of Mexican affairs, from the private information received by our friends. Just for once it may be worth while to give a few details, not because the people engaged were specially interesting, but because the affair may serve to give an idea of the condition of the country.

President Comonfort, not a bad sort of man, as it seemed, but not "strong enough for the place," and with an empty treasury, tried to make a stand against the clergy and the army, who stood firm against any attempt at reform —knowing, with a certain instinct, that, if any real reform once began, their own unreasonable privileges would soon be attacked. So the clergy and part of the army set up an anti-president, one Haro; and he installed himself at Puebla, which is the second city of the Republic, and there Comonfort besieged him. So far I have already described the doings of the "reaccionarios."

The newspapers gave wonderful accounts of attacks and repulses, and reckoned the killed on both sides at 2,500. There were 10,000 regular troops, and 10,000 irregulars (very irregular troops indeed); and these were commanded by a complete regiment of officers, and *forty* generals. This is reckoning both sides; but as, on pretty good authority (Tejada's statistical table), the troops in the Republic are only reckoned at 12,000, no doubt the above numbers are much exaggerated. As for the 2,500 killed, the fact is that the siege was a mere farce; and, judging by what we heard at the time in Mexico, and soon afterwards in Puebla itself, 25 was a much more correct estimate: and some facetious people reduced it, by one more division, to two and a half. The President had managed, by desperate efforts, to borrow some money in Mexico, on the credit of the State, at sixty per cent.; and it seems certain that it was this money, judiciously administered to some of Haro's generals, that brought about the flight of the anti-president, and the capitulation of Puebla. The termination of the affair, according to the newspapers, was, that the rebel army were incorporated with the constitutional troops; that their officers—500 in number—were reduced to the ranks for a term of years; that a hot pursuit was made after the fugitive Haro; and that, as it was notorious that the clergy had found the money for the rebellion, it was considered suitable that they should pay the expenses of the other side too; and an order was made on the church-estates of the district to that effect. Of course, it was an understood thing that the officers thus degraded would desert at the first opportunity, and thus the Government would be rid of them. As for Haro, it is not probable that they ever intended to catch him; and they were very glad when he disguised himself in sailor's clothes, and shipped himself off somewhere. When the Mexicans first took to civil wars, the victorious leader used to finish the contest by having his adversary shot. At the time of our visit, this fashion had gone out; and the victor treated the vanquished with great leniency, not unmindful of the time when he might be in a like situation himself.

Whether the President ever got much of the forced contribution from the clergy, I cannot say. At any rate, they have turned him out since; and for a very poor government have substituted mere chaotic anarchy, as Mr. Carlyle would call it. While the siege was going on, all the commerce between Vera Cruz and the capital was interrupted, and, of course, trade and manufacturing felt the effects severely. Nothing shews the capabilities of the country more clearly than the fact that, in spite of its distracted state and continual wars, its industrial interests seem to be gaining ground steadily, though very slowly. The evil of these ceaseless wars and revolutions is not that great battles are here fought, cities destroyed, and men sacrificed by thousands. Perhaps in no country in the world are "decisive victories," "sanguinary engagements," "brilliant attacks," and the like, got over with less loss of life. Incredible as it may seem to any one who knows how many civil wars and revolutions occur in the history of the country for the last four or five years, I should not wonder if the number of persons killed during that time in actual battle was less than the number of those deliberately assassinated, or killed in private quarrels.

Cheap as Mexican revolutions are in actual bloodshed, we must recollect what they bring with them. Thousands of deserters prowling about the country, robbing and murdering, and spreading everywhere the precious lessons they have learnt in barracks. We know something in England of the good moral influence that garrisons and recruiting sergeants carry about with them; and can judge a little what must be the result of the spreading of numbers of these fellows over a country where there is nothing to restrain their excesses! As for the soldiers themselves, one does not wonder at their deserting, for they are in great part pressed men, earned off from their homes, and shut up in barracks till they have been drilled, and are considered to be tamed; and moreover their pay, as one may judge from the general state of the military finances, is anything but regular. People who understand such matters, say that the Mexicans make very good soldiers, and fight well and steadily when well trained and well officered. They are able to march surprising distances, day after day, to live cheerfully on the very minimum of food, and to sleep anyhow. This we could judge for ourselves. One thing there is, however, that they strongly object to, and that is to be moved much beyond the range of their own climate. The men of the plains are as susceptible as Europeans to the ill effects of the climate of the tierra caliente; and the men of the hot lands cannot bear the cold of the high plateaus.

Travellers in the United States make great fun of the profusion of colonels and generals, and tell ludicrous stories on the subject. There is also talk of the absurd number of officers in the Spanish-American armies, but we should not, by any means, confound the two things. In the United States it is merely a harmless exhibition of vanity, and an amusing comment on their own high-minded abnegation of mere titles. In Spanish America it indicates a very real and serious evil indeed.

Don Miguel Lerdo de Tejada, in his statistical chart for 1856, quoted above, estimates the soldiers in the Republic at 12,000, and the officers at 2,000, not counting those on half-pay. One officer to every six men; and among them sixty-nine generals. These are not mere militia heroes, walking about in fine uniforms, but have actual commissions from some one of the many governments that have come and gone, and are entitled to their pay, which they get or do not get, as may happen. Only a fraction of them know anything whatever about the art of war. They were political adventurers, friends or relatives of some one in power, or simply speculators who bought their commissions as a sort of illegitimate Government Annuities. The continual rebellions or pronunciamientos have increased the number of officers still further. Comonfort's notion of degrading all the officers of the rebel army was a new and bold experiment. A very common course had been, when a pronunciamiento had been made anywhere against the then existing government, and a revolutionary army had been raised, for an amalgamation to take place between the two forces; intrigue and bribery and mutual disinclination to fight bringing matters to this peaceful kind of settlement. In this case, it was usual for the rebel officers to retain their self-conferred dignities.

I think this body of soldierless officers is one of the most troublesome political elements at work in the Republic. The political agitators are mostly among them; and it is they, more than any other class, who are continually stirring up factions and making pronunciamientos (what a pleasant thing it is that we have never had to make an English word for "pronunciamiento"). Several times, efforts have been made to reduce the Army List to decent proportions, but a fresh crop always springs up.

In the "lowest depth" of mismanagement to which Mexican military affairs have sunk, the newspapers still triumphantly refer to countries which surpass them in this respect, and, at the time of our arrival, were citing the statistics of the Peruvian Republic, where there are a general and twenty officers to every sixty soldiers, and as many naval officers as seamen.

These officers are not subject to the civil administration at all, whatever they may do. They have their *fuero,* their private charter, and are only amenable to their own tribunals, just as the clergy are to theirs. To the ill effects of the presence of such armies and such officers in the country, we must add the continual interruptions to commerce arising from the distracted state of the republic, and the uncertain tenure by which every one holds his property, not to say his life; and this, in its effect on the morale of the whole country, is worse than the positive suffering they inflict. So much for soldiering, for the present. We leave the President trying, with the aid of his Congress, to organize the government, and set things straight generally. This August assembly is selected from the people by universal suffrage, in the most approved manner, and ought to be a very important and useful body, but unfortunately can do nothing but talk and issue decrees, which no one else cares about.

In consequence of the alarming increase of highway-robbery, steps are taken to diminish the evil. It is made lawful to punish such offenders on the spot, by Lynch law. This is all. You may do justice on him when caught, but really you must catch him yourself. Sober citizens are even regretting the days of Santa Ana (recollect, I speak now of 1856, and they might regret him still more in 1860.) He was a great scoundrel, it is true; but he sent down detachments of soldiery to where the robbers practised their profession, and garotted them in pairs, till the roads were as safe as ours are in England. A President who sells states and pockets the money may have even that forgiven him in consideration of roads kept free from robbers, and some attempt at an effectual police. There is a lesson in this for Mexican rulers.

The Congress professed to be hard at work cleaning out the Augean stable of laws, rescripts, and proclamations, and making a working constitution. We went to see them one day, and heard talking going on, but it all came to nothing. Of one thing we may be quite sure, that if this unlucky country ever does get set straight, it will not be done by a Mexican Congress sitting and cackling over it.

On our return from the Real, we spent two days at the house of an English friend at Tisapán, at the edge of the great Pedrigal, or lava-field, which lies south of the capital. It was across this lava-field that a part of the American army marched in '47, and defeated a division of the Mexican forces encamped at Contrevas. On the same day the American army attacked the Mexicans who held a strongly fortified position at Churubusco, some four miles nearer Mexico, and routed the main army there. They beat them again at Molino del Rey, carried the hill of Chapultepec by storm, and then entered the city without meeting with further resistance; though the Mexicans, after they had formally yielded possession of the city, disgraced themselves by assassinating stray Americans, stabbing them in the streets, and lazoing them from the tops of the low mud houses in the suburbs.

An acquaintance of ours in Mexico met some American soldiers, with a corporal, in the street close to his house, and asked them in. Presently the corporal sent one of the men off into the next street to execute some commission; but half an hour elapsed, and the man not returning, the corporal went out to see what was the matter. He came back presently, and remarked that some of those cursed Mexicans had stabbed the man as he was turning the corner of the street, and left him lying there. "So," said the corporal, "I may as well finish his brandy and water for him;" he did so accordingly, and the men went home to their quarters.

The American soldiers were, as one may imagine, a rough lot. Only the smaller part of them were born Americans, the rest were emigrants from

Europe; to judge by what we heard of them—both in the States and in Mexico—the very refuse of all the scoundrels in the Republic; but they were well officered, and rigid discipline was maintained. So effectually were they kept in order, that the Mexicans confessed that it was a smaller evil to have the enemy's forces marching through the country, than their own army.

An elaborate account of the American invasion is given in Mayer's 'Mexico.' To those who do not care for details of military operations, there are still points of interest in the history. That ten thousand Americans should have been able to get through the mountain-passes, and to reach the capital at all, is an astonishing thing; and after that, their successes in the valley of Mexico follow as a matter of course. They could never have crossed the mountains but for a combination of circumstances.

The inhabitants generally displayed the most entire indifference; possibly preferring to sell their provisions to the Americans, instead of being robbed of them by their own countrymen. Add to this, that the Mexican officers showed themselves grossly ignorant of the art of war; and that the soldiers, though they do not seem to have been deficient in courage, were badly drilled and insubordinate. One would not have wondered at the army being in such a condition—in a country that had long been in a state of profound peace; but in Mexico a standing army had been maintained for years, at a great expense, and continual civil wars ought to have given people some ideas about soldiering. We may judge, from the events of this war, that Mexico might be kept in good order by a small number of American troops. The mere holding of the country is not the greatest difficulty in the question of American annexation.

One thing that struck our friends at Tisapán, among their experiences of the war, was the number of dead bodies of women and children that were found on the battle-fields. A crowd of women follow close in the rear of a Mexican army; almost every soldier having some woman who belongs to him, and who carries a heavy load of Indian corn and babies, and cooks tortillas for her lord and master. The number of these poor creatures who perished in the war was very great.

We spent much of our time at Tisapán in collecting plants, and exploring the lava-field, and the cañada, or ravine, that leads up into the mountains that skirt the valley of Mexico. I recollect one interesting spot we came to in riding through the pine-forest on the northern slope of the mountains, where the course of a torrent, now dry, ran along a mere narrow trench in the hard porphyritic rock, some ten or fifteen feet wide, until it had suddenly entered a bed of gravel, where it had hollowed out a vast ravine, four hundred feet wide and two hundred deep, the inlet of the water being, in proportion, as small as the pipe that serves to fill a cistern.

Such places are common enough in the south of Europe, but seldom on so grand a scale as one finds them in this country, where the floods come down from the hills with astounding suddenness and violence. Mr. L. had experience of this one day, when he had got inside his waterwheel, to inspect its condition, the water being securely shut off, as he thought. However, an aversada—one of these sudden freshets—came down, quite without notice; and enough water got into the channel to set the wheel going, so as to afford its proprietor a very curious and exciting ride, after the manner of a squirrel in a revolving cage, until the people succeeded in drawing off the water.

It was after our return from Tisapán that we paid a visit to Our Lady of Guadalupe, rather an important personage in the history of Mexican church-matters. The way lies past Santo Domingo, the church of the Holy Office, and down a long street where live the purveyors of all things for the muleteers. Here one may buy mats, ropes, pack-saddles—which the arrieros delight to have ornamented with fanciful designs and inscriptions, lazos, and many other things of the same kind. Passing out through the city-gate, we ride along a straight causeway, which extends to Guadalupe. A dull road enough in itself, but the interminable strings of mules and donkeys, bringing in pig-skins full of pulque, are worth seeing for once; and the Indians, trudging out and in with their various commodities, are highly picturesque.

On a building at the side of the causeway we notice "Estación de Méjico" (Mexico Station) painted in large letters. As far as we could observe, this very suggestive sign-board is the whole plant of the Railway Company at this end of the line. A range of hills ends abruptly in the plain, at a place which the Indians called Tepeyacac, "end of the hill" (literally "at the hill's nose"). Our causeway leads to this spot; and there, at the foot and up the slope of the hill, are built the great cathedral and other churches and chapels, altogether a vast and imposing collection of buildings; and round these a considerable town has grown up, for this is the great place of pilgrimage in the country.

The Spaniards had brought a miraculous picture with them, Nuestra Señora de Remedios, which is still in the country, and many pilgrims visit it; but Our Lady of Guadalupe is a native Mexican, and decidedly holds the first rank in the veneration of the people.

In the great church there is a picture mounted in a gold frame of great value. Its distance from the altar-rails, and the pane of glass which covers it, prevent one's seeing it very well. This was the more unfortunate, as, according to my history, the picture is in itself evidently of miraculous origin, for the best artists are agreed that no human hand could imitate the drawing or the colour! It appears that the Aztecs, long before the arrival of the Spaniards, had been in the habit of worshipping—in this very place—a goddess, who was known as *Teotenantzin*, "mother-god," or *Tonantzin*, "our mother." Ten years after the Conquest, a certain converted Indian, Juan Diego (John James) by name, was passing that way, and to him appeared the Virgin Mary. She told him to go to the bishop, and tell him to build her a temple on the place where she stood, giving him a lapful of flowers as a token. When the flowers were poured out of the garment, in presence of the bishop, the miraculous picture appeared underneath, painted on the apron itself. The bishop accepted the miracle with great unction; the temple was built, and the miraculous image duly installed in it. Its name of "Santa Maria de Guadalupe," was not, as one might imagine, taken from the Madonna of that name in Spain (of course not!), but was communicated by Our Lady herself to another converted Indian. She told him that her title was to be *Santa Maria de Tequatlanopeuh*, "Saint Mary of the rocky hill," of which hard word the Spaniards made "Guadalupe,"—just as they had turned Quauhnahuac into Cuernavaca, and Quauhaxallan into Guadalajara, substituting the nearest word of Spanish form for the unpronounceable Mexican names. This at least is the ingenious explanation given by my author, the Bachelor Tanco, Professor of the Aztec language, and of Astrology, in the University of Mexico, in the year 1666. The bishop who authenticated the miracle was no less a person than Fray Juan de Zumarraga, whose name is well known in Mexican history, for it was he who collected together all the Aztec picture-writings that he could find, "quite a mountain of them," say the chroniclers, and made a solemn bonfire of them in the great square of Tlatelolco. The miracles worked by the Virgin of Guadalupe, and by copies of it, are innumerable; and the faith which the lower orders of Mexicans and the Indians have in it is boundless.

On the 12th of December, the Anniversary of the Apparition is kept, and an amazing concourse of the faithful repair to the sanctuary. Heller, a German traveller who was in Mexico in 1846, saw an Indian taken to the church; he had broken his leg, which had not even been set, and he simply expected Our Lady to cure him without any human intervention at all. Unluckily, the author had no opportunity of seeing what became of him. The great miracle of all was the deliverance of Mexico from the great inundation of 1626, and the fact is established thus. The city was under water, the inhabitants in despair. The picture was brought to the Cathedral in a canoe, through the streets of Mexico; and between one and two years afterwards the inundation subsided. *Ergo*, it was the picture that saved the city!

For centuries a fierce rivalry existed between the Spanish Virgin, called "de Remedios," and Our Lady of Guadalupe; the Spaniards supporting the first, and the native Mexicans the second. A note of Humboldt's illustrates this feeling perfectly. He relates that whenever the country was suffering from drought, the Virjen do Remedios was carried into Mexico in procession, to bring rain, till it came to be said, quite as a proverb, *Hasta el agua nos debe venir de la Gachupina*—"We must get even our water from that Spanish creature." If it happened that the Spanish Madonna produced no effect after a long trial, the native Madonna was allowed to be brought solemnly in by the Indians, and never failed in bringing the wished-for rain, which always came sooner or later. It is remarkable that the Spanish party, who were then all-powerful, should have allowed their own Madonna to be placed at such a disadvantage, in not having the last innings. I need hardly say that the shrine of Guadalupe is monstrously rich. The Chapter has been known to lend such a thing as a million or two of dollars at a time, though most of their property is invested on landed security. They are allowed to have lotteries, and make something handsome out of them; and they even sell medals and prints of their patroness, which have great powers. You may have plenary indulgence in the hour of death for sixpence or less. We drank of the water of the chalybeate spring, bought sacred lottery-tickets, which turned out blanks, and tickets for indulgences, which, I greatly fear, will not prove more valuable; and so rode home along the dusty causeway to breakfast.

As means of learning what sort of books the poorer classes in Mexico preferred, we overhauled with great diligence the book-stalls, of which there are a few, especially under the arcades (Portales) near the great square. The Mexican public have not much cheap literature to read; and the scanty list of such popular works is half filled with Our Lady of Guadalupe, and other miracle-books of the same kind. Father Ripalda's Catechism has a large circulation, and is apparently the one in general use in the country. Zavala speaks of this catechism as containing the maxims of blind obedience to king and pope; but my more modern edition has scarcely anything to say about the Pope, and nothing at all about the government. Of late years, indeed, the Pope has not counted for much, politically, in Mexico; and on one occasion his Holiness found, when he tried to interfere about church-benefices, that his authority was rather nominal than real. On the whole, nothing in the Catechism struck me so much as the multiplication-table, which, to my unspeakable astonishment, turned up in the middle of the book; a table of fractions followed; and then it began again with the Holy Trinity.

To continue our catalogue; there are the almanacks, which contain rules for foretelling the weather by the moon's quarters, but none of the other fooleries which we find in those that circulate in England among the less educated classes. It is curious to notice how the taste for putting sonnets and other dreary poems at the beginnings and ends of books has survived in these Spanish countries. What used to be known in England as "a copy of verses" is still appreciated here, and almanacks, newspapers, religious books, even programmes of plays and bull-fights, are full of such dismal compositions. We ought to be thankful that the fashion has long since gone out with us (except in the religions tract, where it still survives). It is not merely apropos of sonnets, but of thousands of other things, that in these countries one is brought, in a manner, face to face with England as it used to be; and very trifling matters become interesting when viewed in this light. The last item in the list comprises translations, principally of French novels, those being preferred in which the agony is "piled up" to the highest point. German literature is represented by the "Sorrows of Werter." Of course, "Uncle Tom's Cabin" is widely circulated here, as it is everywhere in countries not given to the "particular vanity" attacked in it.

One need hardly say that both literature and education are at a very low ebb in Mexico. Referring to Tejada again, I find that he reckons that in the capital, out of a population of 185,000, there are 12,000 scholars at primary schools; but of course, as in other countries, a large proportion of these children attend so irregularly that they can hardly learn anything. For the country generally, he estimates one child receiving instruction out of thirty-seven inhabitants, a very significant piece of statistics. Efforts are being made, especially in the capital, to raise the population out of this state. Mr. Christy took much trouble in investigating the subject, with the assistance of our friend Don José Miguel Cervantes, the head of the Ayuntamiento, or Municipal Council. This gentleman, with a few others, has been doing much up-hill work of this kind for years past, establishing schools, and trying to make head against the opposition of the priests and the indifference of the people, as yet with but small success.

It seems hard to be always attacking the Roman Catholic clergy, but of one thing we cannot remain in doubt,—that their influence has had more to do than anything else with the doleful ignorance which reigns supreme in Mexico. For centuries they had the education of the country in their hands, and even at this day they retain the greater share of it. The training which the priests themselves receive will therefore give one some idea of what they teach their scholars. Unluckily, their course of instruction was stereotyped ages ago, when learned men devoted themselves to writing huge books on divinity, casuistry, logic, and metaphysics; concealing their ignorance of facts under an affectation of wisdom and clouds of long words; demonstrating how many millions of angels could dance on a needle's point; writing treatises "*de omni re scibili*," and on a good many things unknowable also; and teaching their admiring scholars the art of building up sham arguments on any subject, whether they know anything about it or not. This is a very vicious system of training for a man's mind, the more especially when it is supposed to set him up with a stock of superior knowledge; and this is what the Roman Catholic clergy have been learning, generation after generation, in Mexico and elsewhere. Of course, there are plenty of exceptions, particularly among the higher clergy; but, so far as I have been able to ascertain, education in clerical schools has generally been of this kind. It is instinctive to talk a little, as one occasionally finds an opportunity of doing, to some youth just out of these colleges. I recollect speaking to a young man who had just left the Seminario of Mexico, where he had been through a long course of theology and philosophy. He was astonished to hear that bull-fighting and colearing were not universally practised in Europe; and, when his father began to question me about the Crimean war, the young gentleman's remarks showed that he had not the faintest idea where England and France were, nor how far they were from one another.

I happened, not long ago, to visit a celebrated monastic college in South Italy, where they educated, not ordinary mortals, but only young men of noble birth; and here I took particular care in inspecting the library, judging that, though the scholars need not learn all that was there, yet that no department of knowledge would be taught there that was not represented on the library-shelves. What I saw fully confirmed all that I had previously seen and heard about the monastic learning of the present day. There were to be seen many fine manuscripts, and black-letter books, and curious old editions of great value, good store of classics (mostly Latin, however), works of the Fathers by the hundred-weight, and quartos and folios of canon-law, theology, metaphysics, and such like, by the ton. But it seemed that, in the estimation of the librarians, the world had stood still since the time of Duns Scotus; for, of what we call positive knowledge, except a little arithmetic and geometry, and a few very poor histories, I saw nothing. It is easy to see how one result of the clerical monopoly of education has therefore come about—that the intellectual standard is very low in Mexico. The Holy Office, too, has had its word to say in the matter. This institution had not much work to do in burning Indians, who were anything but sceptical in their turn of mind, and, indeed, were too much like Theodore Hook, and would believe "forty, if you pleased." They even went further, and were apt to believe not only what the missionaries taught them, but to cherish the memory of their old gods into the bargain. It was three centuries after the Conquest, that Mr. Bullock got the goddess Teoyaomiqui dug up in Mexico; and the old Indian remarked to him that it was true the Spaniards had given them three very good new gods, but it was rather hard to take away all their old ones. At any rate, the functions of the Inquisition were mostly confined to working the *Index Expurgatorius*, and suppressing knowledge generally, which they did with great industry until not long ago.

Here, then, are two causes of Mexican ignorance, and a third may be this; that

Mexico was a colony to which the Spaniards generally came to make their fortunes, with a view of returning to their own land; and this state of things was unfavourable to the country as regards the progress of knowledge, as well as in other things.

CHAPTER VI.
TEZCUCO.

Across the lake of Tezcuco is Tezcuco itself, a great city and the capital of a kingdom at the time of the Conquest, and famous for its palaces and its learned men. Now it is an insignificant Spanish town, built, indeed, to a great extent, of the stones of the old buildings. Mr. Bowring, who has evaporating-works at the edge of the lake, and lives in the "Casa Grande"—the Great House, just outside Tezcuco, has invited us to pay him a visit; so we get up early one April morning, and drive down to the street of the Solitude of Holy Cross (Calle de la Soledad de Santa Cruz). There we find Mr. Millard, a Frenchman, who is an *employé* of Mr. Bowling's, and is going back to Tezcuco with us; and we walk down to the canal with him, half a dozen Indian porters with baskets following us, and trotting along in the queer shuffling way that is habitual to them. At the landing-place we find a number of canoes, and a crowd of Indians, men and women, in scanty cotton garments which show the dirt in an unpleasant manner. A canoe is going to Tezcuco, a sort of regular packet-boat, in fact; and of this canoe Mr. Millard has retained for us three the stern half, over which is stretched an awning of aloe-fibre cloth. The canoe itself is merely a large shallow box, made of rough planks, with sloping prow and stern, more like a bread-tray in shape than anything else I can think of. There is no attempt at making the bows taper, and indeed the Indians stoutly resist this or any other innovation. In the fore part of the canoe there is already a heap of other passengers, lying like bait in a box, and when we arrive the voyage begins.

The crew are ten in number; the captain, eight men, and an old woman in charge of the tortillas and the pulque-jar. All these are brown people; in fact, the navigation of the lakes is entirely in the hands of the Indians, and "reasonable people" have nothing to do with it. Reasonable people—"gente de razón"—being, as I have said before, those who have any white blood in them; and republican institutions have not in the least effaced the distinction.

So it comes to pass that the canoe-traffic is carried on in much the same way as it was in Montezuma's time. There is one curious difference, however. These canoes are all poled about the lakes and canals; and I do not think we saw an Indian oar or paddle in the whole valley of Mexico. In the ancient picture-writings, however, the Indians are paddling their canoes with a kind of oar, shaped at the end like one of our fire-shovels. But, as we have seen, the distribution of land and water has altered since those days; and the lakes, far greater in extent, were of course several feet deeper all over the present beds; and even at a short distance from the city poling would have been impossible. I suspect that the Aztecs originally used both poles and paddles, and that the latter went out of use when the water became shallow enough for the pole to serve all purposes. Otherwise, we must suppose that the Mexicans, since the Spanish Conquest, introduced a new invention; which is not easy to believe.

We had first to get out of the canal, and fairly out into the lake. This was the more desirable, as the canal is one of the drains of the city, an office that it fills badly enough, seeing that there is scarcely any fall of water from the lower quarters of the city to the lake. I never saw water-snakes in numbers to compare with those in the canal, and by the side of it. They were swimming in the water, wriggling in and out; and on the banks they were writhing in heaps, like our passengers forward. Two of our crew tow us along, and we are soon clear of the canal, and of the salt-swamp that extends on both sides of it, where the bottom of the lake was in old times. Once fairly out, we look round us. We see Mexico from a new point of view, and begin to understand why the Spaniards called it the Venice of the New World. Even now, though the lake is so much smaller than it was then, the city, with its domes and battlemented roofs, seems to rise from the water itself, for the intervening flat is soon foreshortened into nothing. At the present moment it is evident that the level of the lake is much higher than usual. A little way off, on our right, is the Peñón de los Baños—"the rock of baths"—a porphyritic hill forced up by volcanic agency, where there are hot springs. It is generally possible to reach this hill by land, but the water is now so high that the rock has become an island as it used to be.

When the first two brigantines were launched on the Lake of Tezcuco by the Spaniards, Cortes took Montezuma with him to sail upon the lake, soon leaving the Aztec canoes far behind. They went to a Peñón or rocky hill where Montezuma preserved game for his own hunting, and not even the highest nobility were allowed to hunt there on pain of death. The Spaniards had a regular battue there; killing deer, hares, and rabbits till they were tired. This Peñón may have been the Peñón de los Baños which we are just passing, but was more probably a similar hill a little further off, of larger extent, now fortified and known as El Peñón, the Hill. Both were in those days complete islands at some distance from the shore.

Now that we are out of the canal, our Indians begin to pole us along, thrusting their long poles to the bottom of the shallow lake, and walking on two narrow planks which extend along the sides of the canoe from the prow to the middle point. Four walk on each plank, each man throwing up his pole as he gets to the end, and running back up the middle to begin again at the prow. The dexterity with which they swing the poles about, and keep them out of each other's way, is wonderful; and, as seen from our end of the canoe, looks like a kind of exaggerated quarter-staff playing, only nobody is ever hit.

The great peculiarity of the lake of Tezcuco is that it is a salt lake, containing much salt and carbonate of soda. The water is quite brackish and undrinkable. How it has come to be so is plain enough. The streams from the surrounding mountains bring down salt and soda in solution, derived from the decomposed porphyry; and as the water of the lake is not drained off into the sea, but evaporates, the solid constituents are left to accumulate in the lake.

In England, I think, we have no example of this; but the Dead Sea, the Caspian, the Great Salt Lake of Utah, and even the Mediterranean, have various salts accumulated in solution in the same way. It seems to me, that, by taking into account the proportion of soluble material contained in the water that flows down from the mountains, the probable quantity of water that flows down in the year, and the proportion of salt in the lake itself, some vague guess might be made as to the time this state of things has been lasting. I have no data, unfortunately, even for such a rough calculation as this, or I should like to try it.

In spite of the splendid climate, a great portion of the Valley of Mexico is anything but fertile; for the soil is impregnated with salt and soda, which in many places are so abundant as to form, when the water evaporates, a white efflorescence on the ground, which is called *tequesquite*, and regularly collected by the Indians. Some of it is stopped on its way down from the higher ground, by the evaporation of the water that was carrying it; and some is left by the lake itself, in its frequent floodings of the ground in its neighbourhood. So small is the difference of level between the lake and the plain that surrounds it, that the slightest rise in the height of the water makes an immense difference in the size of the lake; and even a strong wind will drive the water over great tracts of ground, from which it retires when the gale ceases. It must have been this, or something similar, that set Cortes upon writing home to Spain that the lakes were like inland seas, and even had tides like the ocean. Of course, this impregnation with salts is ruinous to the soil, which will produce nothing in such places but tufts of coarse grass; and the shores of the lake are the most dismal districts one can imagine. All the lakes, however, are not so salt as Tezcuco; Chalco, for instance, is a fresh-water lake, and there the fertility of the shores is very great, as I have already had occasion to notice.

As soon as the novelty of this kind of travelling had worn off, we began to find it dull, and retired under our awning to breakfast and bitter beer; which latter luxury, thanks to a suitable climate and an English brewer, is very well understood in Mexico, and is even accepted as a great institution by the Mexicans themselves.

We were just getting into a drowsy state, when an unusual bustle among the crew brought us out of our den, and we found that three hours of assiduous poling had taken us half-way across the lake, just six miles—a good test of the value of the Aztec system of navigation. Here was a wooden cross set up in the water; and here, from time out of mind, the boatmen have been used to sing a little hymn to the Madonna, by whose favour we had got so far, and hoped to get safe to the end of our voyage. Very well they sang it too, and the scene was as striking as it was unexpected to us. It seemed to us, however, to be making a great matter of crossing a piece of water only a few feet deep; but Mr. Millard assured us, that when a sudden gale came on, it was a particularly unpleasant place to be afloat in a Mexican canoe, which, being flat-bottomed, has no hold at all on the water, and from its shape is quite unmanageable in a wind. He himself was once caught in this way, and kept out all night, with a "heavy sea" on the lake, the boat drifting helplessly, and threatening to overturn every moment, and that in places where the water was quite deep enough to drown them all. The Indians lost their heads entirely, and throwing down their poles fell on their knees, and joined in the chorus with the women and children and the rest of the helpless brown people, beating their breasts, and presenting medals and prints of our Lady of Guadalupe to each wave as it dashed into them. The wind dropped, however, and Mr. Millard got safe to Tezcuco next morning; but, instead of receiving sympathy for his misfortunes when he got there, found that the idea of a tempest on the lake was reckoned a mere joke, and that the drawing-room of the Casa Grande had been decorated with a fancy portrait of himself, hanging to the half-way cross, with his legs in the water, and underneath, a poetical description of his sufferings to the tune of "*Malbrouke s'en va-t-en guerre, ne sais quand reviendra.*"

More poling across the lake, and then another little canal, also constructed since the diminishing of the water of the lake (which once came close to the city), and along which our Indians towed us. Then came a short ride, which brought us to the Casa Grande, where Mrs. Bowring received us with overflowing hospitality. We went off presently into the town, to see the glassworks. In a country where all things imported have to be carried in rough waggons, or on mules' backs, and over bad roads, it would be hard if it did not pay to make glass; and, accordingly, we found the works in full operation. The soda is produced at Mr. Bowling's works close by, the fuel is charcoal from the mountains, and for sand they have a substitute, which I never heard of or saw anywhere else. It seems that a short distance from Tezcuco there is a deposit of hydrated silica, which is brought down in great blocks by the Indians; and this, when calcined, answers the purpose perfectly, as there is scarcely any iron in it. In its natural state it resembles beeswax in colour.

It is worth while to describe the Casa Grande, which is strikingly different from our European notions of the "great house" of the village. As we enter by the gate, we find ourselves in a patio—an open quadrangle surrounded by a covered walk—a cloister in fact, into which open the rooms inhabited by the family. The second quadrangle, which opens into the first, is devoted to stables, kitchen, &c. The outer wall which surrounds the whole is very thick, and the entire building is built of mud bricks baked in the sun, and has no upper storey at all. It is a Pompeian house on a large scale, and suits the climate perfectly. The Aztec palaces we read so much of were built in just the same way. The roofs slope inwards from the sides of the quadrangle, and drain into the open space in the middle. One afternoon, a tremendous tropical rain-storm showed us how necessary it was to have the covered walk round the quadrangle raised considerably above this open square in the middle, which a few minutes of such rain converted into a pond.

As for ourselves, we spent many very pleasant days at the Casa Grande, and thoroughly approved of the arrangement of the house, except that the four corners of the patio were provokingly alike, and the doors of the rooms also, so that we were as much bothered as the captain of the forty thieves to find our own doors, or any door except Mr. Millard's, whose name was indicated—with more regard to pronunciation than spelling—with a 1 and nine 0's chalked on it.

In spite of a late evening spent in very pleasant society, we were up early next morning, ready for an excursion to the Pyramids of Teotihuacán, some sixteen miles off, or so, under the guidance of one of Mr. Bowring's men. The road lies through the plain, between great plantations of magueys, for this is the most renowned district in the Republic for the size of its aloes, and the quality of the pulque that is made from them. We stopped sometimes to examine a particularly large specimen, which might measure 30 feet round, and to see the juice, which had collected in the night, drawn out of the great hollow that had been cut to receive it, in the heart of the plant. The Indians have a great fancy for making crosses, and the aloe lends itself particularly to this kind of decoration. They have only to cut off six or eight inches of one leaf, and impale the piece on the sharp point of another, and the cross is made. Every good-sized aloe has two or three of these primitive religious emblems upon it.

Several little torrent-beds crossed the road, and over them were thrown old-fashioned Spanish stone bridges, as steep as the Rialto, or the bridge on the willow-patterned plates.

Before going to see the pyramids, we visited the caves in the hill-side not far from them, whence the stone was brought to build them. It is *tetzontli*, the porous amygdaloid which abounds among the porphyritic hills, a beautiful building-stone, easily worked, and durable. There was a large space that seemed to have been quarried out bodily, and into this opened numerous caves. We left our horses at the entrance, and spent an hour or two in hunting the place over. The ground was covered with pieces of obsidian knives and arrow-heads, and fragments of what seemed to have been larger tools or weapons; and we found numbers of hammer-heads, large and small, mostly made of greenstone, some whole, but most broken.

We find two sorts of stone hammers in Europe. Solid hammers belong to the earliest period. They are made of longish rolled pebbles; some are shaped a little artificially, and are grooved round to hold the handle, which was a flexible twig bent double and with the two ends tied together, so as to keep the stone head in its place. The hammers of a later period of the "stone age" are shaped more like the iron ones our smiths use at the present day, and they have a hole bored in the middle for the handle. In Brittany, where Celtic remains are found in such abundance, it is not uncommon to see stone hammers of the latter kind hanging up in the cottages of the peasants, who use them to drive in nails with. They have an odd way of providing them with handles, by sticking them tight upon branches of young trees, and when the branch has grown larger, and has thus rivetted itself tightly on both sides of the stone head, they cut it off, and carry home the hammer ready for use.

Though the Mexicans carried the arts of knife and arrow-making and sculpturing hard stone to such perfection, I do not think they ever discovered the art of making a hole in a stone hammer. The handles of the axes shown in the picture-writings are clumsy sticks swelling into a large knob at one end, and the axe-blade is fixed into a hole in this knob. Some of the Mexican hammers seem to have had their handles fixed in this way; while others were made with a groove, in the same manner as the earlier kind of European stone hammers just described.

When we consider the beauty of the Mexican stonecutter's work, it seems wonderful that they should have been able to do it without iron tools. It is quite clear that, at the time of the Spanish Conquest, they used bronze hatchets, containing that very small proportion of tin which gives the alloy nearly the hardness of steel. We saw many of these hatchets in museums, and Mr. Christy bought some good specimens in a collection of antiquities which had belonged to an old Mexican, who got them principally from the suburb of Tlatelolco, in the neighbourhood of the ancient market-place of the city. Such axes were certainly common among the ancient Mexicans. One of the items of the hieroglyphic tribute-roll in the Mendoza Codex is eighty bronze hatchets.

A story told by Bernal Diaz is to the point. He says that he and his companions, noticing that the Indians of the coast generally carried bright metal axes, the material of which looked like gold of a low quality, got as many as six hundred such axes from them in the course of three days' bartering, giving them coloured glass-beads in exchange. Both sides were highly satisfied with their bargain; but it all came to nothing, as the chronicler relates with considerable disgust, for the gold turned out to be copper, and the beads were found to be trash when the Indians began to understand them better. Such hard copper axes as these have been found at Mitla, in the State of Oajaca, where the ruined temples seem to form a connecting link between the monuments of Teotihuacán and Xochicalco and the ruined cities of Yucatan and Chiapas.

We want one more link in the chain to show the use of the same kind of tools from Mexico down to Yucatan, and this link we can supply. In Lord Kingsborough's great work on Mexican Antiquities there is one picture-writing, the Dresden Codex, which is not of Aztec origin at all. Its hieroglyphics are those of Palenque and Uxmal; and in this manuscript we have drawings of hatchets like those of Mexico, and fixed in the same kind of handles, but of much neater workmanship.

But here we come upon a difficulty. It is supposed that the pyramids of Teotihuacán, as well as most of the great architectural works of the country, were the work of the Toltec race, who quitted this part of the country several centuries before the Spanish Conquest. It seems incredible that bronze should have been in use in the country for so long a time, and not have superseded so bad a material as stone for knives and weapons. We have good evidence to show that in Europe the introduction of bronze was almost simultaneous with the complete disuse of stone for such purposes. It is true that Herodotus describes the embalmers, in his time, as cutting open the bodies with "an Ethiopic stone" though they were familiar with the use of metal. Indeed the flint knives which he probably meant may be seen in museums. But this peculiar usage was most likely kept up for some mystical reason, and does not affect the general question. Almost as soon as the Spaniards brought iron to Mexico, it superseded the old material. The "bronze age" ceased within a year or two, and that of iron began.

The Mexicans called copper or bronze "tepuztli," a word of rather uncertain etymology. Judging from the analogous words in languages allied to the Aztec, it seems not unlikely that it meant originally *hatchet* or *breaker*, just as "itztli," or obsidian, appears to have meant originally *knife*.

When the Mexicans saw iron in the hands of the Spaniards, they called it also "tepuztli," which thus became a general word for metal; and then they had to distinguish iron from copper, as they do at the present day, by calling them "*tliltic* tepuztli," and "*chichiltic* tepuztli;" that is, "black metal," and "red metal."

When the subject of the use of bronze in stone-cutting is discussed, as it so often is with special reference to Egypt, one may doubt whether people have not underrated its capabilities, when the proportion of tin is accurately adjusted to give the maximum hardness; and especially when a minute portion of iron enters into its composition. Sir Gardner Wilkinson relates that he tried the edge of one of the Egyptian mason's chisels upon the very stone it had evidently been once used to cut, and found that its edge was turned directly; and therefore he wonders that such a tool could have been used for the purpose, of course supposing that the tool as he found it was just as the mason left it. This, however, is not quite certain. If we bury a brass tool in a damp place for a few weeks, it will be found to have undergone a curious molecular change, and to have become quite soft and weak, or, as the workmen call it, dead. We ought to be quite sure whether lying for centimes under ground may not have made some similar change in bronze.

I have seen many prickly pears in different places, but never such specimens as those that were growing among the stones in this old quarry. They had gnarled and knotted trunks of hard wood, and were as big as pollard-oaks; their age must have been immense; but, unfortunately, one could not measure it, or it would have been a good criterion of the age of the quarry, which had not only been excavated but abandoned before their time. In one of the caves was a human skeleton, blanched white and clean, and near it some one has stuck a cross, made of two bits of stick, in the crevices of a heap of stones.

Returning to the entrance of the quarry, well loaded with stone hammers and knives, we sat down to breakfast, in a cave, where our man had established himself with the horses. An attempt on my part to cut German sausage with an obsidian knife proved a decided failure.

We had already been struck by the appearance of the two pyramids of Teotihuacán, when we passed by Otumba on our way to Mexico. The hills which skirt the plain are so near them as to diminish their apparent size; but even at a distance they are conspicuous objects. Now, when we came close to them, and began by climbing to their summits, and walking round their terraces, to measure ourselves against them, we began gradually to realize their vast bulk; and this feeling continually grew upon us. Modern architecture strives to unite the greatest possible effect with the least cost; and the modern churches of southern Europe and Spanish America, with their fine tall facades fronting the street, and insignificant little buildings behind, show this idea in its fullest development. Pyramids are built with no such object, and make but little show in proportion to their vast mass of material; but then one gets from them a sense of solid magnitude that no other building gives, however vast its proportions may be. Neither of us had ever seen the Egyptian pyramids. Even in Mexico these of Teotihuacán are not the largest; for, though the pyramid of Cholula is no higher, it covers far more ground. Were these monuments in Egypt, they would only rank, from their size, in the second class.

As has often been remarked, such buildings as these can only be raised under peculiar social conditions. The ruler must be a despotic sovereign, and the mass of the people slaves, whose subsistence and whose lives are sacrificed without scruple to execute the fancies of the monarch, who is not so much the governor as the unrestricted owner of the country and the people. The population must be very dense, or it would not bear the loss of so large a proportion of the working class; and vegetable food must be exceedingly abundant in the country, to feed them while engaged in this unprofitable labour.

We know how great was the influence of the priestly classes in Egypt, though the pyramids there, being rather tombs than temples, do not prove it. In Mexico, however, the pyramids themselves were the temples, serving only incidentally as tombs; and their size proves that—as respects priestly influence—the resemblance between the two people is fully carried out.

Like the Egyptian pyramids, these fronted the four cardinal points. Their shape was not accurately pyramidal, for the line from base to summit was broken by three terraces, or perhaps four, running completely round them; and at the top was a flat square space, where stood the idols and the sacrificial altars. This construction closely resembled that of some of the smaller Egyptian pyramids. Flights of stone steps led straight up from terrace to terrace, and the procession of priests and victims made the circuit of each before they ascended to the one above.

The larger of the two teocallis is dedicated to the Sun, has a base of about 640 feet, and is about 170 feet high. The other, dedicated to the Moon, is rather smaller.

These monuments were called *teocallis*, not because they were pyramids, but because they were temples; "Teocalli" means "god's house"—(*teotl*, god, *calli*, house), a name which the traveller hears explained for the first time with some wonder; and Humboldt cannot help adverting to its curious correspondence with , *dei cella*. Another odd coincidence is found in the Aztec name for their priests, *papahua*, the root of which *papa*, (the *hua*, is merely a termination). In the Old World the word *Papa*, Pope, or Priest, was connected with the idea of father or grandfather, but the Aztec word has no such origin.

When the Aztecs abandoned their temples, and began to build Christian churches, they called them also "teocallis," and perhaps do so to this day.

The heavy tropical rains have to a great extent broken the sharpness of the outline of these structures, and brought them more nearly to the shape of real pyramids than they were originally; but, as we climbed up their sides, we could trace the terraces without any difficulty, and even flights of steps.

The pyramids consist of an outer casing of hewn stone, faced and covered with smooth stucco, which has resisted the effects of time and bad usage in a wonderful manner. Inside this casing were adobes, stones, clay, and mortar, as one may see in places where the exterior has been damaged, and by creeping into the small passage which leads into the Temple of the Moon. Both pyramids are nearly covered with a coating of debris, full of bits of obsidian arrows and knives, and broken pottery. On the teocalli of the moon we found a number of recent sea-shells, which mystified us extremely; and the only explanation we could give of their presence there was that they might have been brought up as offerings. A passage in Humboldt, which I met with long after, seems to clear up the mystery. Speaking of the great teocalli of the city of Mexico, he says, quoting an old description, that the Moon had a little temple in the great courtyard, which was built of shells. Those that we found may be the remains of a similar structure on the top of the pyramid.

Prickly pears, aloes, and mesquite bushes have overgrown the pyramids in all directions, as though they had been mere natural hills. In Sicily one may see the lava fields of Etna planted with prickly pears: in the ordinary course of things, it requires several centuries before even the surface of this hard lava will disintegrate into soil; but the roots of the cactus soon crack it, and a few years suffice to break it up to a sufficient depth to allow of vineyards being planted upon it. Here the same plant has in the same way affected the porous amygdaloid with which the pyramids are faced, and has cut up the surface sadly; but the vegetation which covers them will at any rate defend them from the rains, and now centuries will make but little change in the appearance of these remarkable buildings.

Near Nice there is a hill which gives a wonderfully correct idea of the appearance of the terraced teocallis of Mexico, as they must have looked before time effaced the sharpness of their lines. Where the valley of the Paglione and that of St. Andre meet, the hill between them terminates in a half pyramid, the angle of which lies toward the south; and the inhabitants—as their custom is in southern Europe, have turned the two slopes to account, by building them up into terraces, to prevent the soil they have laboriously carried up from being swept down by the first heavy rain. Seen from the proper point of view the resemblance is complete.

From the south side of the Temple of the Moon runs an avenue of burial-mounds, the Micaotli, "the path of the dead." On these mounds, and round the foot of the pyramids themselves, the whole population of the once great city of Teotihuacán and its neighbourhood used to congregate, to see the priests and the victims march round the terraces and up the stairs in full view of them all. Standing here, one could imagine the scene that Cortes and his men saw from their camp, outside Mexico, on that dreadful day when the Mexicans had cut off their retreat along the causeways, and taken more than sixty Spanish prisoners. Bernal Diaz was there, and tells the tale how they heard from the city the great drum of Huitzilopochtli sending forth a strange and awful sound, that could be heard for miles, and with it many horns and trumpets; and how, when they had looked towards the great teocalli, they saw the Mexicans dragging up the prisoners, pushing and beating them as they went, till they had got them up to the open space at the top, "where the cursed idols stood." Then they put plumes of feathers on their heads, and fans in their hands, and made them dance before the idol; and when they had danced, they threw them on their backs on the sacrificial stone that stood there, and, sawing open their breasts with knives of stone, they tore out their hearts, and offered them up in sacrifice; and the bodies they flung down the stairs to the bottom. More than this the Spaniards cannot have seen, though Diaz describes the rest of the proceedings as though they had been done in his sight; but it was not the first time they had witnessed such things, and they knew well enough what was happening down below,—how the butchers were waiting to cut up the carcases as they came down, that they might be cooked with chile, and eaten in the solemn banquet of the evening.

The day was closing in by this time; and our man was waiting with the horses at the foot of the great pyramid; and with him an Indian, whom we had caught half an hour before, and sent off with a real to buy pulque, and to collect such obsidian arrows and clay heads as were to be found at the ranchos in the neighbourhood.

Near the place we started from, two or three Indians were diligently at work at their stone-quarry, that is to say, they were laboriously bringing out great hewn stones from the side of the pyramid, to build their walls with; and indeed we could see in every house for miles round stones that had come from the same source, as was proved by the stucco still remaining upon them, smoothed like polished marble, and painted dull red with cinnabar.

As I write this, it brings to my recollection an old Roman trophy in North Italy, built—like these pyramids—of a shell of hewn stone, filled with rough stones and cement, now as hard as the rock itself. There I saw the inhabitants of the town which stands at its foot, carrying off the great limestone blocks, but first cutting them up into pieces of a size that they could move about, and build into their houses. Here and there, in this little Italian town, there were to be seen in the walls letters of the old inscription which were once upon the trophy; and the age of the houses shewed that the monument had served as a quarry for centuries.

As we rode home, we noticed by the sides of the road, and where ditches had been cut, numbers of old Mexican stone-floors covered with stucco. The earth has accumulated above them to the depth of two or three feet, so that their position is like that of the Roman pavements so often found in Europe; and we may guess, from what we saw exposed, how great must be the number of such remains still hidden, and how vast a population must once have inhabited this plain, now almost deserted.

Two days afterwards we came back. In the ploughed fields in the neighbourhood we made repeated trials whether it was possible to stand still in any spot where there was no relic of old Mexico within our reach; but this we could not do. Everywhere the ground was full of unglazed pottery and obsidian; and we even found arrows and clay figures that were good enough for a museum. When we left England, we both doubted the accounts of the historians of the Conquest, believing that they had exaggerated the numbers of the population, and the size of the cities, from a natural desire to make the most of their victories, and to write as wonderful a history as they could, as historians are prone to do. But our examination of Mexican remains soon induced us to withdraw this accusation, and even made us inclined to blame the chroniclers for having had no eyes for the wonderful things that surrounded them.

I do not mean by this that we felt inclined to swallow the monstrous exaggerations of Solis and Gomara and other Spanish chroniclers, who seemed to think that it was as easy to say a thousand as a hundred, and that it sounded much better. But when this class of writers are set aside, and the more valuable authorities severely criticised, it does not seem to us that the history thus extracted from these sources is much less reliable than European history of the same period. There is, perhaps, no better way of expressing this opinion than to say that what we saw of Mexico tended generally to confirm Prescott's History of the Conquest, and but seldom to make his statements appear to us improbable.

There are other mounds near the pyramids, besides the Micaotli. Two sides of the Pyramid of the Sun are surrounded by them; and there are two squares of mounds at equal distances, north and south of it, besides innumerable scattered hillocks. There are some sculptured blocks of stone lying near the pyramids, and inside the smaller one is buried what appears to be a female bust of colossal size, with the mouth like an oval ring, so common in Mexican sculptures.

The same abundance of ancient remains that we found here characterizes the neighbourhood of all the Mexican monuments in the country, with one curious exception. Burkart declares that in the vicinity of the extensive remains of temples known as *Los Edificios*, near Zacatecas, no traces of pottery or of obsidian were to be found.

Before going away, we held a solemn market of antiquities. We sat cross-legged on the ground, and the Indian women and children brought us many curious articles in clay and obsidian, which we bought and deposited in two great bags of aloe-fibre which our man carried at his saddle-bow. Among the articles we bought were various pipes or whistles of pottery, *pitos*, as they are called in Spanish, and just as we were mounting our horses to ride off, a lad ran to the top of one of the mounds, and blew on one of these pipes a long dismal note that could be heard a mile off. Our friends had filled our heads so full of robbers and ambushes, that we made sure it was a signal for some one who was waiting for us, and the more so as the boy ran off as soon as he had blown his blast; and when we looked round for the people whose antiquities we had been buying, they had all disappeared. But nothing came of it, and we got safely back to Tezcuco. As usual, we spent a capital evening, and separated late. The owner of the glass-works, who had been spending the evening with us, had an adventure on his road home. He was peaceably riding along, when two men rushed out from behind the corner of the street, and shouted "*alto ahí*!" (halte-là). He thought they were robbers, and started at a gallop. His hat flew off, and the men sent two bullets singing past his head, which sent him on quicker than ever, till he reached his house. There he got his pistols, and came back armed to the teeth to fetch the hat, which lay where it had fallen. The supposed robbers turned out, on enquiry next day, to have been national guards, patrolling the street; but certainly their proceedings were rather questionable.

We had an unpleasant visit the same night. The custom of the Casa Grande was that after dark a watchman patrolled all night, giving a long blast every quarter of an hour on one of these same doleful Mexican whistles, to show that ho was not sleeping on his rounds. This was for the outside. Inside the house, *pour surcroît de précaution,* a servant came round to see that every one was in his room; and having satisfied himself of this, let loose in the courtyard two enormous bulldogs, which were the terror of the household and of the whole neighbourhood. On this particular night, a noise at our own door woke me from a sound sleep; and I had the pleasure of seeing a creature walk deliberately in, looking huge and terrific in the moonlight. The beast had been into the stable two nights before, and had pinned a cow which was there, keeping his hold upon her till next morning, when he was got off by the keeper. With this specimen of the bulldog's abilities fresh in my recollection, I preferred not making any attempt to resent his impertinent intrusion, but lay still, till he had satisfied himself with walking about the room and sniffing at our beds, when he lay down on my carpet; I soon fell asleep again, and next morning he was gone. The foreigners in Mexico seem to delight in fierce bull-dogs. The Casa Grande at Tezcuco is not by any means the only place where they form part of the garrison. One English acquaintance of ours in the Capital kept two of these beasts up in his rooms, and not even the servants dared go up, unless the master was there.

Every one who has read Prescott's 'Mexico' will recollect Nezahualcoyotl, the king of Tezcuco; and the palaces he built there for his wives, and his poets, and the rest of his great court. These palaces were built chiefly of mud bricks; and time and the Spaniards have dealt so hardly with them, that even their outlines can no longer be traced. Traces of two large teocallis are just visible, and Mr. Bowring has some burial mounds in his grounds which will be examined some day. There is a Mexican calendar built into the wall of one of the churches; and, as we walked about the streets of the present town, we noticed stones that must have been sculptured before the Spaniards brought in their broken-down classic style, and so stopped the development of native art. As for the rest of old Tezcuco, it has "become heaps." Wherever they dig ditches or lay the foundations of houses, you may see the ground full of its remains.

As I said before, when speaking of the stuccoed floors near Teotihuacán, the accumulation of alluvial soil goes on very rapidly and very regularly all over the plains of Mexico and Puebla, where everything favours its deposit; and the human remains preserved in it are so numerous that its age may readily be seen. We noticed this in many places, but in no instance so well as between Tezcuco and the hacienda of Miraflores. There a long ditch, some five feet deep, had just been cut in anticipation of the rainy season. As yet it was dry, and, as we walked along it, we found three periods of Mexican history distinctly traceable from one end to the other. First came mere alluvium, without human remains. Then, just above, came fragments of obsidian knives and bits of unglazed pottery. Above this again, a third layer, in which the obsidian ceased, and much of the pottery was still unglazed; but many fragments were glazed, and bore the unmistakable Spanish patterns in black and yellow.

It is a pity that these alluvial deposits, which give such good evidence as to the order in which different peoples or different states of society succeeded one another on the earth, should be so valueless as a means of calculating the time of their duration; but one can easily see that they must always be so, by considering how the thickness of the deposits is altered by such accidents as the formation of a mud-bank, or the opening of a new channel,—things that must be continually occurring in districts where this very accumulation is going on. The only place where any calculation can be based upon its thickness is on the banks of the Nile, where its accumulations round the ancient monuments may perhaps give a criterion as to the time which has elapsed since man ceased to clear away the deposits of the river.

As an instance of the tendency of alluvial deposits to entomb such monuments of former ages, I must mention the temple of Segeste, which stands on a gentle slope among the hills of northern Sicily. I had heard talk of the graceful proportions of this Doric temple, built by the Greek colonists; and great was my surprise, on first coming in sight of it, to see a pediment supported by two rows of short squat columns, without bases, and rising directly from the ground. A nearer inspection showed the cause of this extraordinary distortion. The whole slope had risen full six feet during the 2500 years, or so, that have elapsed since its desertion; and the temple now stands in a large oblong pit, which has lately been excavated. As we left the spot, and turned to see it again a few yards off, the beautiful symmetry of the whole had disappeared again.

To return to Tezcuco. Some three or four miles from the town stands the hill of Tezcotzinco, where Nezahualcoyotl had his pleasure-gardens; and to this hill we made an excursion early one morning, with Mr. Bowring for our guide. We did not go first to Tezcotzinco itself, but to another hill which is connected with it by an aqueduct of immense size, along which we walked. The mountains in this part are of porphyry, and the channel of the aqueduct was made principally of blocks of the same material, on which the smooth stucco that had once covered the whole, inside and out, still remained very perfect. The channel was carried, not on arches, but on a solid embankment, a hundred and fifty or two hundred feet high, and wide enough for a carriage-road.

The hill itself was overgrown with brushwood, aloes, and prickly pears, but numerous roads and flights of steps cut in the rock were distinguishable. Not far below the top of the hill, a terrace runs completely round it, whence the monarch could survey a great part of his little kingdom. On the summit itself I saw sculptured blocks of stone; and on the side of the hill are two little circular baths, cut in the solid rock. The lower of the two has a flight of steps down to it; the seat for the bather, and the stone pipe which brought the water, arc still quite perfect.

His majesty used to spend his afternoons here on the shady side of the hill, apparently sitting up to his middle in water, like a frog, if one may judge by the height of the little seat in the bath. If, as some writers say, these were only tanks with streams of running water, and not baths at all, why the steps cut in their sides, which are just large enough and high enough for a man to sit in? No water has come there for centuries now; and the morning-sun nearly broiled us, till we got into a sort of cave, excavated in the hill, it is said, with an idea of finding treasure. It seems there was once a Mexican calendar cut in the rock at this spot; and some white people who were interested in such matters, used to come to see it, and poke curiously about in search of other antiquities. Naturally enough, the Indians thought that they expected to find treasure; and with a view of getting the first chance themselves, they cut down the calendar, and made this large excavation behind it.

Here we sat in the shade, breakfasting, and hearing Mr. Bowring's stories of the art of medicine as practised in the northern states of Mexico, where decoction of shirt is considered an invaluable specific when administered internally; and the recognised remedy for lumbago is to rub the patient with the drawers of a man named John. No doubt the latter treatment answers very well!

There is an old Mexican bridge near Tezcuco which seems to be the original *Puente de las Bergantinas*, the bridge where Cortes had the brigantines launched on the lake of Tezcuco. This bridge has a span of about twenty feet, and is curious as showing how nearly the Mexicans had arrived at the idea of the arch. It is made in the form of a roof resting on two buttresses, and composed of slabs of stone with the edges upwards, with mortar in the interstices; the slabs being sufficiently irregular in shape to admit of their holding together, like the stones of a real arch. One may now and then see in Europe the roofs of small stone hovels made in the same way; but twenty feet is an immense span for such a construction. I have seen such buildings in North Italy, in places where the limestone is so stratified as to furnish rough slabs, three or four inches thick, with very little labour in quarrying them out. In Kerry there are ancient houses and churches roofed in the same way. What makes the Tezcuco bridge more curious is that it is set askew, which must have made its construction more difficult.

The brigantines which the Spaniards made, and transported over the mountains in such a wonderful manner, fully answered their purpose, for without them Mexico could hardly have been taken. After the Conquest they were kept for years, for the good service they had done; but vessels of such size do not seem to have been used upon the lake since then; and I believe the only sailing craft at present is Mr. Bowring's boat, which the Indians look at askance, and decidedly decline to imitate. It is true that, somewhere near the city, there is moored a little steamer, looking quite civilized at a distance. It never goes anywhere, however; and I have a sort of impression of having heard that when it was first made they got up the steam once, but the conduct of the machinery under these circumstances was so extraordinary and frantic that no one has ventured to repeat the experiment.

Before we left Tezcuco, we went in a boat to explore Mr. Bowring's salt-works, which are rather like the salines of the South of France. Patches of the lake are walled off, and the water allowed to evaporate, which it does very rapidly under a hot sun, and with only three-fourths of the pressure of air upon it that we have at the sea-level. The lake-water thus concentrated is run into smaller tanks. It contains carbonate and sesquicarbonate of soda, and common salt. The addition of lime converts the sesquicarbonate of soda into simple carbonate, and this is separated from the salt by taking advantage of their different points of crystallization. The salt is partly consumed, and partly used in the extraction of silver from the ore, and the soda is bought by the soap-makers.

Humboldt's remarks on the small consumption of salt in Mexico are curious. The average amount used with food is only a small fraction of the European average. While the Tlascalans were at war with the Aztecs, they had to do without salt for many years, as it was not produced in their district. Humboldt thinks that the chile which the Indians consume in such quantities acts as a substitute. It is to be remembered that the soil is impregnated with both salt and natron in many of these upland districts, and the inhabitants may have eaten earth containing these ingredients, as they do for the same purpose in several places in the Old World.

We disembarked after sailing to the end of these great evaporating pans, and found horses waiting to take us to the Bosque del Contador. This is a grand square, looking towards the cardinal points, and composed of ahuehuetes, grand old deciduous cypresses, many of them forty feet round, and older than the discovery of America. My companion, not content with buying collections at secondhand, wished to have some excavations made on his own account, and very judiciously fixed on this spot, where, though there were no buildings standing, the appearance of the ground and the mounds in the neighbourhood, together with the historical notoriety of the place, made it probable that something would be found to repay a diligent search. This expectation was fully realized, and some fine idols of hard stone were found, with an infinitude of pottery and small objects.

When I look through my notes about Tezcuco, I do not find much more to mention, except that a favourite dish here consists of flies' eggs fried. These eggs are deposited at the edge of the lake, and the Indians fish them out and sell them in the market-place. So large is the quantity of these eggs, that at a spot where a little stream deposits carbonate of lime, a peculiar kind of travertine is forming which consists of masses of them imbedded in tho calcareous deposit.

The flies which produce these eggs are called by the Mexicans "*axayacatl*" or "water-face." There was a celebrated Aztec king who was called Axayacatl; and his name is indicated in the picture-writings by a drawing of a man's face covered with water. The eggs themselves are sold in cakes in the market, pounded and cooked, and also in lumps *au naturel*, forming a substance like the roe of a fish. This is known by the characteristic name of "*ahuauhtli*", that is "water-wheat."

The last thing we did at Tezcuco, was to witness the laying down of a new line of water-pipes for the saltworks. This I mention because of the pipes, which were exactly those introduced into Spain by the Moors and brought here by tho Spaniards. These pipes are of glazed earthenware, taper at one end, and each fitting into the large end of the next. The cement is a mixture of lime, fat, and hair, which gets hard and firm when cold, but can be loosened by a very slight application of heat. A thousand years has made no alteration in the way of making these pipes. Here, however, the ground is so level that one great characteristic of Moorish waterworks is not to be seen. I mean the water-columns which are such a feature in the country round Palermo, and in other places where the system of irrigation introduced by the Moorish invaders is still kept up. These are square pillars twenty or thirty feet high, with a cistern at the top of each, into which the water from the higher level flowed, and from which other pipes carried it on; the sole object of the whole apparatus being to break the column of water, and reduce the pressure to the thirty or forty feet which the pipes of earthenware would bear.

This subject of irrigation is very interesting with reference to the future of Mexico. We visited two or three country-houses in the plateaux, where the gardens are regularly watered by artificial channels, and the result is a vegetation of wonderful exuberance and beauty, converting these spots into oases in the desert. On the lower levels of the tierra templada where the sugar-cane is cultivated, a costly system of water-supply has been established in the haciendas with the best results. Even in the plains of Mexico and Puebla, the grain-fields are irrigated to some small degree. But notwithstanding this progress in the right direction, the face of the country shows the most miserable waste of one of the chief elements of the wealth and prosperity of the country, the water.

In this respect, Spain and the high lands of Mexico may be compared together. There is no scarcity of rain in either country, and yet both are dry and parched, while the number and size of their torrent-beds show with what violence the mountain-streams descend into lakes or rivers, rather agents of destruction than of benefit to the land. Strangely enough, both countries have been in possession of races who understood that water was the very life-blood of the land, and worked hard to build systems of arteries to distribute it over the surface. In both countries, the warlike Spaniards overcame these races, and irrigating works already constructed were allowed to fall to ruin.

When the Moriscos were expelled from their native provinces of Andalusia and Granada, their places were but slowly filled up with other settlers, so that a great part of their aqueducts and watercourses fell into decay within a few years. These new colonists, moreover, came from the Northern provinces, where the Moorish system of culture was little understood; and, incredible as it may seem, though they must have had ocular evidence of the advantages of artificial irrigation, they even neglected to keep in repair the water-channels on their own ground. Now the traveller, riding through Southern Spain, may see in desolate barren valleys remains of the Moorish works which centimes ago brought fertility to grain-fields and orchards, and made the country the garden of Europe.

There was another nation who seem to have far surpassed both Moors and Aztecs in the magnitude of their engineering-works for this purpose. The Peruvians cut through mountains, filled up valleys, and carried whole rivers away in artificial channels to irrigate their thirsty soil. The historians' accounts of these water-works as they were, and even travellers' descriptions of the ruins that still remain, fill us with astonishment. It seems almost like some strange fatality that this nation too should have been conquered by the same race, the ruin of its great national works following immediately upon the Conquest.

Spain is rising again after long centuries of degradation, and is developing energies and resources which seem likely to raise it high among European nations, and the Spaniards are beginning to hold their own again among the peoples of Europe. But they have had to pay dearly for the errors of their ancestors in the great days of Charles the Fifth.

The ancient Mexicans were not, it is true, to be compared with the Spanish Arabs or the Peruvians in their knowledge of agriculture and the art of irrigation; but both history and the remains still to be found in the country prove that in the more densely populated parts of the plains they had made considerable progress. The ruined aqueduct of Tetzcotzinco which I have just mentioned was a grand work, serving to supply the great gardens of Nezahualcoyotl, which covered a large space of ground and excited the admiration of the Conquerors, who soon destroyed them, it is said, in order that they might not remain to remind the conquered inhabitants of their days of heathendom.

Such works as these seem, however, not to have extended over whole provinces as they did in Spain. In the thinly peopled mountain-districts, the Indians broke up their little patches of ground with a hoe, and watered them from earthen jars, as indeed they do to this day.

The Spaniards improved the agriculture of the country by introducing European grain, and fruit-trees, and by bringing the old Roman plough, which is used to this day in Mexico as in Spain, where two thousand years have not superseded its use or even altered it. Against these improvements we must set a heavy account of injury done to the country as regards its cultivation. The Conquest cost the lives of several hundred thousand of the labouring class; and numbers more were taken away from the cultivation of the land to work as slaves for the conquerors in building houses and churches, and in the silver-mines. When the inhabitants were taken away, the ground went out of cultivation, and much of it has relapsed into desert. Even before the Conquest, Mexico had been suffering for many years from incessant wars, in which not only thousands perished on the field of battle, but the prisoners sacrificed annually were to be counted by thousands more, while famine carried off the women and children whose husbands and fathers had perished. But the slaughter and famine of the first years of the Spanish Conquest far exceeded anything that the country had suffered before.

At the time of the Conquest of Mexico the Spaniards let the native irrigating-works fall into decay; and they took still more active measures to deprive the land of its necessary water, by their indiscriminate destruction of the forests on the hills that surround the plains. When the trees were cut down, the undergrowth soon perished, and the soil which had served to check the descending waters in their course was soon swept away. During the four rainy months, each heavy shower sends down a flood along the torrent-bed which flows into a river, and so into the ocean, or, as in the Mexican valley, into a salt lake, where it only serves to injure the surrounding land. In both cases it runs away in utter waste.

In later years the Spanish owners of the soil had the necessity of the system impressed upon them by force of circumstances; and large sums were spent upon the construction of irrigating channels, even in the outlying states of the North.

In the American territory recently acquired from Mexico history has repeated itself in a most curious way. We learn from Froebel, the German traveller, that the new American settlers did not take kindly to the system of irrigation which they found at work in the country. They were not used to it, and it interfered with their ideas of liberty by placing restrictions upon their doing what they pleased on their own land. So they actually allowed many of the water-canals to fall into ruins. Of course they soon began to find out their mistake, and are probably investing heavily in water-supply by this time. We ought not to be too severe upon the Spaniards of the sixteenth century for an economical mistake which we find the Americans falling into under similar circumstances in the nineteenth.

CHAPTER VII.
CUERNAVACA. TEMISCO. XOCHICALCO.

Much too soon, as we thought, the day came when we had arranged to leave Tezcuco and return to Mexico, to prepare for a journey into the tierra caliente. On the evening of our return to the capital there was a little earthquake, but neither of us noticed it; and thus we lost our one chance, and returned to England without having made acquaintance with that peculiar sensation.

The purchase of horses and saddles and other equipments for our journey, gave us an opportunity of poking about into out-of-the-way corners of the city, and seeing some new phases of Mexican life; and certainly we made the most of the chance. We made acquaintance with horse-dealers, who brought us horses to try in the courtyard of the great house of our friends the English merchants in the Calle Seminario, and there showed off their paces, walking, pacing, and galloping. To trot is considered a disgusting vice in a Mexican horse; and the universal substitute for it here is the *paso*, a queer shuffling run, first, the two legs on one side together, and then the other two. You jolt gently up and down without rising in the stirrups; and when once you are used to it the paso is not disagreeable, and it is well suited to long mountain-journeys. Horses in the United States are often trained to this gait, and are known as "pacing" horses. Another peculiarity in the training of Mexican horses is, that many of them are taught to "rayar," that is, to put their fore-feet out after the manner of mules going down a pass; and slide a short distance along the ground, so as to stop suddenly in the midst of a rapid gallop. To practise the horses in this feat, the jockey draws a lino ("*raya*") on the ground, and teaches them to stop exactly as they reach it, and whirl round in the opposite direction. This performance is often to be seen on the paseo, and other places, where smart young gentlemen like to show off themselves and their horses; but it is only a fancy trick, and they acknowledge that it spoils the animal's fore-legs.

After much bargaining and chaffering we bought three horses for ourselves and our man Antonio, giving eight, seven, and four pounds for them. This does not seem much to give for good hackneys, as these were; but they were not particularly cheap for Mexico. While we were at Tezcuco, Mr. Christy used to ride one of Mr. Bowring's horses, a pretty little chestnut, which carried him beautifully, and had cost just eleven dollars, or forty-six shillings. It had been bought of the horse-dealers who come down every year from the almost uninhabited states of Chihuahua, Durango, and Cohahuila, on the American frontier, where innumerable herds of horses, all but wild, roam over boundless prairies, feeding on the tall coarse grass. Their keep costs so little, that the breeders are not compelled, as in England, to break them in and sell them at the earliest possible moment, and they let the young colts roam untamed till they are five or six years old. Their great strength and power of endurance in proportion to their size is in great measure to be ascribed to this early indulgence.

It is very clear that when a horse is to be sold for somewhere between two and six pounds, the breeder cannot afford to spend much time in breaking him in. The rough-rider lazos him, puts on the bridle with its severe bit, and springs upon his back in spite of kicking and plunging. The horse gallops furiously off across country of his own accord, but when his pace begins to flag, the great vaquero spurs come into requisition, and in an hour or two he comes back to the corral dead beat and conquered once for all. It is easy to teach him his paces afterwards. The anquera—as it is called—is put on his haunches, to cure him of trotting, and to teach him the paso instead. It is a leather covering fringed with iron tags, which is put on behind the saddle, and allows the horse to pace without annoying him; but the least approach to a trot brings the pointed tags rattling upon his haunches. We bought one of these anqueras at Puebla. It was very old, and curiously ornamented with carved patterns. In the last century, these anqueras were a regular part of Mexican horse-equipment; but now, except in horse-breaking yards or old curiosity-shops, they are seldom to be seen.

Almost all the Mexican horses descend from the Arab breed—the gentlest and yet the most spirited in the world, which have not degenerated since the Spaniards brought them over in the early days of the Conquest, but retain unchanged their small graceful shape, their swiftness, and their power of bearing fatigue. There seem really to be no large horses bred in the country. Instead of jolting about in a carriage drawn by eight or ten mules, with harness covered with silver and gold—as rich Mexicans used to do, the proper thing now is to have a pair of tall carriage-horses, like ours in England; and these are brought at great expense from the United States, and by the side of the graceful little Mexicans they look as big and as clumsy as elephants.

Our saddles were of the old Moorish pattern, of monstrous size and weight, very comfortable for the rider, but, I fear, much less so for the horse, whose back often gets sadly galled, in spite of the thick padding and the two or three blankets that are put on underneath. These saddles run into high peaks behind and before, so that you can hardly fall out of them, even when you go to sleep in the saddle on a long journey, as many people habitually do. In front, the saddle rises into a pummel which is made of hard wood, and is something like a large mushroom with its stalk. Round this the end of the lazo is wound, after the noose has been thrown. All Mexican saddles are provided with these heads in front, and have, moreover, several pairs of little thongs attached to them on each side, which serve to tie on bags, whips, water-gourds, and other odds and ends. Behind the seat of the saddle are more straps, where cloaks and serapes are fastened; and in case of need even a carpet-bag will travel there. We were in the habit of returning from our expeditions with our horses so covered with the plants and curiosities we had collected, that it became no easy matter to get our legs safely over the horses' backs, into their proper places among the clusters of miscellanea. Our acquaintances used to compare us to the perambulating butchers' shops, which are a feature in Mexican streets, and consist of a horse with a long saddle covered with hooks, and on every hook a joint.

The flaps of our saddles, the great spatterdashes that protected our feet from the mud, and the broad stirrup-straps were covered with carved and embossed patterns; indeed almost all leather-work is decorated in this way, and the saddle-makers delight in ornamenting their wares with silver plates and bosses; so that it was not surprising that our saddles and bridles should have cost, though second-hand, nearly as much as the horses.

In books of travels in Mexico up to the beginning of the present century, one of the staple articles of wondering description was the gorgeous trappings of the horses, and the spurs, bits, and stirrups of gold and silver. The costumes have not changed much, but the taste for such costly ornaments has abated; and it is now hardly respectable to have more than a few pounds worth of bullion on one's saddle or around one's hat, or to wear a hundred or so of buttons of solid gold down the sides of one's leather trousers, with a very questionable cotton calzoncillo underneath.

The horses' bits are made with a ring, which pinches the under-lip when the bridle is tightened, and causes great pain when it is pulled at all hard. At first sight it seems cruel to use such bits, but the system works very well; and the horses, knowing the power their rider has over them, rarely misbehave themselves. One rides along with the loop at the end of the twisted horse-hair bridle hanging loose on one finger, so that the horse's mouth is much less pulled about than with the bridles we are accustomed to in England. When it is necessary to guide the horse, the least pressure is enough; but, as a general rule, the little fellow can find his way as well as his rider can. We used continually to let our reins drop on our horses' necks, and jog on careless of pits and stumbling-blocks. I have even seen my companion take out his pocket-book, and improve the occasion by making notes and sketches as he went.

The distance from Mexico to Vera Cruz is about two hundred and fifty miles, and what the roads are I have in some measure described. Rafael Beraza, the courier of the English Mission at Mexico, used to ride this with despatches regularly once a month in forty hours, and occasionally in thirty-five. He changed horses about every ten or fifteen miles; and now and then, when, overcome by sleep, he would let the boy who accompanied him to the next stage ride first, his own horse following, and the rider comfortably dozing as he went along.

As for our own equipment, Mr. Christy adopted the attributes of the eastern traveller when he came into the country, the great umbrella, the veil, and the felt hat with a white handkerchief over it. As for me, my wardrobe was scanty; so, when my travelling coat wore out at the elbows and my trousers were sat through—like the little bear's chair in the story, I replaced the garments with a jacket of chamois leather, and a pair of loose trousers made of the same, after the manner of the country. Then came a grey felt hat, as stiff as a boiler-plate, and of more than quakerish lowness of crown and broadness of brim, but secularized by a silver serpent for a hatband; also, a red silk sash, which—fastening round the waist—held up my trousers, and interfered with my digestion; lastly, a woollen serape to sleep under, and to wear in the mornings and evenings. This is the genuine ranchero costume, and it did me good service. Indeed, ever since my Mexican journey I have considered that George Fox decidedly showed his good sense by dressing himself in a suit of leather; much more so than the people who laughed at him for it.

In the country, all Mexicans—high and low—wear this national dress; and in this they are distinguished from the Indians, who keep to the cotton shirts and drawers, and the straw hats of their ancestors. In the towns, it is only the lower classes who dress in the ranchero costume, for "nous autres" wear European garments and follow the last Paris fashion, with these exceptions—that for riding, people wear jackets and calzoneras of the national cut, though made of cloth, and that the Mexican hat is often worn even by people who adopt no other parts of the costume. There never were such hats as these for awkwardness. The flat sharp brims of passers-by are always threatening to cut your head off in the streets. You cannot get into a carriage with your hat on, nor sit there when you are in. But for walking and riding under a fierce sun, they are perhaps better than anything else that can be used.

The Mexican blanket—the serape—is a national institution; It is wider than a Scotch plaid, and nearly as long, with a slit in the middle; and it is woven in the same gaudy Oriental patterns which are to be seen on the prayer-carpets of Turkey and Palestine to this day. It is worn as a cloak, with the end flung over the left shoulder, like the Spanish *capa*, and muffling up half the face when its owner is chilly or does not wish to be recognized. When a heavy rain comes down, and he is on horseback, he puts his head through the slit in the middle, and becomes a moving tent. At night he rolls himself up in it, and sleeps on a mat or a board, or on the stones in the open air.

Convenient as it is, the serape is as much tabooed among the "respectable" classes in the cities as the rest of the national costume. I recollect going one evening after dark to the house of our friends in the Calle Seminario with my serape on, and nearly having to fight it out with the great dog Nelson, who was taking charge of his master's room. Nelson knew me perfectly well, and had sat that very morning at the hotel-gate for half an hour, holding my horse, while a crowd of leperos stood round, admiring his size and the gravity of his demeanour as he sat on the pavement, with the bridle in his mouth. But that a man in a serape should come into his master's room at dusk was a thing he could not tolerate, till the master himself came in, and satisfied his mind on the subject.

As I said, the equipment of ourselves and our three horses took us into a variety of strange places, for we bought the things we wanted piece by piece, when we saw anything that suited us. Among other places we went to the Baratillo, which is the Rag-Fair and Petticoat Lane of Mexico, and moreover the emporium for whips, bridles, bits, old spurs, old iron, and odds and ends generally. The little shops are arranged in long lines, after the manner of the eastern bazaar; and the shopkeepers, when they are not smoking cigarettes outside, are sitting in their little dens, within arms-length of all the wares they have to sell. Here we found what we had come for, and much more too, in the way of wonderful old spurs, combs, boxes, and ornaments; so that we came several times more before we left the country, and never without carrying away some curious old relic.

Mexico, as everybody knows, is decidedly a thievish place. The shops are all shut at dark, after the *Oración*, for fear of thieves. Ladies used to wear immense tortoise-shell combs at the back of their heads, where the mantilla is fastened on; but, when it became a regular trade for thieves to ride on horseback through the streets, and pull out the combs as they went, the fashion had to be given up. These curiously carved and ornamented combs are still preserved as curiosities, and we bought several of them.

While we were in Mexico, they knocked a man down in the great square at noon-day, robbed him, and left him there for dead. The square is so large, and the sun was so hot, that the police—whose head-quarters are under the arches in that very square—could not possibly walk across to see what was going on! —*moral*, if you will have the distinction of having the largest square in the world, you must take the consequences.

Of course, where thieving is so general, the market for stolen goods must be a place of considerable trade, and this Baratillo is one of the principal depôts for such wares. One may realize here the story of the citizen, in the old book, who had his wig stolen at the beginning of his walk through London, and found it hanging up for sale a little further on. Here the deserter comes to sell his uniform and his ricketty old flintlock. Small blame to him. I would do the same myself if I were in his place, and were compelled to serve under one rascally political adventurer against another rascally political adventurer—to say nothing of being treated like a dog, half-starved, and not paid at all, except by a sort of half license to plunder. "Those poor soldiers! we can't pay them, you know, and they must live somehow."

I have abused the Mexicans for being thieves, and not without reason, though, as regards ourselves personally, we never lost anything except a great brand-new waterproof coat which my companion had brought with him, promising to himself that under its shelter he should bid defiance to the daily rain-storms of the wet season. As we dismounted from the Diligence in Mexico, in the courtyard of the hotel, some one relieved him of it. We did not know of the Baratillo in those days, or would have gone to look for it there. At the time of our visit it was too late, for if it ever had been there, the Mexicans understand too well the value of an English "ulli," as they call them, to let it hang long for sale. "Ulli" is not a borrowed word, but the genuine Aztec name for India-rubber, which was used to make playing-balls with, long before the time of Columbus.

I mentioned the water-bottles as part of our equipment. They are gourds, which are throttled with bandages while young, so as to make them grow into the shape of bottles with necks. Then they are hung up to dry; and the inside being cleaned out through a small hole near the stalk, they are ready for use, holding two or three pints of water. A couple of inches of a corn-cob (the inside of a ear of Indian corn) makes a capital cork; and the bottle is hung by a loop of string to the pummel of the saddle, where it swings about without fear of breaking. One may see gourds, prepared in just the same way, in Italy, hanging up under the eaves of the little farm-houses, among the festoons of red and yellow ears of Indian corn; and indeed the gourd-bottle is a regular institution of Southern Europe.

We sent Antonio on with the horses to Cuernavaca, and started by the Diligence early one morning, accompanied by one of our English friends, whom I will call—as every-one else did—Don Guillermo. It is the regular thing here, as in Spain, to call everybody by his or her Christian name. You may have known Don Antonio or Don Felipe for weeks before you happen to hear their surnames.

The road ran at first over the plain, among great water-meadows, with herds of cattle pasturing, and fields of wheat and maize. Ploughing was going on, after the primitive fashion of the country, with two oxen yoked to each plough. The yoke is fastened to the horns of the oxen, and to the centre of the yoke a pole is attached. At the other end of this pole is the plough itself, which consists of a wooden stake with an iron point and a handle. The driver holds the handle in one hand and his goad in the other (a long reed with an iron point), and so they toil along, making a long scratch as they go. A man follows the plough, and drops in single grains of Indian corn, about three feet apart. The furrows are three feet from one another, so that each stalk occupies some nine square feet of ground. When the plants are growing up they dig between them, and heap up round each stalk a little mound of earth.

We passed many little houses consisting of one square room, built of mud-bricks, with mud-mortar stuck full of little stones; without windows, but generally possessing the luxury of a chimney, with a couple of bricks forming an arch over it to keep out the rain. Glimpses of men smoking cigarettes at the doors, half-naked brown children rolling in the dirt, and women on their knees inside, hard at work grinding the corn for those eternal tortillas.

At San Juan de Dios Mr. Christy climbed to the top of the Diligence, behind the conductor, who sat with a large black leather bag full of stones on the footboard before him. Whenever one of the nine mules showed a disposition to shirk his work, a heavy stone came flying at him, always hitting him in a tender place, for long practice had made the conductor almost as good a shot as the goat-herds in the mountains, who are said to be able to hit their goats on whichever horn they please, and so to steer them straight when they seem inclined to stray. But our conductor simply threw the stones, whereas the goat-herd uses the aloe-fibre honda, or sling, that one sees hanging by dozens in the Mexican shops.

We pass near Churubusco, and along the line by which the American army reached Mexico. The field of lava which they crossed is close at our right hand; and just on the other side of it lie Tisapán and our friend Don Alejandro's cotton-factory. On our left are the freshwater-lakes of Xochimilco and Chalco, which had risen several feet, and flooded the valley in their neighbourhood. Between us and the great mountain-chain that forms the rim of the valley, lies a group of extinct volcanos, from one of which descends the great lava-field.

Passing in full view of these picturesque craters, now mostly covered with trees and brushwood, we begin to ascend, and are soon among the porphyritic range that forms a wall between us and the land of sugar-canes and palms.

Along the road towards Mexico came long files of Indians, dressed in the national white cotton shirts and short drawers and sandals, made like Montezuma's, though not with plates of gold on the soles, such as that monarch's sandals had. Some of these Indians are bringing on their backs wood and charcoal from the pine-forest higher up among the mountains, and some have fastened to their backs light crates full of live fowls or vegetables; others are carrying up tropical fruits from the tierra caliente below, zapotes and mameis, nisperos and granaditas, tamarinds and fresh sugar-canes. These people are walking with their loads thirty or forty miles to market: but their race have been used as beasts of burden for ages, and they don't mind it.

Bright blue and red birds, and larger and more brilliant butterflies than are seen in Europe, show that, though we are among fields of wheat and maize, we are in the tropics after all. As the road rises we get views of the broad valley, with its lakes and green meadows, and the great white haciendas with their clumps of willows, their church-towers, and the clusters of adobe huts surrounding them—like the peasants' cottages in feudal Europe, crowding up to the baron's castle.

Our mules begin to flag as we toil up the steep ascent; but the conductor rattles the stones in his black bag, and as the ominous sound reaches their ears, they start off again with renewed vigour. We pass San Mateo, a village of charcoal-burners, where a large and splendid stone church, with its tall dark cypresses, stands among the huts of reeds and pine-shingles that form the village.

Trains of mules are continually passing with their heavy loads of wood and charcoal, bales of goods and barrels of aguardiente de caña, which is rum made from the sugar-cane, but not coloured like that which comes to England. The men are continually rushing backwards and forwards among their beasts, which are not content with kicking and biting, and banging against one another, but are always trying to lie down in the road; and one of the principal duties of the arriero is constantly to keep an eye on all his beasts at once, and, when he sees one preparing to lie down, to be beforehand with him, and drive him on by a furious shower of blows, kicks, and curses. Certainly, the Mexican mules are the finest and strongest in the world; and, though they are just as obstinate here as elsewhere, they are worth two or three times as much as horses.

Our road lies through a forest of pines and oaks, which reaches to the summit of the pass, where stands a wretched little village, La Guarda. There we had a thoroughly Mexican breakfast, with pulque in tall tumblers, and endless successions of tortillas, coming in hot and hot from the kitchen, where we could see brown women with bare arms, and black hair plaited in long tails, kneeling by the charcoal fire, and industriously patting out fresh supplies, and baking them rapidly on a hot plate. The *pièce de résistance* was a stew, bright red with tomatas, and hot as fire with chile; and then came the *frijoles*—the black beans—without which no Mexican, high or low, considers a meal complete. The walls of the room were decorated with highly coloured engravings, one of which represented an engagement between a Spanish and an English fleet, in which the English ships are being boarded by the victorious Spaniards, or are being blown up in the background. Where the engagement was I cannot recollect. People in Mexico, to whom I mentioned this remarkable historical event, assured me that there are still to be seen pictures of the destruction of the English fleet by the French and Spaniards in the Bay of Trafalgar!

Mexico was always, until the establishment of the republic, profoundly ignorant of European affairs. In the old times, when the intercourse with the mother-country was by the great ship, "el nao," which came once a year, the government at home could have just such news circulated through the country as seemed proper and convenient to them. We see in our own times how despotic governments can mystify their subjects, and distort contemporary history into what shape they please. But in Spanish America the system was worked to a greater extent than in any other country I have heard of; and the undercurrent of popular talk, which spreads in France and Russia things and opinions not to be found in the newspapers, had in Mexico but little influence. Scarcely any Mexican travelled, scarcely any foreigner visited the country, and the Spaniards who came to hold offices and make fortunes were all in the interest of the old country; so the Mexicans went on, until the beginning of this century, believing that Spain still occupied the same position among the nations of Europe that it had held in the days of Charles the Fifth.

While my companion was outside the Diligence, Don Guillermo and I were left to the conversation of an Italian fellow-passenger. One finds such characters in books, but never before or since have I seen the reality. He might have been the original of the great Braggadoccio. His conversation was like a chapter out of the autobiography of his countryman Alfieri.

He had accompanied the Italian nobleman who was killed in an affray with the Mexican robbers, some years ago, and on that occasion his defence had been most heroic. He himself had shot several of the robbers; till at last, his friend being killed, the rest of the party yielded to the overwhelming numbers of the brigands, and he ran off to fetch assistance!

Whenever he was riding along a Mexican road, and any suspicious-looking person asked him for a light, his habit was to hand him his cigar stuck in the muzzle of a pistol; "and they always take the hint," he said, "and see that it won't do to interfere with us." Alone, he had been attacked by three armed men, but with a pistol in each hand he had compelled them to retreat. But this was not all; our champion was victorious in love as well as in arms. Like the great Alfieri, to whom I have compared him, in every country where he travelled, the most beautiful and distinguished ladies hardly waited for him to ask before they cast themselves at his feet. Refusing the rich jewels that he offered them, they declared that they loved him for himself alone.

Weeks after, we were talking to our friend Mr. Del Pozzo, the Italian apothecary in the Calle Plateros, and happened to ask him if he were acquainted with his heroic countryman. Whereupon the apothecary went off into fits of unextinguishable laughter, and told us how our friend really had been in the skirmish he described, and had nobly run away almost before a shot was fired, leaving his friends to fight it out. An hour or two after, he was found shaking with terror in a ditch.

To return to our road. The forest is on both sides of the Sierra; but it is on the southern slope, over which we look down from the pass, that the pines attain their fullest size and beauty; for here they are as grand as in the Scandinavian forests, with all the beauty of the pine-trees on the Italian hills. The pass, with its deep forest skirting the road, has been a resort of robbers for many years; and the driver pointed out to my companion a little grassy dell by the roadside, from which forty men had rushed out and plundered the Diligence just ten days before. With his mind just prepared, one may imagine his feelings when he caught sight of some twenty wild-looking fellows in all sorts of strange garments, with the bright sunshine gleaming on the barrels of their muskets. A man was riding a little in front of us, and as he approached the others they descended, and ranged themselves by the side of the road. They were only the guard, after all, and such a guard! Their thick matted black hair hung about over their low foreheads and wild brown faces. Some had shoes, some had none, and some had sandals. They had straw hats, glazed hats, no hats, leather jackets and trousers, cotton shirts and drawers, or drawers without any shirt at all; and—what looked worst of all—some had ragged old uniforms on, like deserters from the army, and there are no worse robbers than they. When the Diligence reached them, the guard joined us; some galloping on before, some following behind, whooping and yelling, brandishing their arms, and dashing in among the trees and out into the road again. Every now and then my friend outside got a glimpse down the muzzle of a musket, which did not add to his peace of mind. At last we got through the dangerous pass, and then we made a subscription for the guard, who departed making the forest ring again with war-whoops, and firing off their muskets in our honour until we were out of hearing.

The top of the pass is 12,000 feet above the sea, but the clouds seemed as high as ever above us, and the swallows were flying far up in the air. Three thousand feet lower we were in a warmer region, among oaks and arbutus; and here, as in our higher latitudes, the climate is far hotter than on the northern slope at the same height. Bananas are to be found at an elevation of 9,000 feet, three times the height at which they ceased on the eastern slope, as we came up from Vera Cruz. This difference between the two slopes depends, in part, on the different quantity of sunshine they receive, which is of some importance, although we are within the tropics. But the sheltering of the southern sides from the chilling winds from the north still further contributes to give their vegetation a really tropical character.

We felt the heat becoming more and more intense as we descended, and when we reached Cuernavaca we lay down in the beautiful garden of the inn, among orange-trees and cocoanut-palms, listening to the pleasant cool sound of running water, and looking down into the great barranca with its perpendicular walls of rock, and the luxuriant vegetation of the tierra caliente covering the banks of the stream that flowed far below us. We could easily shout to the people on the other edge of the ravine, but it would have taken hours of toiling down the steep paths and up again before we could have reached them.

Here our horses were waiting for us; and an hour or two's ride brought us to the great sugar-hacienda of Temisco, where we were to pass the night, for towns and inns are few and far between in Mexico when one leaves the more populous mountain-plateaus. So much the better, for my companion had provided himself with letters of introduction, and we had already seen something of hacienda life, and liked it.

As we approached Temisco, we saw upon the slopes, immense fields of sugar-cane, now grown into a dense mass, five or six feet high, most pleasant to look upon for the delicate green tint of the leaves that belongs to no other plant. The colour of our English turf is beautiful, and so are the tints of our English woods in spring, but our fields of grain have a dull and dingy green compared to the sugar-cane and the young Indian corn. In this beautiful valley we cannot charge the inhabitants with entirely neglecting the irrigation of the land. Indeed, the culture of the sugar-cane cannot be carried on without it, and the cost of the watercourses on the large estates has been very great. Unfortunately, even here agriculture is not flourishing. The small number of the white inhabitants, and the distracted state of the country make both life and property very insecure; and the brown people are becoming less and less disposed to labour on the plantations.

It is true that most of these channels were made in old times; little new is done now, and I could make a long list of estates that were once busy and prosperous, giving employment to thousands of the Indian inhabitants, and that are now over-grown with weeds and falling to ruin.

Entering the iron gate of the hacienda, we found ourselves in an immense courtyard, into which open all the principal buildings of the estate, the house of the proprietor, the church—which forms a necessary part of every hacienda —the crushing-mill, and the boiling-houses. Into the same great patio open the immense stables for the many riding-horses and the many hundreds of mules that carry the sugar and rum over the mountains to market, and the tienda, the shop of the estate, through which almost all the money paid to the labourers comes back to the proprietor in exchange for goods. A mountain of fresh-cut canes stood near the door of the trapiche (the crushing-mill); and a gang of Indians were constantly going backwards and forwards carrying them in by armfuls; while a succession of mules were continually bringing in fresh supplies from the plantation to replenish the great heap. The court-yard was littered all over, knee-deep, with dry cane-trash; and mules, just freed from their galling saddles, were rolling on their backs in it, kicking with all their legs at once, and evidently in a state of high enjoyment. Part of one side of the square was a sort of wide cloister, and in it stood chairs and tables.

Here the business of the place was transacted, and the Administrador could look up from his ledger, and see pretty well what was going on all over the establishment.

It is very common for the owners of these haciendas to be absentees, and to leave the entire control of their estates to the administradors; but at Temisco, which is much better managed than most others, this is not the case, and the son of the proprietor generally lives there. He was out riding, so we sent our horses to the stable, and lounged about eating sugar-canes till he should return. Presently he came, a young man in a broad Mexican hat and white jacket and trousers, mounted on a splendid little horse, with his saddle glittering with silver, every inch a planter. He welcomed us hospitably, and we sat down together in the cloister looking out on the courtyard. Evening was closing in, and all at once the church-bell rang. Crowds of Indian labourers in their white dresses came flocking in, hardly distinguishable in the twilight, and the sound of their footsteps deadened as they walked over the dry stubble that covered the ground. All work ceased, every one uncovered and knelt down; while, through the open church-doors, we heard the Indian choir chanting the vesper hymn. In the haciendas of Mexico every day ends thus. Many times I heard the Oración chanted at nightfall, but its effect never diminished by repetition, and to my mind it has always seemed the most impressive of religious services.

Then the Administrador seated himself behind a great book, and the calling over the "raya" began. Every man in turn was called by name, and answered in a loud voice, "I praise God!;" then saying how much he had earned in the day, for the Administrador to write down. "Juan Fernandez!"—"*Alabo a Dios, tres reales y medio*:" "I praise God, one and ninepence." "José Valdes!"—"I praise God, eighteen pence, and sixpence for the boy;" and so on, through a couple of hundred names.

Then came, not unacceptably, a little cup of pasty chocolate and a long roll for each of us. Then Don Guillermo and our host talked about their mutual acquaintances in Mexico, and we asked questions about sugar-planting, and walked about the boiling-house, where the night-gang of brown men were hard at work stirring and skimming at the boiling-pans, and ladling out coarse unrefined sugar into little earthen bowls to cool. This common sugar in bowls is very generally used by the poorer Mexicans. The sugar-boilers were naked excepting a cotton girdle. These men were very strong, and with great powers of endurance, but they did not at all resemble the strong men of Europe with their great muscles standing up under their skin, the men in Michael Angelo's pictures, or the Farnese Hercules. They are equally unlike the thin wiry Arabs, whose strength seems so disproportionate to their lean little bodies.

The pure Mexican Indian is short and sturdy; and, until you have observed the peculiarities of the race, you would say he was too stout and flabby to be strong. But this appearance is caused by the immense thickness of his skin, which conceals the play of his muscles; and in reality his strength is very great, especially in the legs and thighs, and in the muscles that are brought into action in carrying burdens. Sartorius used to observe the Indian miners bringing loads of above five-hundred-weight up a hundred fathoms of mine-ladders, which consist of trunks of trees fixed slanting across the shaft, with notches cut in them for steps.

As I have said before, it is not the mere training of the individual that has produced this remarkable development of the power of carrying loads. The centuries before the Conquest, when there were no beasts of burden, had gradually produced a race whose bodies were admirably fitted for such work; and the persistency with which they have clung to their old habits has done much to prevent their losing this peculiarity.

To complete the description of the Indians which I have been led into by speaking of the sugar-boilers,—they are chocolate-brown in colour, with curved noses, straight black hair hanging flat round their heads and covering their wonderfully low foreheads, and occasionally a scanty black beard. Their faces are broadly oval, their eyes far apart, and they have wide mouths with coarse lips. Not bad faces on the whole, but heavy and unexpressive.

At ten o'clock came a heavy supper, the substantial meal of the day, and immediately afterwards we went to bed, and dreamt such dreams as may be imagined. We were off early in the morning with a wizened old mestizo to guide us to the ruins of Xochicalco, which are on this very estate of Temisco. The estate is forty miles across, however, and it is a long ride to the ruins. After we leave the fields of sugar-cane, we see scarcely a hut, nor a patch of cultivated ground. At last we get to Xochicalco, and find ourselves at the foot of a hill, some four hundred feet in height, extraordinarily regular in its conical shape, more so than any natural hill could be, unless it were the cone of a volcano. At different heights upon this hill, we could see from below broad terraces running round and round it. A little nearer we came upon a great ditch. The sides had fallen in, in many places; sometimes it was quite filled up, and everywhere it was overgrown with thick brushwood, as was the hill itself. It seems that this ditch runs quite round the base of the hill, and is three miles long. Climbing up through the thicket of thorny bushes and out upon the terraces, it became quite evident that the hill had been artificially shaped. The terraces were built up with blocks of solid stone, and paved with the same. On the neighbouring hills we could discern traces of more terrace-roads of the same kind; there must be many miles of them still remaining.

But it was when we reached the summit, that we found the most remarkable part of the structure. The top has been cut away so as to form a large level space, which was surrounded by a stone wall, now in ruins. Inside the inclosure are several mounds of stone, doubtless burial-places, and all that is left of the pyramid. Ruined and defaced as it is, I shall never forget our feelings of astonishment and admiration as we pushed our way through the bushes, and suddenly came upon it. We were quite unprepared for anything of the kind; all we knew of the place when we started that morning being that there were some curious old ruins there.

The pyramid was composed of blocks of hewn stone, so accurately fitted together as hardly to show the joints, and the carving goes on without interruption from one block to another. Some of these blocks are eight feet long, and nearly three feet wide. They were laid together without mortar, and indeed, from the construction of the building, none was required. The first storey is about sixteen feet high, including the plinth at the bottom. Above the plinth comes a sculptured group of figures, which is repeated in panels all round the pyramid, twice on each side. Each panel occupies a space thirty feet long by ten in height, and the bas-reliefs project three or four inches. There is a chief, dressed in a girdle, and with a head-dress of feathers just like those of the Red Indians of the north. Below the girdle he terminates in a scroll. In the middle of the group is what may perhaps be a palm-tree, with a rabbit at its foot. Close to the tree, and reaching nearly to the same height, is a figure with a crocodile's head wearing a crown, and with drapery in parallel lines, like the wings of the creatures in the Assyrian bas-reliefs. Indeed this may very likely be a conventional representation of the robes of feather-work so characteristic of Mexico.

Above these bas-reliefs is a frieze between three and four feet high, with another sculptured panel repeated eight times on each side of the pyramid. This remarkable sculpture represents a man sitting barefoot and crosslegged. On his head is a kind of crown or helmet, with a plume of feathers; and from the front of this helmet there protrudes a serpent, just where in the Egyptian sculptures the royal basilisk is fixed on the crowns of kings and queens. The eyes of this personage are protected by round plates with holes in the middle, held on by a strap round the head, like the coloured glasses used in the United States to keep off the glare of the sun, and known as "goggles." In front of this figure are sculptured a rabbit and some unintelligible ornaments or weapons. "Rabbit" may have been his name.

The frieze is surmounted by a cornice; and above the cornice of the second storey enough remains to show that it was covered with reliefs, in the same way as the first There were five storeys originally: the others have only been destroyed about a century. The former proprietor of the hacienda of Temisco pulled down the upper storeys, and carried away the blocks of stone to build walls and dams with.

The perfect execution of the details in the bas-reliefs and the accuracy with which they are repeated show clearly that it was not so much want of skill as the necessity of keeping to the conventional mode of representing objects that has given so grotesque a character to the Mexican scriptures. Certain figures became associated with religion and astrology in Mexico, as in many other countries; and the sculptor, though his facility in details shows that he could have made far better figures if he had had a chance, never had the opportunity, for he was not allowed to depart from the original rude type of the sacred object. Humboldt remarks that the same undeviating reproduction of fixed models is as striking in the Mexican sculptures done since the Conquest. The clumsy outlines of the rude figures of saints brought from Europe in the 16th century were adopted as models by the native sculptors, and have lasted without change to this day.

It is evident that Xochicalco answered several purposes. It was a fortified hill of great strength, also a sacred shrine, and a burial-place for men of note, whose bodies, no doubt, still lie under the ruined cairns near the pyramid. The magnitude of the ditch and the terraces, as well as the great size of the blocks of stone brought up the hill without the aid of beasts of burden, indicate a large population and a despotic government. The beauty of the masonry and sculpture show that the people who erected this monument had made no small progress in the arts. We must remember, too, that they had no iron, but laboriously cut and polished the hardest granite and porphyry with instruments of stone and bronze; we can hardly tell how.

The resemblances which people find between Assyrian and Egyptian sculptures and the American monuments are of little value, and do not seem sufficient to ground any argument upon. When slightly civilized races copy men, trees, and animals in their rude way, it would be hard if there were not some resemblance among the figures they produce. With reference to their ornamentation, it is true that what is called the "key-border" is quite common in Mexico and Yucatan, and that on this very pyramid the panels are divided by a twisted border, which would not be noticed as peculiar in a "renaissance" building. But the model of this border may have been suggested—on either side of the globe—by creepers twined together in the forest, or by a cord doubled and twisted, such as is represented in one of the commonest Egyptian hieroglyphs.

The cornice which finishes the first storey of the pyramid is a familiar pattern, but nothing can be concluded from these simple geometrical designs, which might be invented over and over again by different races when they began to find pleasure in tracing ornamental devices upon their buildings. Upon the tattooed skins of savages such designs may be seen, and the patterns were certainly in use among them before they had any intercourse with white men. This is the view Humboldt takes of these coincidences. That both the Egyptian king and the Mexican chief should wear a helmet with a serpent standing out from it just above the forehead, is somewhat extraordinary.

Now, who built Xochicalco? Writers on Mexico are quite ready with their answer. They tell us that, according to the Mexican tradition, the country was formerly inhabited by another race, who were called*Toltecâ*, or, as we say, *Toltecs*, from the name of their city, *Tollan*, "the Reed-swamp;" and that they were of the same race as the Aztecs, as shown by the names of their cities and their kings being Aztec words; that they were a highly civilized people, and brought into the country the arts of sculpture, hieroglyphic painting, great improvements in agriculture, many of the peculiar religious rites since practised by other nations who settled after them in Mexico, and the famous astronomical calendar, of which I shall speak afterwards. The particular Toltec king to whom the Mexican historians ascribe the building of Xochicalco was called Nauhyotl, that is to say, "Four Bells," and died A.D. 945.

We are further told that just about the time of our Norman Conquest, the Toltecs were driven out from the Mexican plateau by famine and pestilence, and migrated again southward. Only a few families remained, and from them the Aztecs, Chichemecs, and other barbarous tribes by whom the country was re-peopled, derived that knowledge of the arts and sciences upon which their own civilization was founded. It was by this Toltec nation—say the Mexican writers—that the monuments of Xochichalco, Teotihuacán, and Cholula were built. In their architecture the Aztecs did little more than copy the works left by their predecessors; and, to this day, the Mexican Indians call a builder a *toltecatl* or *Toltec*.

If we consider this circumstantial account to be anything but a mere tissue of fables, the question naturally arises—what became of the remains of the Toltecs when they left the high plains of Mexico? A theory has been propounded to answer this question, that they settled in Chiapas and Yucatan, and built Palenque, Copan, and Uxmal, and the other cities, the ruins of which lie imbedded in the tropical forest.

At the time that Prescott wrote his History of the Conquest, such a theory was quite tenable; but the new historic matter lately made known by the Abbé Brasseur de Bourbourg has given a different aspect to the question. Without attempting to maintain the credibility of this writer's history as a whole, I cannot but think that he has given us satisfactory grounds for believing that the ruined cities of Central America were built by a race which flourished long before the Toltecs; that they were already declining in power and civilization in the seventh century, when the Toltecs began to flourish in Mexico; and that the present Mayas of Yucatan are their degenerate descendants.

What I have seen of Central American and Mexican antiquities, and of drawings of them in books, tends to support the Abbé Brasseur de Bourbourg's view of the history of these countries. Traces of communication between the two peoples are to be found in abundance, but nothing to warrant our holding that either people took its civilization bodily from the other. My excuse for entering into these details must be that some of the facts I have to offer are new.

A bas-relief at Kabah, described in Mr. Stephens' account of his second journey, bears considerable resemblance to that on the so-called "sacrificial stone" of Mexico; and the warrior has the characteristic Mexican *maquahuitl*, or "Hand-wood," a mace set with rows of obsidian teeth.

A curious ornament is met with in the Central American sculptures, representing a serpent with a man's face looking out from between its distended jaws; and we find a similar design in the Aztec picture-writings, sculptures, and pottery.

A remarkable peculiarity in the Aztec picture-writings is that the personages represented often have one or more figures of tongues suspended in mid-air near their mouths, indicating that they are speaking, or that they are persons in authority. Such tongues are to be seen on the Yucatan sculptures.

One of the panels on the Pyramid of Xochicalco seems to have a bearing upon this subject, I mean that of the cross-legged chief, of which I have just spoken.

In the first place, sitting cross-legged is not an Aztec custom. I do not think we ever saw an Indian in Mexico sitting cross-legged. In the picture-writings of the Aztecs, the men sit doubled up, with their chins almost touching their knees; while the women have their legs tucked under them, and their feet sticking out on the left side. On the other hand, this attitude is quite characteristic of the Yucatan sculptures. At Copan there is an altar, with sixteen chiefs sitting cross-legged round it; and, moreover, one of them has a head-dress very much like that of the Xochicalco chief (except that it has no serpent), and others are more or less similar; while I do not recollect anything like it in the Mexican picture-writings. The curious perforated eye-plates of the Xochicalco chief, which he wore—apparently—to keep arrows and javelins out of his eyes, are part of the equipment of the Aztec warrior in the picture-writings, while Palenque and Copan seemed to afford no instance of them; so that in two peculiarities the remarkable sculpture before us seems to belong rather to Yucatan than to Mexico, and in one to Mexico rather than to Yucatan.

It is not even possible in all cases to distinguish Central American sculptures from those of Mexican origin. Among the numerous stone figures in Mr. Christy's museum, some are unmistakably of Central American origin, and some as certainly Mexican; but beside these, there are many which both their owner and myself, though we had handled hundreds of such things, were obliged to leave on the debatable ground between the two classes.

So much for the resemblances. But the differences are of much greater weight. The pear-shaped heads of most of the Central American figures, whose peculiar configuration is only approached by the wildest caricatures of Louis Philippe, are perfectly distinctive. So are the hieroglyphics arranged in squares, found on the sculptures of Central America and in the Dresden Codex. So is the general character of the architecture and sculpture, as any one may see at a glance.

It is quite true that the so-called Aztec Astronomical Calendar was in use in Central America, and that many of the religious observances in both countries, such as the method of sacrificing the human victims, and the practice of the worshippers drawing blood from themselves in honour of the gods, are identical. But there were several ways in which this might have been brought about, and it is no real proof that the civilization of either country was an offshoot from that of the other. To consider it as such would be like arguing that the negroes of Cuba and the Indians of Yucatan had derived their civilization one from the other, because both peoples are Roman Catholics, and use the same almanac. On the whole I am disposed to conclude that the civilizations of Mexico and Central America were originally independent, but that they came much into contact, and thus modified one another to no small extent.

At the risk of being prosy, I will mention the *a priori* grounds upon which we may argue that the civilization of Central America did not grow up there, but was brought ready-made by a people who emigrated there from some other country. There is a theory afloat, that it is only in temperate climates that barbarous nations make much progress in civilizing themselves. In tropical countries the intensity of the heat makes man little disposed for exertion, and the luxuriance of the vegetation supplies him with the little he requires. In such climates—say the advocates of this theory—man acknowledges the supremacy of nature over himself, and gives up the attempt to shape her to his own purposes; and thus, in these countries, the inhabitants go on from generation to generation, lazily enjoying their existence, making no effort, and indeed feeling no desire to raise themselves in the social scale. Upon this theory, therefore, when we find a high civilization in hot countries, as in the plains of India, we have to account for it by supposing an immigration of races bringing their civilization with them from more temperate climates. This theory of civilization favours the idea of the Central American cities having been built by a people from Mexico. The climate of the Mexican highlands, which may be taken in a rough way to correspond with that of North Italy, is well suited to a nation's development. But the cities of Yucatan and Chiapas, though geographically not far removed from the Mexican plateau, are brought by their small elevation above the sea into a very different climate. They are in the land of tropical heat and the rankest vegetation, in the midst of dense forests where pestilential fevers and overwhelming lassitude make it almost impossible for Europeans to live, and where the Indians who still inhabit the neighbourhood of the ruined cities are the merest savages sunk in the lowest depths of lazy ignorance.

If this climate-theory of progress have any truth in it, no barbarous tribe could have raised itself in such a country to the social state which is indicated by the ruins of such temples and cities. They must have been settlers from some more temperate region.

While wandering about the hill of Xochicalco we came upon a spot that strongly excited our curiosity. It was simply a small paved oval space with a little altar at one end, and, lying round about it, some fragments of what seemed to have been a hideous grotesque idol of baked clay. Perhaps it was a shrine dedicated to one of the inferior deities, such as often surrounded the greater temples; for, in Mexico, astronomy, astrology, and religion had become mixed up together, as they have been in other quarters of the globe, and even the astronomical signs of days and months had temples of their own.

Xochicalco means "In the House of Flowers." The word "flower,"—*xochitl*,—is often a part of the names of Mexican places and people, such as the lake of Xochimilco—"In the Flower-plantation."*Tlilxochitl*, literally "black flower," is the Aztec name for vanilla, so that the name of that famous Mexican historian, Ixtlilxochitl, whose name sticks in the throats of readers of Prescott, means "Vanilla-face." Why the place was called "In the House of Flowers" is not clear. The usual explanation seems not unlikely, that it was because offerings of flowers and first-fruits were made upon its shrines. The Toltecs, say the Mexican chroniclers, did not sacrifice human victims; and it was not until long after other tribes had taken possession of their deserted temples, that the Aztecs introduced the custom by sacrificing their prisoners of war. It seems odd, however, that one of the Toltec kings should have been called Topiltzin, which was the title of the chief priest among the Aztecs, whose duty it was to cut open the breasts of the human victims and tear out their hearts.

The Indians always delighted in carrying flowers in their solemn processions, crowning themselves with garlands, and decorating their houses and temples with them; and, while they worshipped their gods according to the simple rites which tradition says their prophet, Quetzalcoatl, ("Feathered Snake,") appointed, before he left them and embarked in his canoe on the Eastern ocean, no name could have been more appropriate for their temple. This pleasant custom did not disappear after the Conquest; and to this day the churches in the Indian districts are beautiful with their brilliant garlands and nosegays, and are as emphatically "houses of flowers" as were the temples in ages long past.

Since writing the above notice of the Pyramid of Xochicalco, I have come upon a new piece of evidence, which, if it may be depended on, proves more about the history of this remarkable monument than all the rest put together. Dupaix made a drawing of the ruins at Xochicalco in 1805, which is to be found in Lord Kingsborough's 'Antiquities of Mexico,' and among the sculptures of the upper tier of blocks is represented a reed, with its leaves set in a square frame, with three small circles underneath; the whole forming, in the most unmistakable way, the sign 3 Acatl (3 Cane) of the Mexican Astronomical Calendar.

Now it must be admitted that Dupaix's drawing of these ruins is most grossly incorrect; but still no amount of mere carelessness in an artist will justify us in supposing him to have invented and put in out of his own head a design so entirely *sui generis* as this. It does not even follow that the drawing is wrong because the sign may not be found there now; for it was in an upper tier, and no doubt many stones have been removed since 1805, for building-purposes.

If the existence of the sign 3 Acatl on the pyramid may be considered as certain, it will fit in perfectly with the accounts of the Mexican historians, who state that Xochicalco was built by a king of the Toltec race, and also that the Aztecs adopted the astronomical calendars of years and days in use among the Toltecs.

It was afternoon when we left Xochicalco and rode on over a gently undulating country, crossing streams here and there, and had our breakfast at Miacatlán under a shed in front of the village shop, where all the activity of the little Indian town seemed to be concentrated. By the road-side were beautiful tamarind-trees with their dark green foliage, and the mamei-tree as large as a fine English horse-chestnut, and not unlike it at a distance. On the branches were hanging the great mameis, just like the inside of cocoa-nuts when the inner shell has been cracked off. It appeared that Nature was not acquainted with M. De La Fontaine's works, or she would probably have got a hint from the fable of the acorn and the pumpkin, and not have hung mameis and cocoa-nuts at such a dangerous height.

CHAPTER VIII.
COCOYOTLA. CACAHUAMILPÁN. CHALMA. OCULAN. TENANCINGO. TOLUCA.

A little before dark we came to the hacienda of Santa Rosita de Cocoyotla, another sugar-plantation which was to be our head-quarters for some days to come. We presented our letter of introduction from the owner of the estate, and the two administradors received us with open arms. We were conducted into the strangers' sleeping-room, a long barrack-like apartment with stone walls and a stone floor that seemed refreshingly dark and cool; we could look out through its barred windows into the garden, where a rapid little stream of water running along the channel just outside made a pleasant gurgling sound. Appearances were delusive, however, and it was only the change from the outside that made us feel the inside cool and pleasant. For days our clothes clung to us as if we had been drowned, and the pocket-handkerchiefs with which we mopped our faces had to be hung on chair-backs to dry. Except in the early morning, there was no coolness in that sweltering place.

In one corner of our room I discerned a brown toad of monstrous size squatting in great comfort on the damp flags. He was as big as a trussed chicken, and looked something like one in the twilight. We pointed him out to the administrador, who brought in two fierce watchdogs, but the toad set up his back and spirted his acrid liquor, and the dogs could not be got to go near him. We stirred him up with a bamboo and drove him into the garden, but he left his portrait painted in slime upon our floor.

The Indian choir chanted the Oración as we had heard it the night before at Temisco, and then came the calling over of the raya. After that we walked about the place, and sat talking in the open corridor. Owners of estates, and indeed all white folks living in this part of the country were beginning to feel very anxious about their position, and not without reason. Ordinary political events excite but little interest in these Indian districts, and so trifling a matter as a revolution and a change of people in power does not affect them perceptibly. The Indians are absolutely free, and have their votes and their civil privileges like any other citizens. All that the owners of the plantations ask of them is to work for high wages, and hitherto they have done this, but for years it has been becoming more and more difficult to get them to work. All they do with the money when they get it, is to spend it in drinking and gambling, if they are of an extravagant turn of mind; or to bury it in some out-of-the-way place, if they are given to saving. If they were whites or half-caste Mexicans they would spend their money upon fine clothes and horses, but the Indian keeps to the white cotton dress of his fathers, and is never seen on horseback. Now this being the case, it does not seem unreasonable that they should not much care about working hard for money that is of so little use to them when they have got it, and that they should prefer living in their little huts walled with canes and thatched with palm-leaves, and cultivating the little patch of garden-ground that lies round it—which will produce enough fruit and vegetables for their own subsistence, and more besides, which they can sell for clothes and tobacco. A day or two of this pleasant easy work at their own ground will provide this, and they do not see why they should labour as hired servants to get more. This is bad enough, think the hacendados, but there is worse behind. The Indians have been of late years becoming gradually aware that the government of the country is quite rotten and powerless, and that in their own districts at least, the power is very much in their own hands, for the few scattered whites could offer but slight resistance. The doctrine of "America for the Americans" is rapidly spreading among them, and active emissaries are going about reminding them that the Spaniards only got their lands by the right of the strongest, and that now is the time for them to reassert their rights.

The name of Alvarez is circulated among them, as the man who is to lead them in the coming struggle—Alvarez the mulatto general, whose hideous portrait is in every print-shop in Mexico. He was President before Comonfort, and is now established with his Indian regiments in the hot pestilential regions of the Pacific coast.

The undisguised contempt with which the Indians have been treated for ages by the whites and the mestizos has not been without its effect. The revolution, and the abolition of all legal distinctions of caste still left the Indians mere senseless unreasoning creatures in the eyes of the whiter races; and, if the original race once get the upper hand, it will go hard with the whites and their estates in these parts. Only a day or two before we came down from Mexico, the government had endeavoured to quarter some troops in one of the little Indian towns which we passed through on our way from Temisco. But the inhabitants saluted them with volleys of stones from the church-steeple and the house-tops, and they had to retreat most ignominiously into their old quarters among "reasonable people."

I have put down our notions on the "Indian Question," just as they presented themselves to us at the time. The dismal forebodings of the planters seem to have been fulfilled to some extent at least, for we heard, not long after our return to Europe, that the Indians had plundered and set fire to numbers of the haciendas of the south country, and that our friends the administradors of Cocoyotla had escaped with their lives. The hacienda itself, if our information is correct, which I can hardly doubt, is now a blackened deserted ruin.

At supper appeared two more guests besides ourselves, apparently traders carrying goods to sell at the villages and haciendas on the road. In such places the hacienda offers its hospitality to all travellers, and there was room in our caravanserai for yet more visitors if they had come. Our beds were like those in general use in the tropics, where mattresses would be unendurable, and even the pillows become a nuisance. The frame of the bed has a piece of coarse cloth stretched tightly over it; a sheet is laid upon this, and another sheet covers the sleeper. This compromise between a bed and a hammock answers the purpose better than anything else, and admits of some circulation of air, especially when you have kicked off the sheet and lie fully exposed to the air and the mosquitos.

I cannot say that it is pleasant to wake an hour or two after going to bed, with your exact profile depicted in a wet patch on the pillow; nor is it agreeable to become conscious at the same time of an intolerable itching, and to find, on lighting a candle, that an army of small ants are walking over you, and biting furiously. These were my experiences during my first night at Cocoyotla; and I finished the night, lying half-dressed on my bed, with the ends of my trousers-legs tied close with handkerchiefs to keep the creatures out. But when we got into our saddles in the early morning, we forgot all these little miseries, and started merrily on our expedition to the great stalactitic cave of Cacahuamilpán.

Our day's journey had two objects; one was to see the cave, and the other to visit the village close by,—one of the genuine unmixed Indian communities, where even the Alcalde and the Cura, the temporal and spiritual heads of the society, are both of pure Indian blood, and white influence has never been much felt.

A ride of two or three hours from the hacienda brought us into a mountainous district, and there we found the village of Cacahuamilpán on the slope of a hill. In the midst of neat trim gardens stood the little white church, and the ranches of the inhabitants, cottages of one room, with walls of canes which one can see through in all directions, and roofs of thatch, with the ground smoothed and trodden hard for a floor. Everything seemed clean and prosperous, and there was a bright sunny look about the whole place; but to Englishmen, accustomed to the innumerable appliances of civilized life, it seems surprising how very few and simple are the wants of these people. The inventory of their whole possessions will only occupy a few lines. The *metate* for grinding or rubbing down the maize to be patted out into tortillas, a few calabashes for bottles, and pieces of calabashes for bowls and cups, prettily ornamented and painted, and hanging on pegs round the walls. A few palm-leaf mats (petates) to sleep upon, some pots of thin unglazed earthenware for the cooking, which is done over a wood-fire in the middle of the floor. A chimney is not necessary in houses which are like the Irishman's coat, consisting principally of holes. A wooden box, somewhere, contains such of the clothes of the family as are not in wear. There is really hardly anything I can think of to add to this catalogue, except the agricultural implements, which consist of a wooden spade, a hoe, some sharp stakes to make the drills with, and the machete—which is an iron bill-hook, and serves for pruning, woodcutting, and now and then for less peaceful purposes. Sometimes one sees women weaving cotton-cloth, or *manta*, as it is called, in a loom of the simplest possible construction; or sitting at their doors in groups, spinning cotton-thread with the *malacates*, and apparently finding as much material for gossip here as elsewhere.

The Mexicans spun and wove their cotton-cloth just in this way before the Conquest, and malacates of baked clay are found in great numbers in the neighbourhood of the old Mexican cities. They are simple, like very large button-moulds, and a thin wooden skewer stuck in the hole in the middle makes them ready for use. Such spindles were used by the lake-men of Switzerland, but the earthen heads were not quite the same in shape, being like balls pierced with a hole, as are those at present used in Mexico.

The Indians here had not the dull sullen look we saw among those who inhabit the colder regions; and, though belonging to the same race, they were better formed and had a much freer bearing than their less fortunate countrymen of the colder districts.

Our business in the village was to get guides for the cavern. While some men were gone to look for the Alcalde, we walked about the village, and finally encamped under a tree. One of our men had got us a bag full of fruit,—limes, zapotes, and nisperos, which last are a large kind of medlar, besides a number of other kinds of fruit, which we ate without knowing what they were. Though rather insipid, the limes are deliciously refreshing in this thirsty country; and they do no harm, however enormously one may indulge in them. The whole neighbourhood abounds in fruit, and its name *Cacahuamilpán* means "the plantation of *cacahuate* nuts."

It soon became evident that the Alcalde was keeping us waiting as a matter of dignity, and to show that, though the white men might be held in great estimation elsewhere, they did not think so much of them in this free and independent village. At last a man came to summon us to a solemn audience. In a hut of canes, the Alcalde, a little lame Indian, was sitting on a mat spread on the ground in the middle, with his escribano or secretary at his left hand. Other Indians were standing outside at the door. The little man scarcely condescended to take any notice of us when we saluted him, but sat bolt upright, positively bursting with suppressed dignity, and the escribano inquired in a loud voice what our business was. We told him we wanted guides to the cave, which he knew as well as we did; but instead of answering, he began to talk to the Alcalde. We quite appreciated the pleasure it must have been to the two functionaries to show off before us and their assembled countrymen, who were looking on at the proceedings with great respect; and we had not minded affording them this cheap satisfaction; but at last the joke seemed to be getting stale, so we proceeded some to sit and some to lie down at full length, and to go on eating limes in the presence of the August company. Thereupon they informed us what would be the cost of guides and candles, and we eventually made a bargain with them and started on foot.

On looking at the map of the State of Mexico, there is to be seen a river which stops suddenly on reaching the mountains of Cacahuamilpán, and begins again on the other side, having found a passage for itself through caves in the mountain for six or seven miles. Not far from the place where this river flows out of the side of the hill, is a path which leads to the entrance of the cave. A long downward slope brought us into the first great vaulted chamber, perhaps a quarter of a mile long and eighty feet high; then a long scramble through a narrow passage, and another hall still grander than the first. At the end of this hall is another passage leading on into another chamber. Beyond this we did not go. As it was, we must have walked between one and two miles into the cavern, but people have explored it to twice this distance, always finding a repetition of the same arrangement, great vaulted chambers alternating with long passages almost choked by fallen rocks. In one of the passages, I think the last we came to, the roaring of the river in its subterranean bed was distinctly audible below us.

Excepting the great cave of Kentucky, I believe there is no stalactitic cavern known so vast and beautiful as this. The appearance of the largest hall was wonderful when some twenty of our Indian guides stationed themselves on pinnacles of stalagmite, each one holding up a blazing torch, while two more climbed upon a great mass at one end called the altar, and burnt Bengal lights there; the rest stood at the other extremity of the cave sending up rockets in rapid succession into the vaulted roof, and making the millions of grotesque incrustations glitter as if they had been masses of diamonds: All the quaint shapes that are found in such caverns were to be seen here on the grandest scale, columns, arched roof, organ-pipes, trees, altars, and squatting monsters ranged in long lines like idols in a temple. There may very well be some truth in the notion that the origin of Gothic architecture was in stalactites of a limestone cavern, so numerous and perfect are the long slender columns crowned with pointed Gothic arches.

Our procession through the cave was a picturesque one. We carried long wax altar-candles and our guides huge torches made of threads of aloe-fibre soaked in resin and wrapped round with cloth, in appearance and texture exactly like the legs and arms of mummies. As we went, the Indians sang Mexican songs to strange, monotonous, plaintive tunes, or raced about into dark corners shouting with laughter. They talked about adventures in the cave, to them of course the great phenomenon of the whole world; but it did not seem, as far as we could hear, that they associated with it any recollections of the old Aztec divinities and the mystic rites performed in their honour.

No fossil bones have been found in the cavern, nor human remains except in one of the passages far within, where a little wooden cross still marks the spot where the skeleton of an Indian was found. Whether he went alone for mere curiosity to explore the cave, or, what is more likely, with an idea of finding treasure, is not known; nothing is certain but that his candle was burnt out while he was still far from the entrance, and that he died there. I said no fossil remains had been found, but the level floors of the great halls are continually being raised by fresh layers of stalagmite from the water dropping from the roof, and no one knows what may lie under them. These floors are in many places covered with little loose concretions like marbles, and these concretions in the course of time are imbedded in the horizontal layers of the same material.

As we left the entrance hall and began to ascend the sloping passage that leads to daylight, we saw an optical appearance which, had we not seen it with our own eyes, we could never have believed to be a natural effect of light and shade. To us, still far down in the cave, the entrance was only illuminated by reflected light; but as the Indians reached it, the direct rays of sunlight fell upon them, and their white dresses shone with an intense phosphoric light, as though they had been self-luminous. It is just such an effect that is wanting in our pictures of the Transfiguration, but I fear it is as impossible to paint it upon canvas as to describe it in words.

Next morning our friend Don Guillermo said good-bye to us, and started to return post-haste to his affairs in the capital. We stayed a few days longer at Cocoyotla, never tiring of the beautiful garden with its groves of orange-trees and cocoanut-palms, and the river which, running through it, joins the stream that we heard rushing along in the cavern, to flow down into the Pacific.

On Sunday morning the priest arrived on an ambling mule, the favourite clerical animal. They say it is impossible to ride a mule unless you are either an arriero or a priest. Not that it is by any means necessary, however, that he should ride a mule. I shall not soon forget the jaunty young monk we saw at Tezcuco, just setting out for a country festival, mounted on a splendid little horse, with his frock tucked up, and a pair of hairy goat-skin *chaparreros* underneath, a broad Mexican hat, a pair of monstrous silver spurs, and a very large cigar in his mouth. The girls came out of the cottage doors to look at him, as he made the fiery little beast curvet and prance along the road; and he was evidently not insensible to the looks of admiration of these young ladies, as they muffled up their faces in their blue rebozos and looked at him through the narrow opening.

Nearly two hundred Indians crowded into the church to mass, and went through the service with evident devotion. There are no more sincere Catholics in the world than the Indians, though, as I have said, they are apt to keep up some of their old rites in holes and corners. The administradors did not trouble themselves to attend mass, but went on posting up their books just outside the church-door; in this, as in a great many other little matters, showing their contempt for the brown men, and adding something every day to the feeling of dislike they are regarded with.

We speak of the Indians still keeping up their ancient superstitious rites in secret, as we often heard it said so in Mexico, though we ourselves never saw anything of it. The Abbé Clavigero, who wrote in the last century, declares the charge to be untrue, except perhaps in a few isolated cases. "The few examples of idolatry," he says, "which can be produced are partly excusable; since it is not to be wondered at that rude uncultured men should not be able to distinguish the idolatrous worship of a rough figure of wood or stone from that which is rightly paid to the holy images." (There are people who would quite agree with the good Abbé that the distinction is rather a difficult one to make.)

"But how often has prejudice against them declared things to be idols which were really images of the saints, though shapeless ones! In 1754 I saw some images found in a cave, which were thought to be idols; but I had no doubt that they were figures representing the mystery of the Holy Nativity."

A good illustration of the wholesale way in which the early Catholic missionaries went about the work of conversion is given in a remark of Clavigero's. There is one part of the order of baptism which proceeds thus: "Then the Priest, wetting his right thumb with spittle from his mouth, and touching therewith in the form of a cross the right ear of the person to be baptized, &c." The Mexican missionaries, it seems, had to leave out this ceremony, from sheer inability to provide enough of the requisite material for their crowds of converts.

After mass we rode out to a mound that had attracted our attention a day or two before, and which proved to be a fort or temple, or probably both combined. There were no remains to be found there except the usual fragments of pottery and obsidian. Then we returned to the hacienda to say good-bye to our friends there, before starting on our journey back to Mexico. All the population were hard at work amusing themselves, and the shop was doing a roaring trade in glasses of aguardiente. The Indian who had been our guide for some days past had opened a Monté bank with the dollars we had given him, and was sitting on the ground solemnly dealing cards one by one from the bottom of a dirty pack, a crowd of gamblers standing or sitting in a semicircle before him, silently watching the cards and keeping a vigilant eye upon their stakes which lay on the ground before the banker. Other parties were busy at the same game in other parts of the open space before the shop, which served as the great square for the colony.

Under the arcades in front of the shop a fandango was going on, though it was quite early in the afternoon. A man and a woman stood facing each other, an old man tinkled a guitar, producing a strange, endless, monotonous tune, and the two dancers stamped with their feet, and moved their arms and bodies about in time to the music, throwing themselves into affected and voluptuous attitudes which evidently met with the approval of the bystanders, though to us, who did not see with Indian eyes, they seemed anything but beautiful. When the danseuse had tired out one partner, another took his place. An admiring crowd stood round or sat on the stone benches, smoking cigarettes, and looking on gravely and silently, with evident enjoyment. Just as we saw it, it would go on probably through half the night, one couple, or perhaps two, keeping it up constantly, the rest looking on and refreshing themselves from time to time with raw spirits. Though inferior to the Eastern dancing, it resembled it most strikingly, my companion said. It has little to do with the really beautiful and artistic dancing of Old Spain, but seems to be the same that the people delighted in long before they ever saw a white man. Montezuma's palace contained a perfect colony of professional dancers, whose sole business was to entertain him with their performances, which only resembled those of the Old World because human nature is similar everywhere, and the same wants and instincts often find their development in the same way among nations totally separated from each other.

We left the natives to their amusement, and started on our twenty miles ride. By the time the evening had fairly begun to close in upon us, we crossed the crest of a hill and had a dim view of a valley below us, but there were no signs of Chalma or its convent. We let our horses find their way as well as they could along the rocky path, and got down into the valley. A light behind us made us turn round, and we saw a grand sight. The coarse grass on a large hill further down the valley had been set fire to, and a broad band of flame stretched right across the base of the hill, and was slowly moving upwards towards its top, throwing a lurid glare over the surrounding country, and upon the clouds of smoke that were rising from the flames. Every now and then we turned to watch the line of fire as it rose higher and higher, till at last it closed in together at the summit with one final blaze, and left us in the darkness. We dismounted and stumbled along, leading our horses down the precipitous sides of the deep ravines that run into the valley, mounting again to cross the streams at the bottom, and clambering up on the other side to the level of the road. At last a turn in the valley showed lights just before us, and we entered the village of Chalma, which was illuminated with flaring oil-lamps in the streets, where men were hard at work setting up stalls and booths of planks. It seemed there was to be a fair next day.

They showed us the way to the *meson* and there we left Antonio with the horses, while the proprietor sent an idiot boy to show us the way to the convent, for our inspection of the meson decided us at once on seeking the hospitality of the monks for the night. We climbed up the hill, went in at the convent-gate, across a courtyard, along a dim cloister, and through another door where our guide made his way out by a different opening, leaving us standing in total darkness. After a time another door opened, and a good-natured-looking friar came in with a lamp in his hand, and conducted us upstairs to his cell. I think our friend was the sub-prior of the convent. His cell was a very comfortable bachelor's apartment, in a plain way, vaulted and whitewashed, with good chairs and a table and a very comfortable-looking bed.

We sat talking with him for a long while, and heard that the fair next day would be attended by numbers of Indians from remote places among the mountains, and that at noon there would be an Indian dance in the church. It is not the great festival, however, he said. That is once a year; and then the

Indians come from fifty miles round, and stay here several days, living in the caves in the rock just by the town, buying and selling in the fair, attending mass, and having solemn dances in the church. We asked him about the ill feeling between the Indians and the whites. He said that among the planters it might be as we said, but that in the neighbourhood of his convent the respect and affection of the Indians for the clergy, whether white or Indian, was as great as ever. Then we gossipped about horses, of which our friend was evidently an amateur, and when the conversation flagged, he turned to the table in the middle of the room and handed us little bowls made of calabashes, prettily decorated and carved, and full of sweetmeats. There were ten or twelve of these little bowls on the table, each with a different kind of "tuck" in it. We inquired where all those good things came from, and learnt that making them was one of the favourite occupations of the Mexican nuns, who keep their brethren in the monasteries well supplied. At last the good monk went away to his duties and left us, when I could not resist the temptation of having a look at the little books in blue and green paper covers which were lying on the table with the sweetmeat-bowls and the venerable old missal. They proved to be all French novels done into Spanish, and "Notre-Dame de Paris" was lying open (under a sheet of paper); so I conclude that our visit had interrupted the sub-prior while deep in that improving work.

Presently a monk came to conduct us down into the refectory, and there they gave us an uncommonly good supper of wonderful Mexican stews, red-hot as usual, and plenty of good Spanish wine withal. The great dignitaries of the cloister did not appear, but some fifteen or twenty monks were at table with us, and never tired of questioning us—exactly in the same fashion that the ladies of the harem questioned Doña Juana. We delighted them with stories of the miraculous Easter fire at Jerusalem, and the illumination of St. Peter's, of the Sistine chapel and the Pope, and we parted for the night in high good humour.

Next morning a monk attached himself to us as our cicerone, a fine young fellow with a handsome face, and no end of fun in him.

Now that we saw the convent by daylight, we were delighted with the beauty of its situation. The broad fertile valley grows narrower and narrower until it becomes a gorge in the mountains; and here the convent is built, with the mountain-stream running through its beautiful gardens, and turning the wheel of the convent-mill before it flows on into the plain to fertilize the broad lands of the reverend fathers.

When we had visited the gardens and the stables, our young monk brought us back to the great church of the convent, where we took our places near the monks, who had mustered in full force to be present at the dancing. Presently the music arrived, an old man with a harp, and a woman with a violin; and then came the dancers, eight Indian boys with short tunics and head-dresses of feathers, and as many girls with white dresses, and garlands of flowers on their heads. The costumes were evidently intended to represent the Indian dresses of the days of Montezuma, but they were rather modernized by the necessity of wearing various articles of dress which would have been superfluous in old times. They stationed themselves in the middle of the church, opposite the high altar, and, to our unspeakable astonishment, began to dance the polka. Then came a waltz, then a schottisch, then another waltz, and finally a quadrille, set to unmitigated English tunes. They danced exceedingly well, and behaved as though they had been used to European ball-rooms all their lives. The spectators looked on as though it were all a matter of course for these brown-skinned boys and girls to have acquired so singular an accomplishment in their out-of-the-way village among the mountains. As for us we looked on in open-mouthed astonishment; and when, in the middle of the quadrille, the harp and violin struck up no less a tune than "The King of the Cannibal Islands," we could hardly help bursting out into fits of laughter. We restrained ourselves, however, and kept as grave a countenance as the rest of the lookers-on, who had not the faintest idea that anything odd was happening. The quadrille finished in perfect order; each dancer took his partner by the hand and led her forward; and so, forming a line in front of the high altar, they all knelt down, and the rest of the congregation followed their example; there was a dead silence in the church for about the space of an Ave Maria, then everyone rose, and the ceremony was over.

Our young monk asked permission of his superior to take us out for a walk, and we went down together to the convent-mill. There we saw the mill, which was primitive, and the miller, who was burly; and also something much more worth seeing, at least to our young acquaintance, who tucked up his skirts and ran briskly up a ladder into the upper regions, calling to us to follow him. A door led from the granary into the miller's house, and the miller's daughter happened, of course entirely by chance, to be coming through that way. A very pretty girl she was too, and I never in my life saw anything more intensely comic than the looks of intelligence that passed between her and the young friar when he presented us. It was decidedly contrary to good monastic discipline it is true, and we ought to have been shocked, but it was so intolerably laughable that my companion bolted into the granary to examine the wheat, and I took refuge in a violent fit of coughing. Our nerves had been already rudely shaken by the King of the Cannibal Islands, and this little scene of convent-life fairly finished us.

We asked our young friend what his day's work consisted of, and how he liked convent-life. He yawned, and intimated that it was very slow. We enquired whether the monks had not some parochial duties to perform, such as visiting the sick and the poor in their neighbourhood. He evidently wondered whether we were really ignorant, or whether we were "chaffing" him, and observed that that was no business of their's, the curas of the villages did all that sort of thing. "Then, what have you to do?" we said. "Well," he said, "there are so many services every day, and high mass on Sundays and holidays; and besides that, there's—well, there isn't anything particular. It's rather a dull life. I myself should like uncommonly to go and travel and see the world, or go and fight somewhere." We were quite sorry for the young fellow when we shook hands with him at parting, and he left us to go back to his convent.

We had been clambering about the hill, seeing the caves with which it is honeycombed, but at present they were uninhabited. At the time of the great festival, when they are full of Indian families, the scene must be a curious one.

The monks had hospitably pressed us to stay till their mid-day meal, but we preferred having it at the shop down in the village, so as to start directly afterwards. Here the people gave us a regular reception, entertained us with their best, and could not be prevailed upon to accept any payment whatever. The proprietor of the meson sat down before the barley-bin which served him for a desk, and indited a long and eloquent letter of introduction for us to a friend of his in Oculan, who was to find a night's lodging for us. Before he sealed up the despatch he read it to us in a loud voice, sentence by sentence. It might have been an autograph letter from King Philip to some foreign potentate. Armed with this important missive, we mounted our horses, shook hands with no end of well-wishers, and rode off up the valley.

For a little while our path lay through a sort of suburb of Chalma, houses lying near one another, each surrounded by a pleasant garden, and both houses and people looking prosperous and cheerful. Our directions for finding the way were simple enough. We were to go up the valley past the Cerra de los Atambores, "the hill of drums," and the great *ahuehuete*. What the Cerra de los Atambores might be, we could not tell, but when we had followed the valley for an hour or so, it came into view. On the other side of the stream rose a precipitous cliff, several hundred feet high, and near the top a perpendicular wall of rock was carved with rude designs. People have supposed, it seems, that these carvings represented drums, and hence the name.

Had we known of the place before, we should have made an effort to explore it, and copy the sculptured designs; but now it was too late, and from the other side of the valley we could not make out more than that there seemed to be a figure of the sun among them.

A little further on we came to the "Ahuehuete." The name means a deciduous cypress, a common tree in Mexico, and of which we had already seen such splendid specimens in the grove near Tezcuco, and in the wood of Chapoltepec. This was a remarkable tree as to size, some sixty feet round at the lower part where the roots began to spread out. A copious spring of water rose within the hollow trunk itself, and ran down between the roots into the little river. All over its spreading branches were fastened votive offerings of the Indians, hundreds of locks of coarse black hair, teeth, bits of coloured cloth, rags, and morsels of ribbon. The tree was many centuries old, and had probably had some mysterious influence ascribed to it, and been decorated with such simple offerings long before the discovery of America. In Brittany the peasants still keep up the custom of hanging up locks of their hair in certain chapels, to charm away diseases; and there it is certain that the Christians only appropriated to their own worship places already held sacred in the estimation of the people.

Oculan is a dismal little place. We found the great man of the village standing at his door, but our letter to him was dishonoured in the most decided manner. He read the epistle, carefully folded it up and pocketed it, then pointed in the direction of two or three houses on the other side of the way, and saying he supposed we might get a lodging over there, he wished us good-day and retired into his own premises. The landlord of "over there" was very civil. He had a shed for the horses, and could give us palm-mats to sleep upon on the floor, or on the shop-counter, which was very narrow, but long enough for us both; and this latter alternative we chose.

We walked up to the top of a hill close by the village, and were surveying the country from thence, keeping a sharp look-out all the while for Mexican remains in the furrows. For a wonder, we found nothing but some broken spindle-heads; but, while we were thus occupied, two Indians suddenly made their appearance, each with his *machete* in his hands, and wanted to know what we were doing on their land. We pacified them by politeness and a cigar apiece, but we were still evidently objects of suspicion, and they were quite relieved to see us return to the village. There, an old woman cooked us hard-boiled eggs and tortillas, and then we went tranquilly to bed on our counter, with our saddles for pillows, and our serapes for bed-clothes.

All the way from Cocoyotla our height above the sea had been gradually increasing; and soon after we started from Oculan next morning, we came to the foot of one of the grand passes that lead up into the high lands, where the road mounts by zig-zag turns through a splendid forest of pines and oaks, and at the top of the ascent we were in a broad fertile plain as high or higher than the valley of Mexico. It was like England to ride between large fields of wheat and barley, and to pick blackberries in the hedges. It was only April, and yet the grain was almost ready for the sickle, and the blackberries were fully ripe. Fresh green grass was growing in the woods under the oak-trees, and the banks were covered with Alpine strawberries.

We are in the great grain-district of the Republic. Wheat is grown for the supply of the large towns, and barley for the horses. Green barley is the favourite fodder for the horses in the Mexican highlands, and in the hotter districts the leaves of young Indian corn. Oats are to be seen growing by chance among other grain, but they are never cultivated. Though wheat is so much grown upon the plains, it is not because the soil and climate are more favourable than elsewhere for such culture. In the plains of Toluca and Tenancingo the yield of wheat is less than the average of the Republic, which is from 25- to 30-fold, and in the cloudy valleys we passed through near Orizaba it is much greater. Labour is tolerably cheap and plentiful here, however; and then each large town must draw its supplies of grain from the neighbouring districts, for, in a country where it pays to carry goods on mules' backs, it is clear that grain cannot be carried far to market.

In the question of the population of Mexico, one begins to speculate why—in a country with a splendid climate, a fertile soil, and almost unlimited space to spread in, the inhabitants do not increase one-half so fast as in England, and about one-sixth as fast as their neighbours of the United States. One of the most important causes which tend to bring about this state of things is the impossibility of conveying grain to any distance, except by doubling and trebling its price. The disastrous effects of a failure of the crop in one district cannot be remedied by a plentiful harvest fifty miles off; for the peasants, already ruined by the loss of their own harvest, can find neither money nor credit to buy food brought from a distance at so great an expense. Next year may be fruitful again, but numbers die in the interval, and the constitutions of a great proportion of the children never recover the effects of that one year's famine.

We left the regular road and struck up still higher into the hills, riding amongst winding roads with forest above and below us, and great orchids of the most brilliant colours, blue, white, and crimson, shining among the branches of the oak-trees. The boughs were often breaking down with the bulbs of such epiphytes; but as yet it was early in the season, and only here and there one was in flower. At the top of the hill, still in the midst of the woods, is the Desierto, "the desert," the place we had selected for our noon-day halt. There are many of these Desiertos in Mexico, founded by rich people in old times. They are a kind of convent, with some few resident ecclesiastics, and numbers of cells for laymen who retire for a time into this secluded place and are received gratuitously. They spend a week or two in prayer and fasting, then confess themselves, receive the sacrament, and return into the world. The situation of this quiet place was well chosen in the midst of the forest, and once upon a time the cells used to be full of penitents; but now we saw no one but the old porter, as we walked about the gardens and explored the quadrangle and the rows of cells, each with a hideous little wood-cut of a martyr being tortured, upon the door.

Thence we rode down into the plain, looking down, as we descended, upon a hill which seemed to be an old crater, rising from the level ground; and then our path lay among broad fields where oxen were ploughing, and across marshes covered with coarse grass, until we came to the quaint little town of Tenancingo. There we found the *meson*; and the landlord handed us the key of our room, which was square, whitewashed, and with a tiled floor. There was no window, so we had to keep the door open for light. The furniture consisted of three articles,—two low tables on four legs, made of rough planks, and a bracket to stick a candle in. The tables were beds after the manner of the country; but, as a special attention to us, the patron produced two old mattresses; the first sight of them was enough for us, and we expelled them with shouts of execration. We had to go to a shop in the square to get some supper; and on our return, about nine o'clock, our man Antonio remarked that he was going to sleep, which he did at once in the following manner. He took off his broad-brimmed hat and hung it on a nail, tied a red cotton handkerchief round his head, rolled himself up in his serape, lay down on the flags in the courtyard outside our door, and was asleep in an instant. We retired to our planks inside and followed his example.

The next afternoon we reached Toluca, a large and prosperous town, but with little noticeable in it except the arcades (portales) along the streets, and the hams which are cured with sugar, and are famous all over the Republic. Our road passed near the Nevado de Toluca, an extinct snow-covered volcano, nearly 15,000 feet above the sea. It consists entirely of grey and red porphyry, and in the interior of its crater are two small lakes. We were not sorry to take up our quarters in a comfortable European-looking hotel again, for roughing it is much less pleasant in these high altitudes—where the nights and mornings are bitterly cold—than in the hotter climate of the lower levels.

Our next day's ride brought us back to Mexico, crossing the corn-land of the plain of Lerma, where the soil consists of disintegrated porphyry from the mountains around, and is very fertile. Lerma itself is the worst den of robbers in all Mexico; and, as we rode through the street of dingy adobe houses, and saw the rascally-looking fellows who were standing at the doors in knots, with their horses ready saddled and bridled close by, we got a very strong impression that the reputation of the place was no worse than it deserved. After Lerma, there still remained the pass over the mountains which border the valley of Mexico; and here in the midst of a dense pine-forest is Las Cruzes, "the crosses," a place with an ugly name, where several robberies are done every week. We waited for the Diligence at some little glass-works at the entrance of the pass, and then let it go on first, as a sop to those gentlemen if they should be out that day. I suppose they knew pretty accurately that no one had much to lose, for they never made their appearance.

CHAPTER IX.
ANTIQUITIES. PRISON. SPORTS.

It was like getting home again to reach Mexico, we had so many friends there, though our stay had been so short. We were fully occupied, for weeks of hard sight-seeing are hardly enough to investigate the objects of interest to be found in the city. We saw these things under the best auspices, for Mr. Christy had letters to the Minister of Public Instruction and other people in authority, who were exceedingly civil, and did all they could to put us in the way of seeing everything we wished. Among the places we visited, the Museum must have some notice. It is in part of the building of the University; but we were rather surprised, when we reached the gate leading into the court-yard, to be stopped by a sentry who demanded what we wanted. The lower storey had been turned into a barrack by the Government, there being a want of quarters for the soldiers. As the ground-floor under the cloisters is used for the heavier pieces of sculpture, the scene was somewhat curious. The soldiers had laid several of the smaller idols down on their faces, and were sitting on the comfortable seat on the small of their backs, busy playing at cards. An enterprising soldier had built up a hutch with idols and sculptured stones against the statue of the great war-goddess Teoyaomiqui herself, and kept rabbits there. The state which the whole place was in when thus left to the tender mercies of a Mexican regiment may be imagined by any one who knows what a dirty and destructive animal a Mexican soldier is.

The guardians of the Museum have treated it even worse. People who know how often the curators of the Museums of southern Europe are ready to sell anything not very likely to be missed will not be astonished to hear of the same thing being done to a great extent some six or eight years before our visit.

The stone known as the statue of the war-goddess is a huge block of basalt covered with sculptures. The antiquaries think that the figures on it stand for different personages, and that it is three gods,—Huitzilopochtli the god of war, Teoyaomiqui his wife, and Mictlanteuctli the god of hell. It has necklaces of alternate hearts and dead man's hands, with death's heads for a central ornament. At the bottom of the block is a strange sprawling figure, which one cannot see now, for it is the base which rests on the ground; but there are two shoulders projecting from the idol, which show plainly that it did not stand on the ground, but was supported aloft on the tops of two pillars. The figure carved upon the bottom represents a monster holding a skull in each hand, while others hang from his knees and elbows. His mouth is a mere oval ring, a common feature of Mexican idols, and four tusks project just above it. The new moon laid down like a bridge forms his forehead, and a star is placed on each side of it. This is thought to have been the conventional representation of Mictlanteuctli (Lord of the Land of the Dead), the god of hell, which was a place of utter and eternal darkness. Probably each victim as he was led to the altar could look up between the two pillars and see the hideous god of hell staring down upon him from above.

There is little doubt that this is the famous war-idol which stood on the great teocalli of Mexico, and before which so many thousands of human victims were sacrificed. It lay undisturbed underground in the great square, close to the very site of the teocalli, until sixty years ago. For many years after that it was kept buried, lest the sight of one of their old deities might be too exciting for the Indians, who, as I have mentioned before, had certainly not forgotten it, and secretly ornamented it with garlands of flowers while it remained above ground.

The "sacrificial stone," so called, which also stands in the court-yard of the Museum, was not one of the ordinary altars on which victims were sacrificed. These altars seem to have been raised slabs of hard stone with a protuberant part near one end, so that the breast of the victim was raised into an arch, which made it more easy for the priest to cut across it with his obsidian knife. The Breton altars, where the slab was hollowed into the outline of a human figure, have some analogy to this; but, though there were very many of these altars in different cities of Mexico, none are now known to exist. The stone we are now observing is quite a different thing, a cylindrical block of basalt nine feet across and three feet high: and Humboldt considers it to be the stone described by early Spanish writers, and called *temalacatl*(spindle-stone) from its circular shape, something like a distaff-head. Upon this the captive chiefs stood in the gladiatorial fights which took place within the space surrounding the great teocalli. Slightly armed, they stood upon this raised platform in the midst of the crowd of spectators; and six champions in succession, armed with better weapons, came up to fight with them. If the captive worsted his assailants in this unequal contest, he was set free with presents; but this success was the lot of but few, and the fate of most was to be overpowered and dragged off ignominiously to be sacrificed like ordinary prisoners. On the top of the stone is sculptured an outline of the sun with its eight rays, and a hollow in the centre, whence a groove runs to the edge of the stone, probably to let the blood run down. All round it is an appropriate bas-relief repeated several times. A vanquished warrior is giving up his stone-sword and his spears to his conqueror, who is tearing the plumed crest from his head.

The above explanation by Humboldt is a plausible one. But in Central America altars not unlike this, and with grooves upon the top, stand in front of the great stone idols; and this curious monument may have been nothing after all but an ordinary altar to sacrifice birds and small animals upon.

Señor Leon Ramirez, the curator, had come to the Museum to meet us, and we went over the collection of smaller objects, which are kept up stairs in glass-cases,—at any rate out of the way of the soldiers.

Here are the stone clamps shaped like the letter U, which were put over the wrists and ankles of the victims, to hold them down on the sacrificial stone. They are of hard stone, very heavy and covered with carvings. It is remarkable that, though the altars for human sacrifices are no longer to be found, these accessory stone clamps, or yoke-like collars, are not uncommon. A fine one from Mr. Christy's collection is figured. *(See opposite page.)*

The obsidian knives and arrow-heads are very good, but these I have spoken of already, as well as of the stone hammers. The axes and chisels of stone are so exactly like those found in Europe that it is quite impossible to distinguish them. The bronze hatchet-blades are thin and flat, slightly thickened at the sides to give them strength, and mostly of a very peculiar shape, something like a T, but still more resembling the section of a mushroom cut vertically through the middle of the stalk.

The obsidian mask is an extraordinary piece of work, considering the difficulty of cutting such a material. It was chipped into a rude outline, and finished into its exact shape by polishing down with jeweller's sand. The polish is perfect, and there is hardly a scratch upon it. At least one of the old Spanish writers on Mexico gives the details of the process of cutting precious stones and polishing them with *teoxalli* or "god's sand." Masks in stone, wood, and terra-cotta are to be seen in considerable number in museums of Mexican antiquities. Their use is explained by passages in the old Mexican writers, who mention that it was customary to mask the idols on the occasion of the king being sick, or of any other public calamity; and that men and women wore masks in some of the religious ceremonies. A fine mask of brown lava (from Mr. Christy's collection), which has been coloured, is here figured. *(See illustration.)* The mirrors of obsidian have the same beautifully polished surface as the obsidian mask shows; and those made of nodules of pyrites, cut and polished, are worth notice.

The Mexicans were very skilful in making pottery; and of course there is a good collection here of terra-cotta vases, little altars and incense-dishes, rattles, flageolets, and whistles, tobacco-pipes and masks. Some of the large vases, which were formerly filled with skulls and bones, are admirable in their designs and decorations; and many specimens are to be seen of the red and black ware of Cholula, which was famous at the time of the Conquest, and was sent to all parts of the country. The art of glazing pottery seems only to have been introduced by the Spaniards, and to this day the Indians hardly care to use it. The terra-cotta rattles are very characteristic. They have little balls in them which shake about, and they puzzled us much as the apple-dumpling did good King George, for we could not make out very easily how the balls got inside. They were probably attached very slightly to the inside, and so baked and then broken loose. We often got little balls like schoolboys' marbles, among lots of Mexican antiquities, and these were most likely the balls out of broken rattles.

Burning incense was always an important part of the Mexican ceremonies. When the white men were on their march to the capital, the inhabitants used to come out to meet them with such plates as we saw here, and burn copal before the leaders; and in Indian villages to this day the procession on saints' days would not be complete without men burning incense, not in regular censers, but in unglazed earthen platters such as their forefathers used.

Our word *copal* is the Mexican *copalli*. There are a few other Mexican words which have been naturalized in our European languages, of course indicating that the things they represent came from Mexico.*Ocelotl* is *ocelot*; *Tomatl* is *tomata*; *Chilli* is the Spanish *chile* and our *chili*; *Cacahuatl* is *cacao* or cocoa; and *Chocolatl*, the beverage made from the cacao-bean with a mixture of vanilla, is our chocolate.

Cacao-beans were used by the Mexicans as money. Even in Humboldt's time, when there was no copper coinage, they were used as small change, six for a halfpenny; and Stephens says the Central Americans use them to this day. A mat in Mexican is *petlatl*, and thence a basket made of matting was called *petlacalli*—"mathouse." The name passed to the plaited grass cigar-cases that are exported to Europe; and now in Spain any kind of cigar-case is called a *petaca*.

The pretty little ornamented calabashes—used, among other purposes, for drinking chocolate out of—were called by the Mexicans *xicalli*, a word which the Spaniards made into *jícara*, and now use to mean a chocolate-cup; and even the Italians have taken to it, and call a tea-cup a *chicchera*.

There is a well-known West Indian fruit which we call an *avocado* or *alligator-pear*, and which the French call *avocat* and the

Spaniards *aguacate*. All these names are corruptions of the Aztec name of the fruit, *ahuacatl*.

Vanilla and cochineal were first found in Mexico; but the Spaniards did not adopt the unpronounceable native names, *tlilxochitl* and *nocheztli*. Vanilla, *vainilla*, means a little bean, from *vaina*, which signifies a scabbard or sheath, also a pod. *Cochinilla* is from *coccus*, a berry, as it was at first supposed to be of vegetable origin. The Aztec name for cochineal, *nocheztli*, means "cactus-blood," and is a very apt description of the insect, which has in it a drop of deep crimson fluid, in which the colouring matter of the dye is contained.

The turkey, which was introduced into Europe from Mexico, was called *huexolotl* from the gobbling noise it makes. (It must be remembered that x and j in Spanish are not the same letters as in English, but a hard guttural aspirate, like the German ch). The name, slightly altered into *guajalote*, is still used in Mexico; but when these birds were brought to Europe, the Spaniards called them peacocks (*pavos*). To get rid of the confusion, it became necessary to call the real peacock "*pavón*" (big peacock), or "*pavo real*" (royal peacock). The German name for a turkey, "Wälscher Hahn," "Italian fowl," is reasonable, for the Germans got them from Italy; but our name "turkey" is wonderfully absurd.

There may be other Mexican words to be found in our language, but not many. The Mexicans were cultivating maize and tobacco when the Spaniards invaded the country, and had done so for ages; but these vegetables had been found already in the West India islands, and had got their name from the language of Hayti, *mahiz* and *tabaco*; the latter word, it seems, meaning not the tobacco itself, but the cigars made of it.

I do not recollect anything else worthy of note that Europe has borrowed from Ancient Mexico, except Botanic Gardens, and dishes made to keep hot at dinner-time, which the Aztecs managed by having a pan of burning charcoal underneath them.

To return to the Museum. There are stamps in terra-cotta with geometrical patterns, for making lines and ornaments on the vases before they were baked, and for stamping patterns upon the cotton cloth which was one of their principal manufactures, as it is now. Connected with the same art are the *malacates*, or winders, which I have already described. Little grotesque heads made of baked clay, like those I have mentioned as being found in such immense numbers on the sites of old Mexican cities, are here by hundreds. I think there were, besides, some of the moulds, also in terra-cotta, in which they were formed; at any rate, they are to be seen, so that making the little heads must have been a regular trade. What they were for is not so easy to say.

Some have bodies, and are made with flat backs to stand against a wall, and these were probably idols. The ancient Mexicans, we read, had household-gods in great numbers, and called them *Tepitotons*, "little ones." The greatest proportion, however, are mere heads which never had had bodies, and will not stand anyhow. They could not have been personal ornaments, for there is nothing to fasten them on by. They are rather a puzzle. I have seen a suggestion somewhere, that when a man was buried, each surviving member of his family put one of these heads into his grave. This sounds plausible enough, especially as both male and female heads are found.

One shelf in the museum is particularly instructive. We called it the "Chamber of Horrors," after the manner of Marlborough House, and it contains numbers of the sham antiquities, the manufacture of which is a regular thing in Mexico, as it is in Italy. They are principally vases and idols of earthenware, for the art of working obsidian is lost, and there can be no trickery about that; and as to the hammers, chisels, and idols in green jade, serpentine, and such like hard materials, they are decidedly cheaper to find than to make. The Indians in Mexico make their unglazed pottery just as they did before the Conquest, so that, if they imitate real antiques exactly, there is no possibility of detecting the fraud; but when they begin to work from their own designs, or even to copy from memory, they are almost sure to put in something that betrays them.

As soon as the Spaniards came, they began to introduce drawing as it was understood in Europe; and from that moment the peculiarities of Mexican art began to disappear. The foreheads of the Mexican races are all very low, and their painters and sculptors even exaggerated this peculiarity, to make the faces they depicted more beautiful,—so producing an effect which to us Europeans seems hideously ugly, but which is not more unnatural than the ideal type of beauty we see in the Greek statues. After the era of the Spaniards we see no more of such foreheads; and the eyes, which were drawn in profiles as one sees them in the full face, are put in their natural position. The short squat figures become slim and tall; and in numberless little details of dress, modelling, and ornament, the acquaintance of the artist with European types is shown; and it is very seldom that the modern counterfeiter can keep clear of these and get back to the old standard.

Among the things on the condemned shelf were men's faces too correctly drawn to be genuine, grotesque animals that no artist would ever have designed who had not seen a horse, head-dresses and drapery that were European and not Mexican. Among the figures in Mayer's *Mexico*, a vase is represented as a real antique, which, I think, is one of the worst cases I ever noticed. There is a man's head upon it, with long projecting pointed nose and chin, a long thin pendant moustache, an eye drawn in profile, and a cap. It is true the pure Mexican race occasionally have moustaches, but they are very slight, not like this, which falls in a curve on both sides of the mouth; and no Mexican of pure Indian race ever had such a nose and chin, which must have been modelled from the face of some toothless old Spaniard.

Mention must be made of the wooden drums—*teponaztli*—of which some few specimens are still to be seen in Mexico. Such drums figured in the religious ceremonies of the Aztecs, and one often hears of them in Mexican history. I have mentioned already the great drum which Bernal Diaz saw when he went up the Mexican teocalli with Cortes, and which he describes as a hellish instrument, made with skins of great serpents; and which, when it was struck, gave a loud and melancholy sound, that could be heard at two leagues' distance. Indeed, they did afterwards hear it from their camp a mile or two off, when their unfortunate companions were being sacrificed on the teocalli.

The Aztec drums, which are still to be seen, are altogether of wood, nearly cylindrical, but swelling out in the middle, and hollowed out of solid logs. Some have the sounding-board made unequally thick in different parts, so as to give several notes when struck. All are elaborately carved over with various designs, such as faces, head-dresses, weapons, suns with rays, and fanciful patterns, among which the twisted cord is one of the commonest.

Besides the drums which are preserved in museums, there are others, carefully kept in Indian villages, not as curiosities, but as instruments of magical power. Heller mentions such a *teponaztli*, which is still preserved among the Indians of Huatusco, an Indian village near Mirador in the tierra templada, where the inhabitants have had their customs comparatively little altered by intercourse with white men. They keep this drum as a sacred instrument, and beat it only at certain times of the year, though they have no reason to give for doing so. It is to be regretted that Heller did not take a note of the particular days on which this took place; for the times of the Mexican festivals are well known, and this information would have settled the question whether the Indians of the present day have really any definite recollection of their old customs.

Drums of this kind do not belong exclusively to Mexico. Among all the tribes of North America they were one of the principal "properties" used by the Medicine-men in their ceremonies; and among the tribes which have not been christianized they are still to be found in use. After we left Mexico, Mr. Christy visited some tribes in the Hudson's Bay Territory; and on one occasion, happening to assist at a festival in which just such a wooden drum was used, he bought it of the Medicine-man of the tribe, and packed it off triumphantly to his museum.

A few picture-writings are still to be seen in the Museum, which, with the few preserved in Europe, are all we have left of these interesting records, of which there were thousands upon thousands in Mexico and Tezcuco. Some were burnt or destroyed during the sieges of the cities, some perished by mere neglect, but the great mass was destroyed by archbishop Zumarraga, when he made an attempt—and, to some extent, a successful one—to obliterate every trace of heathenism, by destroying all the monuments and records in the country. One of the picture-writings hanging on the wall is very probably the same that was sent up from Vera Cruz to Montezuma, with figures of the newly-arrived white men, their ships and horses, and their cannons with fire and smoke issuing from their mouths. Another shows a white man being sacrificed, of course one of the Spanish prisoners. The pictorial history of the migration of the Aztecs is here, and a list of tributes paid to the Mexican sovereign; the different articles being drawn with numbers against each, to show the quantities to be paid, as in the Egyptian inscriptions. Lord Kingsborough's great work contains fac-similes of several Mexican manuscripts, and in Humboldt's *Vues des Cordillères* some of the most remarkable are figured and described.

One of the most curious of the Aztec picture-writings is in the Bodleian Library, and in fac-simile in Lord Kingsborough's *Antiquities of Mexico*. In it are shown, in a series of little pictures, the education of Mexican boys and girls, as prescribed by law. The child four days old is being sprinkled with water, and receiving its name. At four years old they are to be allowed one tortilla a meal, which is indicated by a drawing above their heads, of four circles representing years, and one cake; and the father sends the son to carry water, while the mother shows the daughter how to spin. A tortilla is like an oat-cake, but is made of Indian corn.

At seven years old the boy is taken to learn to fish, while the girl spins; and so on with different occupations for one year after another. At nine years old the father is allowed to punish his son for disobedience, by sticking aloe-points all over his naked body, while the daughters only have them stuck into their hands; and at eleven years old, both boy and girl were to be punished by holding their faces in the smoke of burning capsicums.

At fifteen the youth is married by the simple process of tying the corner of his shirt to the corner of the bride's petticoat (thus literally "splicing" them, as my companion remarked). And so on; after scenes of cutting wood, visiting the temples, fighting and feasting, we come to the last scene of all, headed "*seventy years*," and see an old man and woman reeling about helplessly drunk with pulque; for drunkenness, which was severely punished up to that age, was tolerated afterwards as a compensation for the sorrows and infirmities of the last period of life.

Astrological charts formed a large proportion of these picture-writings. Here, as elsewhere, we may trace the origin of astrology. The signs of the days and years were represented, for convenience sake, by different animals, and objects, like the signs of the Zodiac which we still retain. The signs remained after the history of their origin was lost; and then—what more natural than to imagine that the symbols handed down by their wise ancestors had some mysterious meaning, connected with the days and years they stood for; and then, that a man's destiny had to do with the names of the signs that "prevailed" at his birth?

There is little to be seen here or elsewhere, of one kind of work in which the Mexicans excelled perhaps more than in any other, the goldsmith's work. Where are the calendars of solid gold and silver—as big as great wheels, and covered with hieroglyphics, and the cups and collars, the golden birds, beasts, and fishes? The Spaniards who saw them record how admirable their workmanship was, and they were good judges of such matters. Benvenuto Cellini saw some of these things, and was filled with admiration. They have all gone to the melting-pot centuries ago! How important the goldsmith's trade was accounted in old times is shown by a strange Aztec law. It was no ordinary offence to steal gold and silver. Criminals convicted of this offence were not treated as common thieves, but were kept till the time when the goldsmiths celebrated their annual festival, and were then solemnly sacrificed to their god Xipe; the priests flaying their bodies, cooking and eating them, and walking about dressed in their skins, a ceremony which was called *tlacaxipehualiztli*, "the man-flaying."

Museums of Mexican antiquities are so much alike, that, in general, one description will do for all of them. Mr. Uhde's Museum at Heidelberg is a far finer one than that at Mexico, except as regards the picture-writings. I was astonished at the enormous quantity of stone idols, delicately worked trinkets in various hard stones and even in obsidian, terra-cotta tobacco-pipes, figures, and astronomical calendars, &c., displayed there.

Mr. Christy's collection is richer than any other in small sculptured figures from Central America. It contains a squatting female figure in hard brown lava, like the one in black basalt which is drawn in Humboldt's *Vues des Cordillères*, and there called (I cannot imagine why) an Aztec priestess. Above all, it contains what I believe to be the three finest specimens of Aztec decorative art which exist in the world. One of these is the knife of which the figure at page 101 gives some faint idea, the other two being a wooden mask overlaid with mosaic, and a human skull decorated in the same manner, of which a more particular description will be found in the Appendix. There are two kinds of Aztec articles in Mr. Christy's collection which I did not observe either at Mexico or Heidelberg. These are bronze needles, resembling our packing-needles, and little cast bronze bells, called in Aztec *yotl*, not unlike small horse-bells made in England at the present day; these are figured in the tribute-lists in the picture-writings.

Apropos of the mammoth bones preserved in the Mexican Museum, I must insert a quotation from Bernal Diaz. It is clear that the traditions of giants which exist in almost every country had their origin in the discovery of fossil bones, whose real character was not suspected until a century ago; but I never saw so good an example of this as in the Tlascalan tradition, which my author relates as follows.—"And they" (the Tlascalan chiefs) "said that their ancestors had told them that, in times past, there lived amongst them in settlements men and women of great size, with huge bones; and, as they were wicked and of evil dispositions, they (the ancestors of the Tlascalans) fought against them and killed them; and those who were left died out. And that we might see what stature they were of, they brought a bone of one of them, and it was very big, and its height was that of a man of reasonable stature; it was a thigh-bone, and I (Bernal Diaz) measured myself against it, and it was as tall as I am, who am a man of reasonable stature; and they brought other pieces of bones like the first, but they were already eaten through and rotted by the earth; and we were all amazed to see those bones, and held that for certain there had been giants in that land; and our captain, Cortes, said to us that it would be well to send the great bone to Castile, that His Majesty might see it; and so we did send it by the first messengers who went."

Among other things belonging to the Spanish period is the banner, with the picture of the Virgin, which accompanied the Spanish army during the Conquest. Authentic or not, it is certainly very well painted. There is a suit of armour said to have belonged to Cortes. Its genuineness has been doubted; but I think its extreme smallness seems to go towards proving that it is a true relic, for Bullock saw the tomb of Cortes opened some thirty years ago, and was surprised at the small proportions of his skeleton. Specimens of the pottery and glass now made in the country, and other curiosities, complete the catalogue of this interesting collection.

The Mexican calendar is not in the Museum, but is built into the wall of the cathedral, in the Plaza Mayor. It is sculptured on the face of a single block of basalt, which weighs between twenty and thirty tons, and must have been transported thirty miles by Mexican labourers, for the stone is not found nearer than that distance from the city; and this transportation was, of course, managed by hand-labour alone, as there were no beasts of burden.

We know pretty well the whole system of Mexican astronomy from this calendar-stone and a few manuscripts which still exist, and from the information given in the work of Gama the astronomer and other writers. The Aztecs and Tezcucans who used it, did not claim its invention as their own, but said they had received it from the Toltecs, their predecessors. The year consisted of 365 days, with an intercalation of 13 days for each cycle of 52 years, which brought it to the same length as the Julian year of 365 days 6 hours. The theory of Gama, that the intercalation was still more exact, namely, 12-1/2 days instead of 13, seems to be erroneous.

Our reckoning only became more exact than this when we adopted the Gregorian calendar in 1752, and the people marched about the streets in procession, crying "Give us back our eleven days!" Perhaps this is not quite a fair way of putting the case, however, for the new style would have been adopted in our country long before, had it not been a Romish institution. It was the deliberate opinion of the English, as of people in other Protestant countries, that it was much better to have the almanack a few days wrong than to adopt a Popish innovation. One often hears of the Papal Bull which settles the question of the earth's standing still. The history of the Gregorian calendar is not a bad set-off against it on the other side. At any rate, the new style was not introduced anywhere until sixty or seventy years after the discovery of Mexico, and five hundred years after the introduction of the Toltec calendar in Mexico.

The Mexican calendar-stone should be photographed on a large scale, and studied yet more carefully than it has been, for only a part of the divided circles which surround it have been explained. It should be photographed, because, to my certain knowledge, Mayer's drawing gives the year, above the figure of the sun which indicates the date of the calendar, quite wrongly; and yet, presuming on his own accuracy, he accuses another writer of leaving out the hieroglyph of the winter solstice. What is much more strange is, that Humboldt's drawing in the small edition of the *Vues des Cordillères* is wrong in both points. The drawing in Nebel's great work is probably the best. As to the wax models which Mr. Christy and I bought in Mexico, in the innocence of our hearts, a nearer inspection showed that the artist, observing that the circle of days would divide more neatly into sixteen parts than into twenty, had arranged his divisions accordingly; apparently leaving out the four hieroglyphics which he considered the ugliest.

The details made out at present on the calendar are as follows:—the summer and winter solstices, the spring and autumn equinoxes, the two passages of the Sun over the zenith of Mexico, and some dates which possibly belong to religious festivals. The dates of the two zenith-transits are especially interesting; for, as they vary with the latitude, they must have been made out by actual observation in Mexico itself, and not borrowed from some more civilised people in the distant countries through which the Mexicans migrated. This fact alone is sufficient to prove a considerable practical knowledge of astronomy.

Besides this, the Mexican cycle of fifty-two years seems to be indicated in the circle outside the signs of days, and also the days in the priestly year of 260 days; but to make these numbers, we must allow for the compartments supposed to be hidden by the projecting rays of the sun.

The arrangement of the Mexican cycle of fifty-two years is very curious. They had four signs of years, *tochtli, acatl, tecpatl,* and *calli,*—rabbit, canes, flint, and *house*; and against these signs they ranged numbers, from 1 to 13, so that a cycle exactly corresponds to a pack of cards, the four signs being the four suits, thirteen of each. Now, any one would suppose that in making such a reckoning, they would first take one suit, count *one, two, three,* &c. in it, up to 13, and then begin another suit. This is not the Mexican idea, however. Their reckoning is 1 *tochtli,* 2 *acatl,* 3 *tecpatl,* &c., just as it may be made with the cards thus: ace of hearts, two of diamonds, 3 of spades, 4 of clubs, 5 of hearts, 6 of diamonds, and so on through the pack. The correspondence between the cycle of 52 years, divided among 4 signs, and our year of 52 weeks, divided among 4 seasons, is also curious, though as entirely accidental as the resemblance to the pack of cards, for the Mexican week (if we may call it so) consisted of 5 days instead of 7, which to a great extent nullifies the comparison.

The reckoning of days is still more cumbrous. It consists of the days of the week written in succession from 1 to 13, underneath these the 20 signs of days, and underneath these again another series of 9 signs; so that each day was distinguished by a combination of a number and two signs, which combination could not belong to any other day.

The date of the year at the top of the calendar is 13 *acatl* (13 canes), which stands for 1479, 1427, 1375, 1323, and so on, subtracting 52 years each time. Now, why was this year chosen? It was not the beginning of a cycle, but the 26th year; and so, in ascertaining the meaning of the dates on the calendar, allowance has to be made for six days which have been gained by the leap-years only being adjusted at the end of the cycle; but this certainly offers no advantage whatever; and if an arbitrary date had been chosen to start the calendar with, of course it would have been the first year of a cycle. The year may have been chosen in commemoration of the foundation of Mexico or Tenochtitlán, which historians give as somewhere about 1324 or 1325. The sign 13 *acatl* would stand for 1323. It is more likely that the date merely refers to the year in which the calendar was put up. As such a massive and elaborate piece of sculpture could only belong to the most flourishing period of the Aztec empire, the year indicated would be 1279, nine years before the building of the great pyramid close by.

Baron Humboldt's celebrated argument to prove the Asiatic origin of the

Mexicans is principally founded upon the remarkable resemblance of this system of cycles in reckoning years to those found in use in different parts of Asia. For instance, we may take that described by Hue and Gabet as still existing in Tartary and Thibet, which consists of one set of signs, *wood, fire, earth*, &c., combined with a set of names of animals, *mouse, ox, tiger*, &c. The combination is made almost exactly in the same way as that in which the Aztecs combine their signs and numbers, as for instance, the year of the fire-pig, the iron-hare, &c. If these were simple systems of counting years, or even if, although difficult, they had some advantages to offer, we might suppose that two different races in want of a system to count their years by, had devised them independently. But, in fact, both the Asiatic and the Mexican cycles are not only most intricate and troublesome to work, but by the constant liability to confound one cycle with another, they lead to endless mistakes. Hue says that the Mongols, to get over this difficulty, affix a special name to all the years of each king's reign, as for instance, "the year Tao-Kouang of the fire-ram;" apparently not seeing that to give the special name and the number of the year of the reign, and call it the 44th year of Tao-Kouang, would answer the same purpose, with one-tenth of the trouble.

Not only are the Mexican and Asiatic systems alike in the singular principle they go upon, but there are resemblances in the signs used that seem too close for chance. The other arguments which tend to prove that the Mexicans either came from the Old World or had in some way been brought into connexion with tribes from thence, are principally founded on coincidences in customs and traditions. We must be careful to eliminate from them all such as we can imagine to have originated from the same outward causes at work in both hemispheres, and from the fact that man is fundamentally the same everywhere. To take an instance from Peru. We find the Incas there calling themselves "Child of the Sun," and marrying their own sisters, just as the Egyptian kings did. But this proves nothing whatever as to connexion between the two people. The worship of the Sun, the giver of light and heat, may easily spring up among different people without any external teaching; and what more natural, among imperfectly civilized tribes, than that the monarch should claim relationship with the divinity? And the second custom was introduced that the royal race might be kept unmixed.

Thus, when we find the Aztecs burning incense before their gods, kings, and great men, and propitiating their deities with human sacrifices, we can conclude nothing from this. But we find them baptizing their children, anointing their kings, and sprinkling them with holy water, punishing the crime of adultery by stoning the criminals to death, and practising several other Old World usages of which I have already spoken. We must give some weight to these coincidences.

Of some of the supposed Aztec Bible-traditions I have already spoken in no very high terms. There is another tradition, however, resting upon unimpeachable evidence, which relates the occurrence of a series of destructions and regenerations of the world, and recalls in the most striking manner the Indian cosmogony; and, when added to the argument from the similarity of the systems of astronomical notation of Mexico and Asia, goes far towards proving a more or less remote connection between the inhabitants of the two continents.

There is another side to the question, however, as has been stated already. How could the Mexicans have had these traditions and customs from the Old World, and not have got the knowledge of some of the commonest arts of life from the same source? As I have said, they do not seem to have known the proper way of putting the handle on to a stone-hammer; and, though they used bronze, they had not applied it to making such things as knives and spearheads. They had no beasts of burden; and, though there were animals in the country which they probably might have domesticated and milked, they had no idea of anything of the kind. They had oil, and employed it for various purposes, but had no notion of using it or wax for burning. They lighted their houses with pine-torches; and in fact the Aztec name for a pine-torch—*ocotl* —was transferred to candles when they were introduced.

Though they were a commercial people, and had several substitutes for money —such as cacao-grains, quills of gold-dust, and pieces of tin of a particular shape, they had no knowledge of the art of weighing anything, but sold entirely by tale and measure. This statement, made by the best authorities, their language tends to confirm. After the Conquest they made the word *tlapexouia* out of the Spanish "peso," and also gave the meaning of weighing to two other words which mean properly *to measure* and *to divide equally*. Had they had a proper word of their own for the process, we should find it. The Mexicans scarcely ever adopted a Spanish word even for Spanish animals or implements, if they could possibly make their own language serve. They called a sheep an *ichcatl*, literally a "*thread-thing*," or "*cotton*": a gun a "*fire-trumpet*:" and sulphur "*fire-trumpet-earth*." And yet, a people ignorant of some of the commonest arts had extraordinary knowledge of astronomy, and even knew the real cause of eclipses, and represented them in their sacred dances.

Set the difficulties on one side of the question against those on the other, and they will nearly balance. We must wait for further evidence.

Our friend Don José Miguel Cervantes, the President of the Ayuntamiento, took us one day to see the great prison of Mexico, the Acordada. As to the prison itself, it is a great gloomy building, with its rooms and corridors arranged round two courtyards, one appropriated to the men, the other to the women. A few of the men were at work making shoes and baskets, but most were sitting and lying about in the sun, smoking cigarettes and talking together in knots, the young ones hard at work taking lessons in villainy from the older hands; just the old story.

Offenders of all orders, from drunkards and vagrants up to highway robbers and murderers, all were mixed indiscriminately together. But we should remember that in England twenty years ago it was usual for prisons to be such places as this; and even now, in spite of model prisons and severe discipline, the miserable results of our prison-system show, as plainly as can be, that when we have caught our criminal we do not in the least know how to reform him, now that our colonists have refused him the only chance he ever had.

It is bad enough to mix together these men under the most favourable circumstances for corrupting one another. Every man must come out worse than he went in; but this wrong is not so great as that which the untried prisoners suffer in being forced into the society of condemned criminals, while their trials drag on from session to session, through the endless technicalities and quibbles of Spanish law.

We made rather a curious observation in this prison. When one enters such a place in Europe, one expects to see in a moment, by the faces and demeanour of the occupants, that most of them belong to a special criminal class, brought up to a life of crime which is their only possible career, belonging naturally to police-courts and prisons, herding together when out of prison in their own districts and their own streets, and carefully avoided by the rest of society. You may know a London thief when you see him; he carries his profession in his face and in the very curl of his hair. Now in this prison there was nothing of the kind to be seen. The inmates were brown Indians and half-bred Mexicans, appearing generally to belong to the poorest class, but just like the average of the people in the streets outside. As my companion said, "If these fellows are thieves and murderers, so are our servants, and so is every man in a serape we meet in the streets, for all we can tell to the contrary." There was positively nothing at all peculiar about them.

If they had been all Indians we might have been easily deceived. Nothing can be more true than Humboldt's observation that the Indian face differs so much from ours that it is only after years of experience that a European can learn to distinguish the varieties of feature by which character can be judged of. He mistakes peculiarities which belong to the race in general for personal characteristics; and the thickness of the skin serves still more to mask the expression of their faces. But the greater part of these men were Mexicans of mixed Indian and Spanish blood, and their faces are pretty much European.

The only explanation we could give of this identity of character inside the prison and outside is not flattering to the Mexican people, but I really believe it to be true. We came to the conclusion that the prisoners did not belong to a class apart, but that they were a tolerably fair specimen of the poorer population of the table-lands of Mexico. They had been more tempted than others, or they had been more unlucky, and that was why they were here.

There were perhaps a thousand prisoners in the place, two men to one woman. Their crimes were—one-third, drunken disturbance and vagrancy; another third, robberies of various kinds; a fourth, wounding and homicides, mostly arising out of quarrels; leaving a small residue for all other crimes.

Our idea was confirmed by many foreigners who had lived long in the country and had been brought into personal contact with the people. Every Mexican, they said, has a thief and a murderer in him, which the slightest provocation will bring out. This of course is an exaggeration, but there is a great deal of truth in it. The crimes in the prison-calendar belong as characteristics to the population in general. Highway-robbery, cutting and wounding in drunken brawls, and deliberate assassination, are offences which prevail among the half-white Mexicans; while stealing is common to them and the pure Indian population. We noticed several instances of bigamy, a crime which Mexican law is very severe upon. As far as we could judge by the amount of punishment inflicted, it is a greater crime to marry two women than to kill two men. In one gallery are the cells for criminals condemned to death, but the occupants were allowed to mix freely with the rest of the prisoners, and they seemed comfortable enough.

Everybody knows how much in England the condition of a prisoner depends on the disposition of the governor in office and the system in vogue for the moment. The mere words of his sentence do not indicate at all what his fate will be. He comes in—under Sir John—to light labour, much schoolmaster and chaplain, and the expectation of a ticket-of-leave when a fraction of his time is expired. All at once Sir James supersedes Sir John, and with him comes in a régime of hard work, short rations, and the black hole. If he had been "in" a month sooner, he would have been "out" now with those more fortunate criminals, his late companions.

Things ought not to be so in England, but we need hardly wonder at their being still worse in Mexico in this respect as in all others. There have been twenty changes of government in ten years, and sometimes extreme severity has been the rule, which may change at a day's notice into the extreme of mildness. In Santa Ana's time the utmost rigour of the law prevailed. Our friends in the Calle Seminario, as they came back from their morning's ride in the Paseo, had to pass through the great square; and used to see there, day after day, pairs of garotted malefactors sitting bolt upright in the high wooden chairs they had just been executed in, with a frightful calm look on their dead faces.

For the last year or so all this had ceased, and there had scarcely been an execution. It seems that one principal reason of this lenity is that the government is too weak to support its judges; and that the ministers of justice are actually intimidated by threats mysteriously conveyed to witnesses and authorities, that, if such or such a criminal is executed, his friends have sworn to avenge his death, and are on the look-out, every man with his knife ready. To political offences the same mercy is extended. In the early times of the war of independence, and for years afterwards, when one leader caught an officer on the other side, he had him tried by a drum-head court-martial, and shot. Since then it has come to be better understood that civil war is waged for the benefit of individuals who wish for their turn of power and their pull at the public purse; and the successful leader spares his opponent, not caring to establish a precedent which might prove so very inconvenient to himself.

We were taken to see the garotte by the President, who took it out of its little mahogany case, into which it was fitted like any other surgical instrument. We noticed that it was rusty, and indeed it had not been used for many months. It is not worth while to describe it.

Mexican law well administered is bad enough, not essentially unjust, but hampered with endless quibbles and technicalities, quite justifying the Spanish proverb, "*Mas vale una mala composición que un buen pleito*,"—a bad compromise is better than a good lawsuit. As things stand now, the law of any case is the least item in the account, there are so many ways of working upon judges and witnesses. Bribery first and foremost; and—if that fails—personal intimidation, political influence, private friendship, and the *compadrazgo*. Naturally, if you have a lawsuit or are tried for a crime, you should lay a good foundation. This is done by working upon the *Juez de primera instancia*, who corresponds in some degree to the *Juge d'instruction* in France. This functionary is wretchedly paid, so that a small sum is acceptable to him; and, moreover, the records of the case, as tried by him, form the basis of all future litigation, so that it is very bad economy not to get him into proper order. If you do not, it will cost you three times as much afterwards. If your suit is with a soldier or a priest, the ordinary tribunals will not help you. These two classes —the most influential in the community—have their *fuero*, their special jurisdiction; and woe to the unfortunate civilian who attacks them in their own courts!

Don Miguel Lerdo do Tejada, whose sense of humour occasionally peeps out from among his statistics, remarks gravely that "the clergy has its special legislation, which consists of the Sacred Volumes, the decision of General and Provincial Councils, the Pontifical Decretals, and doctrines of the Holy Fathers." Of what sort of justice is dealt out in that court, one may form some faint idea.

One of our friends in Mexico had a house which was too large for him, and in a moment of weakness he let part of it to a priest. Two years afterwards, when we made his acquaintance, he was hard at work trying, not to get his rent, he had given up that idea long before, but to get the priest out. I believe that, eventually, he gave him something handsome to take his departure.

I have often quoted Don Miguel Lerdo de Tejada, and shall do so again. His statistics of the country for 1856 are given in a broad sheet, and seem to be generally reliable. The annual balance-sheet of the country he sums up in three lines—

Annual Expenditure . . . . . . 25,000,000 dollars.
Annual Revenue . . . . 15,000,000 dollars.
———
Annual Deficit . . . . 10,000,000 dollars.

The President of the Ayuntamiento was a pleasant person to know, among the dishonest, intriguing Mexican officials. He received but little pay in return for a great deal of hard work; but he liked to be in office for the opportunities it afforded him of improving the condition of the poor of the city. It was a sight to see the prisoners crowd round him as he entered the court. They all knew him, and it was quite evident they all considered him as a friend. In what little can be done for the ignorant and destitute under the unfavourable circumstances of the country, Don Miguel has had a large share; but until an orderly government, that is, a foreign one, succeeds to the present anarchy, not very much can be done.

I mentioned the word "*compadrazgo*" a little way back. The thing itself is curious, and quite novel to an Englishman of the present day. The godfathers and godmothers of a child become, by their participation in the ceremony, relations to one another and to the priest who baptizes the child, and call one another ever afterwards *compadre* and *comadre*. Just such a relationship was once expressed by the word "gossip," "God-sib," that is "akin in God." Gossip has quite degenerated from its old meaning, and even "sib," though good English in Chaucer's time, is now only to be found in provincial dialects; but in German "sipp" still means "kin."

In Mexico this connexion obliges the compadres and comadres to hospitality and honesty and all sorts of good offices towards one another; and it is wonderful how conscientiously this obligation is kept to, even by people who have no conscience at all for the rest of the world. A man who will cheat his own father or his own son will keep faith with his *compadre*. To such an extent does this influence become mixed up with all sorts of affairs, and so important is it, that it is necessary to count it among the things that tend to alter the course of justice in the country.

The French have the words *compère* and *commère*; and it is curious to observe that the name of *compère* is given to the confederate of the juggler, who stands among the crowd, and slyly helps in the performance of the trick.

We went one day to the Hospital of San Lazaro. I have mentioned the word "*lepero*" as applied to the poor and idle class of half-caste Mexicans. It is only a term of reproach, exactly corresponding to the "*lazzarone*" of Naples, who resembles the Mexican lepers in his social condition, and whose name implies the same thing; for, of course, Saint Lazarus is the patron saint of lepers and foul beggars. There are some few real lepers in Mexico, who are obliged by law to be shut up in this hospital. We rather expected to see something like what one reads of the treatment of lepers which prevailed in Europe until a few years ago—shutting them up in dismal dens cut off from communication with other human beings. We were agreeably disappointed. They were confined, it is true, but in a spacious building, with court-yard and garden; their nurses and attendants appeared to be very kind to them; and it seems that many charitable people come to visit the inmates, and bring them cigars and other small luxuries, to relieve the monotony of their dismal lives. Some had their faces horribly distorted by the falling of the corners of the eyes and mouth, and the disappearance of the cartilage of the nose; and a few, in whom the disease had terminated in a sort of gangrene, were frightful objects, with their features scarcely distinguishable; but in the majority of cases the leprosy had caused a gradual disappearance of the ends of the fingers and toes, and even of the whole hands and feet. The limbs thus mutilated looked as though the parts which were wanting had been amputated, and the wound had quite healed over, but it is caused by a gradual absorption without wound and without pain. As every one knows, leprosy of these kinds was held until quite lately to be dangerously contagious; but, fortunately for the poor creatures themselves, this is quite clearly proved to be false, and the lepers are only shut up that they may have no children, for the affection appears to be hereditary.

It was early one morning, when we were going out to breakfast at Tisapán, that Don Juan recounted to us his experience of garrotted malefactors sitting dead in their chairs in the great square across which we were riding. "It was really almost enough to spoil a fellow's breakfast," he added pathetically. Though an Englishman, and only arrived in the country a few years before, Don Juan was as clever with the lazo as most Mexicans, and could *colear* a bull in great style. Indeed, we had started early that morning in order to have time enough to look at the bulls in the *potreros*—the great grass-meadows—that lie for miles outside the city, and which are made immensely fertile by flooding from time to time. Wherever we saw a bull in the distance, Don Juan and his grand little horse *Pancho* plunged over a bank and through a gap, and we after him. No one ever leaps anything in this country, indeed the form of the saddle puts it out of the question. One or two bulls looked up as we entered the enclosure, and bolted into other fields, pushing in among the thorns of the aloes which formed close hedges of fixed bayonets round the meadows. At last Don Juan cut off the retreat of an old bull, and galloping after him like mad, flung the running loop of the lazo over his horns, at the same time winding the other end round the pummel of his saddle. The bull was still standing on all four legs, pulling with all its might against Pancho. Galloping after him, so as to slacken the end of the lazo, we contrived to transfer it from Don Juan's saddle to mine. Now my own horse happened to be a little lame, and I was riding a poor little black beast whose bones really seemed to rattle in his skin. Our acquaintances in the Paseo had been quite facetious about him, recommending us to be careful and not to smoke up against him, for fear we should blow him over, and otherwise whetting their wit upon him. He acquitted himself very creditably, however, and when the bull began to pull against him, he leant over on the other side, as if he had been galloping round a circus; and the bull could not move him an inch. It was quite evident that it was not his first experiment. In the mean time Don Juan had dropped the noose of my lazo just before the bull's nose, and presently that animal incautiously put his foot into it, when Don Juan whipped it up round his leg and went off at full gallop. My little black horse knew perfectly well what had happened, though his head was exactly in the opposite direction; and he tugged with all his might, and leant over more than ever. The two lazos tightened with a twang, as though they had been guitar-strings; and in a moment the unfortunate bull was rolling with all his legs in the air, in the midst of a whirlwind of dust. Having thus humiliated him we let him go, and off he went at full speed. All this time the proprietor of the field was tranquilly standing on a bank, looking on. Far from raging at us for treating his property in this free and easy manner, he returned our salutation when we rode up to him, and, addressing our sporting countryman, said, "Well done, old fellow, come another day and try again."

Our whole ride to Tisapán was enlivened by a series of Don Juan's exploits. He raced after bulls, got hold of their tails, and coleared them over into the dust. He lazo'd everything in the road, from milestones and trunks of trees upwards; and I shall never forget our meeting with a great mule which was trotting along the road without a burden,—just as he passed us, our companion slipped the noose round his hind leg, and the beast went down as if he had been shot, the muleteers pulling up on purpose to have a good open-mouthed laugh at the incident.

We seemed to be in rather a sporting line that day, for, after our return from Tisapán, Don Juan and I went to see a cockfight. In Mexico, as in Cuba and all Spanish America, this is the favourite sport of the people. In Cuba, the principal shopkeeper in every village keeps the cockpit—the "*plaza de gallos*." The people from the whole district round about come in on Sunday to the village, with a triple object; *first*, to hear mass; *secondly*, to buy their supplies for the ensuing week; and *thirdly*, to spend the afternoon in cockfighting, at which amusement it is easy to win or lose two or three hundred pounds in an afternoon. The custom that the cockpit brings to the shop more than repays the proprietor for the expense and trouble of keeping it. In Cuba, the spurs of the cock are artificially pointed by paring with a penknife, but the Mexican way of arming them is even more abominable.

Each bird has a sharp steel knife three or four inches long, just like a little scythe-blade, fastened over the natural spur before the fight commences. A leather sheath covers the weapon while the cocks are being put into the ring, and held with their beaks almost touching till they are furious. Then they are drawn back to opposite sides of the ring, the sheaths are taken off, and they fly at one another, giving desperate cuts with the steel blades.

The cockpit was a small round wooden shed, with the ring in the middle, and circular benches round it, rising one above another. The place was full of people, mostly Mexicans of the lower orders, smoking, betting, and talking sporting-slang. The betting was surprising, when one compared its amount with the appearance of the spectators, among whom there was hardly a decent coat to be seen. Every now and then, a dirty scoundrel in a shabby leather jacket would walk round the ring with a handful of gold, offering the odds—ten to five, ten to seven, ten to nine, or whatever they might be, in gold ounces, which coins are worth above three pounds apiece.

Cockfighting is such a passion here that we thought it as well to see it for once. Santa Ana, now he has retired from politics, spends his time at Carthagena pretty much entirely in this his favourite sport, which forms one of the great items among the pleasures and excitements of a Mexican life. We saw a couple of mains fought, in which the victorious birds were dreadfully mangled, while the vanquished were literally cut to pieces; as much money changed hands as we should have thought sufficient to buy up the whole of the people present, cockpit and all. Then, being both agreed that it was a disgusting sight, we went away.

Before we left Mexico we were taken by our man Antonio to a cutler's shop, where the principal trade seemed to be the making of these *cuchillos* to arm the cocks with. We bought a couple of pairs of them, and had them carefully fitted up. The old cutler was quite delighted, and remarked that foreigners must acknowledge that there were some things which were done better in Mexico than anywhere else. I fear we left him under the pleasing impression that we were taking home the blades to introduce as models in our own benighted country.

The Mexican is a great gambler. Bad fortune he bears with the greatest equanimity. You never hear of his committing suicide after being ruined at play; he just goes away, and sets to work to earn enough for a fresh stake. The government have tried to put down gambling in the State of Mexico, but not with much success. For three days in the year, however, at the festival of San Agustín de las Cuevas, public gambling-tables are tolerated, though soldiers and officials are strictly forbidden to play, an injunction which they carefully set at nought. Oddly enough, the government, while doing all it could to keep its own functionaries away from the *monte* table, did not scruple to send a military escort to convoy the bankers with their bags of gold from Mexico to San Agustín. On one of the three days, Mr. Christy and I went there. There was a great crowd, this time mostly a well-dressed one, and the cockpit was on a large scale. But of course the great attraction was the *monte*, which was being played everywhere, the stakes in some places being coppers, in others silver, while more aristocratic establishments would allow no stake under a gold ounce. Dead silence prevailed in these places, and the players seemed to pride themselves upon not showing the slightest change in their countenances, whether they won or lost. The game itself is very simple, and has some points of resemblance to that of lansquenet, known in Europe. The first two cards in the pack, say a four and a king, are laid down, face up, on the table, and the gamblers put down their money against one or the other. Then the *croupier* deals the cards out slowly and solemnly one after another, calling out their names as they fall, until he comes—say to a king; when those who have betted on the king have their stakes doubled, and the others lose theirs. The banker has a great advantage to compensate him for his expense and risk. If the first card which is thrown out be one of the two numbers on the table, the banker withholds a quarter of the stake he would otherwise have lost, paying only a stake and three-quarters, instead of two stakes. Now, as there are forty cards in a Spanish pack, two of which have been already thrown out, the chances for a throw favourable to the banker are about one in six, so that he may reckon on an average profit of about two per cent, on all the money staked.

As for the players, they sat round the table, carefully noticing the course of the games, and regulating their play accordingly, as they do at Baden-Baden and Hombourg. I suppose that now and then these scientific calculators must be told that their whole theory of chances is the most baseless delusion, but they certainly do not believe it; and at any rate this curious pseudo-science of winning by skill at games of pure chance will last our time, if not longer.

On some tables there were as much as three or four thousand gold ounces. This struck us the more because we had often tried to get gold coin for our own use, instead of the silver dollars, the general currency of the country, of which twenty pounds' worth to carry home on a hot day was enough to break one's heart. We often tried to get gold, but the answer was always that what little there was in the country was in the hands of the gamblers, whose operations could not be worked on a large scale without it.

The prevalence of mining, as a means of getting wealth, has contributed greatly to make the love of gambling an important part of the national character. Silver-mining in the old times was a most hazardous speculation, and people engaged in it used to make and lose great fortunes a dozen times in their lives. The miners worked not on fixed wages, but for a share of the produce, and so every man became a gambler on his own account. To a great extent the same evils prevail now, but two things have tended to lessen them. Poor ores are now worked profitably which used to be neglected by the miners; and, as these ores occur in almost inexhaustible masses, their mining is a much less speculative affair than the old system of mining for rich veins. Moreover, the men are, in some of the largest mines, paid by the day, so that their life has become more regular. In many places, however, the work is still done on shares by the miners, who pass their lives in alternations of excessive riches and all kinds of extravagance, succeeded by times of extreme poverty.

An acquaintance of ours was telling us one day about the lives of these men. One week, a party of three miners had come upon a very rich bit of ore, and went away from the *raya*, each man with a handkerchief full of dollars. This was on Saturday evening. On Monday morning our informant went out for a ride, and on the road he met three dirty haggard-looking men, dressed in some old rags; one of the three came forward, taking off the sort of apology for a hat which he had on, and said, "Good morning, Señor Doctor, would you mind doing us the favour of lending us half a dollar to get something to eat?" They were the three successful miners; and when, a few days afterwards, the man who had asked for the money came back to return it, the Doctor inquired what had happened.

It seemed that the three, as soon as they had received their money on Saturday, got a lift to the nearest town, and there rigged themselves out with new clothes, silver buttons, five-pound serapes, and a horse for each, with magnificent silver mountings to the saddle and spurs. Here they have dinner, and lots of pulque, and swagger about outside the door, smoking cigarettes. There, quite by chance, an acquaintance meets them, and admires the horses, but would like to see their paces tried a little outside the town. So they pace and gallop along for half a mile or so; when, also quite accidentally, they find two men sitting outside a rancho, playing at cards. The two men—strangely enough—are old acquaintances of the curious friend, and they produce a bowl of cool pulque from within, which our miners find quite refreshing after the ride. Thereupon they sit down to have a little game at *monte*, then more pulque, then more cards; and when they awake the next morning, they find themselves possessed of a suit of old rags, with no money in the pockets. They had dim recollections of losing—first money, then horses, and lastly clothes, the night before; but—as they were informed by the old woman, who was the only occupant of the place besides themselves—their friends had been obliged to go away on urgent business, and could not be so impolite as to disturb them. So they walked back to the mines, ragged and hungry, and borrowed the doctor's half-dollar.

CHAPTER X.
TEZCUCO. MIRAFLORES. POPOCATEPETL. CHOLULA.

The wet season was fast coming on when we left Mexico for the last time. We had to pass through Vera Cruz, where the rain and the yellow fever generally set in together; so that to stay longer would have been too great a risk.

Our first stage was to Tezcuco, across the lake in a canoe, just as we had been before. We noticed on our way to the canoes, a church, apparently from one to two centuries old, with the following doggerel inscription in huge letters over the portico, which shows that the dogma of the Immaculate Conception is by no means a recent institution in Mexico:

Antes de entrar afirma con tu vida, S. Maria fué sin pecado concebida:

Which may be translated into verse of equal quality,

Confess on thy life before coming in, That blessed Saint Mary was conceived without sin.

Nothing particular happened on our journey, except that a well-dressed Mexican turned up at the landing-place, wanting a passage, and as we had taken a canoe for ourselves, we offered to let him come with us. He was a well-bred young man, speaking one or two languages besides his own; and he presently informed us that he was going on a visit to a rich old lady at Tezcuco, whose name was Doña Maria Lopez, or something of the kind. When we drove away from the other end of the lake, towards Tezcuco, we took him as far as the road leading to the old lady's house; when he rather astonished us by hinting that he should like to go on with us to the Casa Grande, and could walk back. At the same time, it struck us that the youth, though so well dressed, had no luggage; and we began to understand the queer expression of the coachman's face when he saw him get into the carriage with us. So we stopped at the corner of the road, and the young gentleman had to get out.

At the Casa Grande, our friends laughed at us immensely when we told them of the incident, and offered us twenty to one that he would come to ask for money within twenty-four hours. He came the same evening, and brought a wonderful story about his passport not being *en règle,* and that unless we could lend him ten dollars to bribe the police, he should be in a dreadful scrape. We referred him to the master of the house, who said something to him which caused him to depart precipitately, and we never saw him again; but we heard afterwards that he had been to the other foreigners in the neighbourhood with various histories. We made more enquiries about him in the town, and it appeared that his expedition to Tezcuco was improvised when he saw us going down to the boat, and of course the visit to the rich old lady was purely imaginary. Now this youth was not more than eighteen, and looked and spoke like a gentleman. They say that the class he belonged to is to be counted rather by thousands than by hundreds in Mexico. They are the children of white Creoles, or nearly white mestizos; they get a superficial education and the art of dressing, and with this slender capital go out into the world to live by their wits, until they get a government appointment or set up as political adventurers, and so have a chance of helping themselves out of the public purse, which is naturally easier and more profitable than mere sponging upon individuals. One gets to understand the course of Mexican affairs much better by knowing what sort of raw material the politicians are recruited from.

We saw some good things in a small collection of antiquities, on this second visit to Tezcuco. Among them was a nude female figure in alabaster, four or five feet high, and—comparatively speaking—of high artistic merit. Such figures are not common in Mexico, and they are supposed to represent the Aztec Venus, who was called *Tlazolteocihua,* "Goddess of Pleasure." A figure, laboriously cut in hard stone, representing a man wearing a jackal's head as a mask, was supposed to be a figurative representation of the celebrated king of Tezcuco, *Nezahualcoyotl,* "hungry jackal," of whom Mexican history relates that he walked about the streets of his capital in disguise, after the manner of the Caliph in the Arabian Nights. The explanation is plausible, but I think not correct. The *coyote* or jackal was a sacred animal among the Aztecs, as the Anubis-jackal was among the Egyptians. Humboldt found in Mexico the tomb of a coyote, which had been carefully interred with an earthen vase, and a number of the little cast-bronze bells which I noticed in the last chapter. The Mexicans used actually to make a kind of fetish—or charm—of a jackal's skin, prepared in a peculiar way, and called by the same name, *nezahualcoyotl*, and very likely they do so still. From this fetish the king's name was, no doubt, borrowed; and it is not improbable that the whole story of the king's walking in disguise may have grown up out of his name being the same as that of the figure we saw, muffled up in a jackal's skin.

It is curious that the jackal, or the human figure in a jackal-mask, should have been an object of superstitious veneration both in Mexico and in Egypt. This, the extraordinary serpent-crown of Xochicalco, and the pyramids, are the three most striking resemblances to be found between the two countries; all probably accidental, but not the less noteworthy on that account.

The collection contained a number of spherical beads in green jade, highly polished, and some as large as pigeon's eggs. They were found in an alabaster box, of such elaborate and beautiful workmanship that the owner deemed it worthy to be presented as a sort of peace-offering to the wife of President Santa Ana.

The word *coyotl* in the name of the Tezcucan king is the present word *coyote*—a jackal. Though unknown in English, it has passed, with several Spanish words, into what we may call the American dialect of our language. Prairie-hunters and Californians have introduced several other words in this way, such as *ranch, gulch, corral,* &c.

The word *lariat* one is constantly meeting with in books about American prairies. A horse-rope, or a lazo, is called in Spanish *reata*; and, by absorbing the article, *la reata* is made into lariat, just as such words as *alligator, alcove,* and *pyramid* were formed. The flexible leather riding-whip or *cuarta* is apparently the *quirt* that some American politicians use in arguing with their opponents.

Our last day at Tezcuco was spent in packing up antiquities to be sent to England, the express orders of the Government against such exportation to the contrary notwithstanding. Next morning we rode off to Miraflores, passing on our way the curious stratum of alluvial soil containing pottery, &c., which I have described already. Miraflores is a cotton-factory, in the opening of a picturesque gorge just at the edge of the plain of Mexico. The machinery is American, for the mill dates from the time when it was considered expedient to prohibit the exportation of cotton-mill machinery from England; and having begun with American work, it naturally suits them to go on with it. It is driven by a great Barker's mill, which works in a sort of well, having an outlet into the valley, and roars as though it would tear the place down. It is not common to see this kind of machine working on a large scale; but here, with a great fall of water, it does very well. Otherwise the place was like an ordinary cotton-factory, and one cannot be surprised at people thinking that such establishments are a source of prosperity to the country. They see a population hard at work and getting good wages, masters making great profits, and no end of bales going off to town; and do not consider that half the price of the cloth is wasted, and that the protection-duty sets the people to work which they cannot do to advantage, while it takes them away from occupations which their country is fit for.

Next morning took us to Amecameca, a town in a little plain at the foot of Popocatepetl, whose snow-covered top towers high up in the clouds, like Mont Blanc over Sallanches. We had at one time cherished hopes of getting to the top of this grand volcano, but had heard such frightful reports of difficulties and dangers that we had concluded not to do more than look at it from a distance, the more especially as there had been a heavy fall of snow upon it a day or two before. We presented our letter to the Spaniard who kept the great shop at Amecameca, and asked him, casually, about the mountain. He assured us that the surface of the snow would be frozen over, and that instead of being a disadvantage the fall of snow was in our favour, for it was easier to climb over frozen snow than up a loose heap of volcanic ashes. So we sent for the guide, a big man, who used to manage the sulphur-workings in the crater until that undertaking was given up. He set to work to get things ready for the expedition, and we strolled out for a walk.

Close by the town is a "sacred mount," with little stations, and on one day in the year numbers of pilgrims come to visit the place. Near the top, the Indian lad who came with us showed us the mouth of a cavern, which leads by subterranean passages under the sea to Rome—as caverns not unfrequently do in Roman Catholic countries! What was more worth noticing was that here there was a cypress-tree, covered with votive offerings, like the great ahuchuete in the valley above Chalma; so that it is likely that the place was sacred long before chapels and stations were built upon it. Our guide told us that whenever a man touched the tree, all feeling of weariness left him. How characteristic this superstition is of a nation of carriers of burdens!

In the afternoon we started—ourselves, our guide, and an Indian to carry cloaks, &c. up the mountain. We soon left the cultivated region, and entered upon the pine-forest, which we never left during our afternoon journey. One of the first showers of the rainy season came down upon us as we rode through the forest. It only lasted half an hour, but it was a deluge. In a shower of the same kind at Tezcuco, a day or two before, rain to the amount of 1-1/10 inches fell in the hour. By dusk we reached the highest habitation in North America, the place where the sulphur used to be sublimed from the pumice brought down from the crater. This place was shut up, for the undertaking has been abandoned; but in a *rancho* close by we found some Indian women and children, and there we took up our quarters. The *rancho* was a circular hut, built and thatched with reeds, though in the midst of a pine-forest; and presently a smart shower began, which came in upon us as though the roof had been a sieve.

The Indian women were kneeling all the evening round the wood-fire in the centre of the hut, baking *tortillas* and boiling beans and coffee in earthen pots. The wood was green, and the place was full of suffocating smoke, except within eighteen inches of the ground, where lay a stratum of purer air. We were obliged to lie down at once, upon mats and serapes, for we could not exist in the smoke; and as often as we raised ourselves into a sitting posture, we had to dive down again, half suffocated. The line of demarcation was so accurately drawn that it was like the Grotto del Cane, only reversed.

After a primitive supper in earthen bowls, we lay round the fire, listening to the talk of our men and the Indian women. It was mostly about adventures with wolves, and about the sulphur-workings, now discontinued. The weather had cleared, and as we lay we could see the stars shining in through the roof. About three in the morning I awoke, feeling bruised all over, as was natural after sleeping on a mat on the ground. Moreover, the fire had gone out, and it was horribly cold, as well it might be at 13,000 feet above the sea. I shook some one up to make up the fire, and went out into the open air. It was nearly full moon; but the moonlight was very different from what we can see in England, even on the clearest nights. On the plateau of Mexico, the rarity and dryness of the air are such that distant objects are seen far more distinctly than at the level of the sea, and the European traveller's measurements of distance by the eye are always too small. The sunlight and moonlight, for the same reason, are more intense than at lower levels. Here, at about the same elevation as the top of the Jungfrau, the effect was far more striking, and I shall never forget the brilliant flood of light that illuminated that grand scene. Far down below I could see the plain, with houses and fields dimly visible. At the bottom of the slope began the dark pine-forest, which enveloped the mountains up to the level at which I stood, and there broke into an uneven line, with straggling patches running up a few hundred feet higher in sheltered crevices. Above the forest came a region of bare volcanic sand, and then began the snow. The highest peak no longer looked steep and pointed as from below, but seemed to rise from the darker line of sand in a gentle swelling curve up into the sky. There did not seem to be a speck or a wrinkle on this smooth snowy dome, the brilliant whiteness of which contrasted so wonderfully with the dark pine-forest below.

About seven in the morning we started on horseback, rode up across the sandy district, and entered upon the snow. After we left the pines, small bushes and tufts of coarse Alpine grass succeeded. Where rocks of basaltic lava stood out from the heaps of crumbling ashes, after the grass had ceased, lichens—the occupants of the highest zone—were still to be seen. Before we reached the snow, we were in the midst of utter desolation, where no sign of life was visible. From this point we sent back the horses, and started for the ascent of the cone. On our yesterday's ride we had cut young pine-trees in the forest, for alpenstocks; and we tied silk handkerchiefs completely over our faces, to keep off the glare of the sun. Our guide did the same; but the Indian, who had been many times before up to the crater to get sulphur, had brought no protection for his face. We marched in a line, the guide first, sounding the depth of the snow with his pole, and keeping as nearly as he could along ridges just covered with snow, where we did not sink far. It was from the lower part of the snow that we began to understand the magnificent proportions of Iztaccihuatl—the "White Woman," the twin mountain which is connected with Popocatepetl by an immense col, which stretches across below the snow-line. This mountain is not conical like Popocatepetl, but its shoulders are broader, and break into grand peaks, like some of the *Dents* of Switzerland, and it has no crater. Indeed, the two mountains, joined together like Siamese twins, look as though they had been set up, side by side, to illustrate the two contending theories of the formation of volcanos. Von Buch and Humboldt might have made Iztaccihuatl on the "upheaval theory," by a force pushing up from below, without breaking through the crust to form a crater; while Poulett Scrope was building Popocatepetl on the "accumulation theory," by throwing up lava and volcanic ashes out of an open vent, until he had formed a conical heap some five thousand feet high, with a great crater at the top.

As we toiled slowly up the snow, we took off our veils from time to time, to look more clearly about us. The glare of the sun upon the snow was dazzling, and its intense whiteness contrasted wonderfully with the cloudless dark indigo-blue of the sky. Between twelve and one we reached the edge of the crater, 17,884 feet above the sea. The ridge upon which we stood was only a few feet wide, and covered with snow; but it seemed that there was still heat enough to keep the crater itself clear, for none lay on the bottom, or in clefts on the steep sides.

The crater was oval, full a mile in its longest diameter, and perhaps 700 to 800 feet in depth; and its almost perpendicular walls of basaltic lava are covered with red and yellow patches of sublimed sulphur. We climbed a little way down into it to get protection from the wind, but to descend further unassisted was not possible, so we sat there, with our legs dangling down into the abyss. Part of the *malacate*, or winder, used by the Indians in descending, was still there; but it was not complete, and even if it had been, so many months had elapsed since it was last used that we should not have cared to try it. It consisted of a rope of hide, descending into the bottom of the crater in a slanting direction; and the sulphur-collectors were lowered and drawn up it by a windlass, in a basket to which another rope was attached. A few years back, the volcano used to send up showers of ashes, and even large stones; but now it has sunk to the condition of a mere *solfatara*, sending out, from two crevices in the floor, great volumes of sulphurous acid and steam, with a loud roaring noise. The sulphur-working merely consisted in looking for places where the pumice-stone was fully impregnated with sulphur, and breaking out pieces, which were hauled up in the basket. The chief risk which the labourers ran was from the terrific snow-storms, which come on suddenly and without the slightest notice. Men at work collecting sulphur have once or twice been caught by such storms in parts of the crater at a distance from the rope, and buried in the snow.

The appearance of the "White Woman," but little lower than the point where we stood, was very grand, but all other objects looked small. The two great plains of Mexico and Puebla, with their lakes and towns, were laid out like a map; and the ranges of mountains which hem them in made them look like Roman encampments surrounded by earthworks. Even now that the lakes have shrunk to a fraction of their former size, we could see the fitness of the name given in old times to the Valley of Mexico, *Anahuac*, that is, "By the Water-side." The peaks of Orizaba and Perote were conspicuous to the east; to the north lay the silver-mountains of Pachuca; and to the south-west a darker shade of green indicated the forests and plantations of the *tierra caliente*, below Cuernavaca.

It was a novel sensation to be at an altitude where the barometer stands at 15-1/2 inches, so that the pressure on our lungs was hardly more than one-half what we are accustomed to in England; but we did not experience much inconvenience from it. The last thousand feet or so had been very hard work, and we were obliged to stop every few steps, but on the comparatively level edge of the crater we felt no difficulty in moving about.

Popocatepetl means "Smoking Mountain." The Indians naturally enough considered it to be the abode of evil spirits, and told Cortes and his companions that they could never reach the top. One of the Spaniards, Diego Ordaz, tried to climb to the summit, and got as far as the snow; whereupon he returned, and got permission to put a burning mountain in his coat of arms, in commemoration of the exploit! If, as he declared, a high wind was blowing, and showers of ashes falling, his turning back was excusable, though his bragging was not. He seems to have afterwards told Bernal Diaz that he got to the top, which we know, by Cortes' letters to Spain, was not true. A few years later, Francesco Montano went up, and was lowered into the crater to get sulphur. When Humboldt relates the story, in his *New Spain*, he seems incredulous about this; but since the *Essai Politique* was written the same thing has been regularly done by the Indians, as the merest matter of business, until the crater has been fairly worked out.

We took our last look at Mexico from the ridge of the crater, and, descending twenty feet at a stride, soon reached the bottom of the cone. As far as we could see, the substance of the hill seemed to be of basaltic lava, which was mostly covered with the *lapilli* which I have spoken of before as ashes and volcanic sand. Even before we reached the pine-forest there was evidence of the action of water, which had covered the slope of the mountain with beds of thick compact tufa, composed of these lapilli mixed with fragments of lava. The water-courses had cut deep channels through these beds, and down into the rock below; so that the streams from the melted snow rushed down between walls of lava, in which traces of columnar structure were observable.

The snow we had travelled over was sometimes dry and powdery, and sometimes hard and compact. There were no glaciers, and no glacier-ice, properly so called. It never rains at this elevation; and, though evaporation goes on rapidly with half the pressure taken off the air, and a great increase in the intensity of the sun's rays, the snow either passes directly into vapour, or carries the water off instantaneously, as it is formed. Only so much water seems to be produced and re-frozen as suffices to make the snow hard, and in some favourable places near the rocks to form lumps of ice, and some of those great icicles which the Spaniards brought down from the mountain on their first expedition, so greatly astonishing their companions.

When we reached the rancho we thought of passing another night there; but the Indians who had gone down to the valley for corn had not returned, and everything was eaten up except beans, which are all very well as accessories to dinner, but our English digestions could not stand living upon them; so we started at once for San Nícolas de los Ranchos. Our ride was down a deep ravine, by the side of a mountain-torrent coming down from the snows of Popocatepetl; and, when we stopped now and then to look behind us, we had one of the grandest views which I have ever witnessed. The elements of the picture were simple enough. A deep gorge at our feet, with a fierce torrent rushing down it, dark pine-trees all round us, and above us—on either side—a snow-covered mountain towering up into the sky. We were just in the track of the Spanish invaders, who crossed most likely by this very road between the two volcanos; and they record the amazement which they felt that in the tropics snow should be unmelted upon the mountains.

A few hours riding down the steep descent, and we were in the flat plain of Puebla. There were our two mountains behind us, but now they looked as we had so often seen them before from a distance. The power of realizing their size was gone, and with it most of their grandeur and beauty. Nothing was left us but a vivid recollection of the wonderful scenes that were before us a few hours ago, impressions not likely to be ever effaced from our minds, where the picture of the great snowy cone seen in the bright moonlight, and the descent between the mountains, remain indelibly impressed as the types of all that is most grand and impressive in the scenery of lofty mountains.

We slept at San Nícolas de los Ranches, "St. Nicholas of the huts," where the shopkeeper, to whom we had a letter, insisted upon turning out of his own room for us, and treated us like princes. The reason of our often being provided with letters to the shopkeepers in small places, was, that they are the only people who have houses fit for entertaining travellers. Many of them are very rich, and in the United States they would call themselves merchants. Next morning our Indian carrier, who had ascended the mountain without a veil, was brought in by our guide, a pitiful object. All the skin of his face was peeling off, and his eyes were frightfully inflamed, so that he was all but blind, and had to be led about. Fortunately, this blindness only lasts for a time, and no doubt he got well in a few days.

We rode through the plain to Cholula. Our number was now four; for, besides Antonio, we had engaged another servant a few days before. We wanted some one who knew this district well; and when a friend of ours mentioned that there was a young man to be had who had a good horse and was a smuggler by profession, we engaged him directly, and he proved a great acquisition. Of course, from the nature of his trade, he knew every bypath between Mexico and the tobacco-districts towards which we were going; he was always ready with an expedient whenever there was a difficulty, he was never tired and never out of temper. As for the morality of his peculiar profession, it probably does harm to the honesty of the people; but, considering it as a question of abstract justice, we must remember that almost the whole of the taxes which the Mexicans are compelled to pay to the general government are utterly wasted upon paying officials who do nothing but intrigue, and keeping up armies which—far from being a protection to life and property—are a permanent and most destructive nuisance. The contract between government and subject ought to be a two-sided one; and when the government so entirely misuses the taxes paid by the people, I am quite inclined to sympathize with the subjects who will not pay them if they can help it.

We scarcely entered the town of Cholula, which is a poor place now, though it was a great city at the time of the Spanish Conquest. The Spanish city of Puebla, only a few miles off, quite ruined it.

We went straight to the great pyramid, which lies close to the town, and which had been rising before us like a hill during the last miles of our journey. This extraordinary structure is perhaps the oldest ruin in Mexico, and certainly the largest. A close examination of its structure in places where the outline is still to some extent preserved, and a comparison of it with better preserved structures of the same kind, make it quite clear that it was a terraced *teocalli*, resembling the drawing called the "Pyramid of Cholula," in Humboldt's *Vues des Cordillères*. But let no one imagine that the well-defined and symmetrical structure represented in that drawing is in the least like what we saw, and from which Humboldt made the rough sketch, which he and his artist afterwards "idealized" for his great work. At the present day, the appearance of the structure is that of a shapeless tree-grown hill; and until the traveller comes quite close to it he may be excused for not believing that it is an artificial mound at all.

The pyramid is built of rows of bricks baked in the sun, and cemented together with mortar in which had been stuck quantities of small stones, fragments of pottery, and bits of obsidian knives and weapons. Between rows of bricks are alternate layers of clay. It was built in four terraces, of which traces are still to be distinguished; and is about 200 feet high. Upon the platform at the top stand some trees and a church. The sides front the four cardinal points, and the base line is of immense length, over thirteen hundred feet, so that the ascent is very gradual.

When we reached Cholula we sent the two men to enquire in the neighbourhood for antiquities, of which numbers are to be found in every ploughed field round. At the top of the pyramid we held a market, and got some curious things, all of small size however. Among them was a mould for making little jackal-heads in the clay, ready for baking; the little earthen heads which are found in such quantities in the country being evidently made by wholesale in moulds of this kind, not modelled separately. We got also several terra-cotta stamps, used in old times for stamping coloured patterns upon the native cloth, and perhaps also for ornamenting vases and other articles of earthenware. Cholula used to be a famous place for making pottery, and its red-and-black ware was famous at the time of the Conquest, but the trade now seems to have left it. We were struck by observing that, though there was plenty of coloured pottery to be found in the neighbourhood of the pyramid, the pyramid itself had only fragments of uncoloured ware imbedded in its structure; which seems to prove that it was built before the art of colouring pottery was invented.

They have cut a road through one corner of the pyramid, and this cutting exposed a chamber within. Humboldt describes this chamber as roofed with blocks, each overlapping the one before, till they can be made to meet by a block of ordinary size. This is the false arch so common in Egypt and Peru, and in the ruined cities of Central America. Every child who builds houses with a box of bricks discovers it for himself. The bridge at Tezcuco, already described, is much more remarkable in its structure. Whether our inspection was careless, or whether the chamber has fallen in since Humboldt's time, I cannot say, but we missed this peculiar roof.

There are several legends about the Pyramid of Cholula. That recorded by Humboldt on the authority of a certain Dominican friar, Pedro de los Rios, I mention—not because of its intrinsic value, which is very slight, but because it will enable us to see the way in which legends grew up under the hands of the early missionaries, who were delighted to find fragments of Scripture-history among the traditions of the Ancient Mexicans, and who seem to have taken down from the lips of their converts, as native traditions, the very Bible-stories that they had been teaching them, mixed however with other details, of which it is hard to say whether they were imagined on purpose to fill up gaps in the story, or whether they were really of native traditional origin.

Pedro de los Rios' story tells us that the land of Anahuac was inhabited by giants; that there was a great deluge, which devastated the earth; that all the inhabitants were turned into fishes, except seven who took refuge in a cave (apparently with their wives). Years after the waters had subsided, and the earth had been re-peopled by these seven men, their leader began to build a vast pyramid, whose top should reach to heaven. He built it of bricks baked in the sun, which were brought from a great distance, passing them from hand to hand by a file of men. The gods were enraged at the presumption of these men, and they sent down fire from heaven upon the pyramid, which caused its building to be discontinued. It is stated that at the time of the Spanish Conquest, the inhabitants of Cholula preserved with great veneration a large aerolite, which they said was the thunderbolt that fell upon the top of the pyramid when the fire struck it.

The history of the confusion of tongues seems also to have existed in the country, not long after the Conquest, having very probably been learnt from the missionaries; but it does not seem to have been connected with the Tower-of-Babel legend of Cholula. Something like it at least appears in the Gemelli table of Mexican migrations, reproduced in Humboldt, where a bird in a tree is sending down a number of tongues to a crowd of men standing below.

I think we need not hesitate in condemning the legend of Cholula, which I have just related, as not genuine, or at least as partly of late fabrication. But we fortunately possess another version of it, which shows the legend to have developed itself farther than was quite discreet. A MS. history, written by Duran in 1579, and quoted by the Abbé Brasseur de Bourbourg, relates that people built the pyramid to reach heaven, finding clay or mud *("terre glaise")* and a very sticky *bitumen ("bitume fort gluant")*, with which they began at once to build, &c. This is evidently the slime or bitumen of the Book of Genesis; but I believe I may safely assert that the Mexicans never used bitumen for any such purpose, and that it is not found anywhere near Cholula.

The Aztec historians ascribe the building of the Pyramid of Cholula to the prophet Quetzalcoatl. The legends which relate to this celebrated personage are to be found in writers on Mexican history, and, more fully than elsewhere, in the Abbé Brasseur de Bourbourg's work.

I am inclined to consider Quetzalcoatl a real personage, and not a mythical one. He is said to have been a white, bearded man, to have come from the East, to have reigned in Tollan, and to have been driven out from thence by the votaries of human sacrifices, which he opposed. He took refuge in Chololan, now called Cholula (which means the "place of the fugitive"), and taught the inhabitants to work in metals, to observe various fasts and festivals, to use the Toltec calendar of days and years, and to perform penance to appease the gods.

A relic of the father of Quetzalcoatl is said to have been kept until after the Spanish Conquest, when it was opened, and found to contain a quantity of fair human hair. The prophet himself departed from Cholula, and put to sea in a canoe, promising to return. So strong was the belief in the tradition of these events among the Aztecs, that when the Spaniards appeared on the coast, they were supposed to be of the race of the prophet, and the strange conduct of Montezuma to Cortes is to be ascribed to the influence of this belief.

There is a singular legend, mentioned by the Abbé Brasseur de Bourbourg, of a white man, with a hooded robe and white beard, bearing a cross in his hand, who lands at Tehuantepec (on the Pacific coast of Mexico), and introduces among the Indians auricular confession, penance, and vows of chastity.

The coming of white, bearded men from the East, centuries before the Spanish invasion in the 16th century, and the introduction of new arts and rites by them in Mexico, is as certain as most historical events of which we have only legendary knowledge. As to who they were I cannot offer an opinion. There are, however, one or two points connected with the presence of the Irish and Northmen in America in the 9th and following centuries—a period not very far from that ascribed to Quetzalcoatl—which are worthy of notice.

The Scandinavian antiquarians make the "white-man's land" *(Hvitramannaland)* extend down as far as Florida, on the very Gulf of Mexico. It is curious to notice the coincidence between the remark of Bernal Diaz, that the Mexicans called their priests *papa* (more properly *papahua*), and that in the old Norse Chronicle, which tells of the first colonization of Iceland by the Northmen, and relates that they found living there "Christian men whom the Northmen call *Papa*." These latter are shown by the context to have been Irish priests. The Aztec root *teo (teo-tl, God)* comes nearer to the Greek and Latin, but is not unlike the Irish *dia*, and the Norse *ty-r*. The Aztec root *col* (charcoal) is exactly the Norse *kol* (our word *coat*), but not so near to the Irish *gual*. It is desirable to notice such coincidences, even when they are too slight to ground an argument upon.

This seems to be the proper place to mention the many Christian analogies to be found in the customs of the ancient Aztecs.

Children were sprinkled with water when their names were given to them. This is certainly true, though the statement that they believed that the process purified them from original sin is probably a monkish fiction. Water was consecrated by the priests, and was supposed thus to acquire magical qualities. In the coronation of kings, anointing was part of the ceremony, as well as the use of holy water. The festival of All Souls' Day reminds us of the Aztec feasts of the Dead in the autumn of each year; and in Mexico the Indians still keep up some of their old rites on that day. There was a singular rite observed by the Aztecs, which they called the *teoqualo,* that is, "the eating of the god." A figure of one of their gods was made in dough, and after certain ceremonies they made a pretence of killing it, and divided it into morsels, which were eaten by the votaries as a kind of sacred food.

We may add to the list the habitual use of incense in the ceremonies: the existence of monasteries and nunneries, in which the monks wore long hair, but the nuns had their hair cut off: and the use of the cross as a religious emblem in Mexico and Central America.

Less certain is the recorded use of knotted scourges in performing penance, and the existence of a peculiar kind of auricular confession.

It is difficult to ascribe this mass of coincidences to mere chance, and not to see in them traces of connexion, more or less remote, with Christians. Perhaps these peculiar rites came, with the Mexican system of astronomy, from Asia; or perhaps the white, bearded men from the East may have brought them. It is true that such a supposition runs quite counter to the argument founded on the ignorance of the Mexicans of common arts known in Europe and Asia. We should have expected Christian missionaries to have brought with them the knowledge of the use of iron, and the alphabet. Perhaps our increasing knowledge of the ancient Mexicans may some day allow us to adopt a theory which shall at least have the merit of being consistent with itself; but at present this seems impossible.

CHAPTER XI.
PUEBLA. NOPALUCÁN. ORIZABA. POTRERO.

We reached Puebla in the afternoon, and found it a fine Spanish city, with straight streets of handsome stone houses, and paved with flag-stones. We rather wondered at the *pasadizos*, a kind of arched stone-pavement across the streets at short intervals, very much impeding the progress of the carriages, which had to go up and down them upon inclined planes. In the evening we saw the use of them however, for a shower of rain came down which turned every street into a furious river within five minutes after the first drop fell. For half an hour the pasadizos did their duty, letting the water pass through underneath, while passengers could get across the streets dryshod. At last, the flood swept clear along, over bridges and all; but this only lasted a few minutes, and then the way was practicable again. The moveable iron bridges on wheels, which are to be seen standing in the streets of Sicilian cities, ready to be wheeled across them for the benefit of foot-passengers whenever the carriage-way is flooded, are on the whole a better arrangement.

We should never have thought, from looking at Puebla, that it had just been undergoing a siege; for, beyond a few patches of whitewash in the great square, where the cannon-balls had knocked the houses about, there were no traces of it.

We made many enquiries about the siege, and found nothing to invalidate our former estimate of twenty-five killed,—one per cent of the number stated in the government manifestos. Among the casualties we heard of an Englishman who went out to see the fun, and was wounded in a particularly ignominious manner as he was going back to his house.

Revolutions and sieges form curious episodes in the life of the foreign merchants in the Republic. Their trade is flourishing, perhaps,—plenty of buyers and good prices; and hundreds of mules are on the road, bringing up their wares from the coast. All at once there is a pronunciamiento. The street-walls are covered with proclamations. Half the army takes one side, half the other; and crowds of volunteers and self-made officers join them, in the hope of present pillage or future emolument. Barricades appear in the streets; and at intervals there is to be heard the roaring of cannon, and desultory firing of musketry from the flat roofs, killing a peaceable citizen now and then, but doing little execution on the enemy.

Trade comes to a dead stop. Our merchant gets his house well furnished with provisions, shuts the outer shutters, locks up the great gates, and retires into seclusion for a week or a fortnight, or a month or two, as may be. At the time we were there he used to run no great risk, for neither party was hostile to him; and if a stray cannon-ball did hit his house, or the insurgents shot his cook going out on an expedition in search of fresh beef, it was only by accident.

Having no business to do, the counting-house would probably take stock, and balance the books; but when this is finished there is little to be done but to practice pistol-shooting and hold tournaments in the court-yard, and to teach the horses to rayar; while the head of the house sits moodily smoking in his arm-chair, reckoning up how many of his debtors would be ruined, and wondering whether the loaded mules with his goods had got into shelter, or had been seized by one party or the other.

At last the revolution is over. The new president is inaugurated with pompous speeches. The newspapers announce that now the glorious reign of justice, order, and prosperity has begun at last. If the millennium had come, they could not make much more talk about it. Our unfortunate friend, coming out of his den only to hear dismal news of runaway debtors and confiscated bales, has to illuminate his house, and set to getting his affairs into something like order again.

Since we left the country things have got even worse. Formerly, all that the foreign merchants had to suffer were the incidental miseries of a state of civil war. Now, the revolutionary leaders put them in prison; and, if threats are not sufficient, they get forced loans out of them, much as King John did out of his Jews.

Even in times of peace, foreign goods must be dear in Mexico. In a country where they have to be carried nearly three hundred miles on mules' backs, and where credit is so long that the merchant can never hope to see his money again in less than two years, he cannot be expected to sell very cheaply. But the continual revolutions and the insecurity of property make things far worse, and one almost wonders how foreign trade can go on at all.

One of our friends in Mexico had three or four hundred mules coming up the country laden with American cotton for his mill, just when Haro's revolution began. He got off much better than most people, however; for, greatly to the disgust of the legitimate authorities, he went down into the enemy's camp, and gave the revolutionary chief a dollar a bale to let them go.

As may be supposed, commercial transactions have often very curious features here. Strange things happen in the eastern states; but people there say that they are nothing to the doings on the Pacific coast, where the merchants get up a revolution when their ships appear in the offing, and turn out the Custom-house officers, who do not enter upon their functions again until the rich cargos have started for the interior.

One little incident, which happened——I think—at Vera Cruz, rather amused us. When the Government is hard-up, a favourite way of raising ready money is to sell—of course at a very low price—orders upon the Custom-house, to pass certain quantities of goods, duty-free. Such a transaction as this was concluded between the Minister of Finance and a merchant's house who gave hard dollars in exchange for an order to pass so many hundred bales of cotton, free of duty. When the ship arrived at port, however, the Yankee captain brought in his manifest with a broad grin upon his face. The inspectors went down to the ship, and stood aghast. There were the bales of cotton, but such bales! They had to be shoved and coaxed to get them up through the hatchways at all. The Customhouse officials protested in vain. The order was for so many bales of cotton, and these overgrown monsters were bales of cotton, and the merchants sent them up to Mexico in triumph.

To us, Puebla was not an interesting city. It was built by the Spaniards, and called *Puebla de los Angeles*, because angels assisted in building the cathedral, which does no great credit to their good taste. Its costly ornaments of gold, silver, jewels, and variegated marbles, are most extraordinary. One does not know which to wonder at most, the value and beauty of the materials, or the unmitigated ugliness of the designs.

We saw the festival of Corpus Christi while we were in Puebla; but were to a certain extent disappointed in the display of plate and jewelled vestments for the clergy, whose attempt to overthrow Comonfort's government had only resulted in themselves being heavily fined, and who were in consequence keeping their wealth in the background, and making as little display as possible. The most interesting part of the ceremonial to us was to see the processions of Indians from the surrounding villages, walking crowned with flowers, and carrying Madonnas in bowers of green branches and blossoms.

At the head of each procession walked an Indian beating a drum, *tap, tap, tap,* without a vestige of time. The other processions with stoles and canopies, and the officials of the city in dress-coats and yellow kid gloves, were paltry affairs enough.

Neither during this ceremonial, nor at Easter in the Capital were any miracles exhibited, like the performances of the Madonna at Palermo, which the coachmen of the city carry about at Easter, weeping real tears into a cambric pocket-handkerchief; nor is anything done in the country like the lighting of the Greek fire, or the melting of the blood of St. Januarius.

Puebla pretty much belongs to the clergy, who are paramount there. A population of some sixty thousand has seventy-two churches, some of them very large. It is the focus of the church-party, whose steady powerful resistance to reform is one of the causes of the unhappy political state of the country. As is usual in cathedral-towns, the morality of the people is rather lower than elsewhere. I have said already that the revenues of the Mexican Church are very large. Tejada estimates the income at twenty millions of dollars yearly, more than the whole revenue of the State; but this calculation far exceeds that given by any other authority. He remarks that the Church has always tried as much as possible to conceal its riches, and probably he makes a very large allowance for this. At any rate, I think we may reasonably estimate the annual income of the Church at $10,000,000, or £2,000,000, two-thirds of the income of the State.

There is nothing extraordinary in the Church having become very rich by the accumulations of three centuries in a Spanish colony, where the manners and customs remained in the 18th century to a great extent as they were in the 16th, and the practice of giving and leaving great properties to the Church was in full vigour—long after it had declined in Europe. It is considered that half the city of Mexico belongs to the Church. This seems an extraordinary statement; but, if we remember that in Philip the Second's time half the freehold property of Spain belonged to the Church, we shall cease to wonder at this. The extraordinary feature of the case is that, counting both secular and regular clergy, there are only 4600 ecclesiastics in the country. The number has been steadily decreasing for years. In 1826 it was 6,000; in 1844 it had fallen to 5,200, in 1856 to 4,600, giving, on the lowest reckoning, an average of over £200 a year for each priest and monk. A great part of this income is probably left to accumulate; but, when we remember that the pay of the country curas is very small, often not more than £30 to £50, there must be fine incomes left for the church-dignitaries and the monks. Now any one would suppose that a profession with such prizes to give away would become more and more crowded. Why it is not so I cannot tell. It is true that the lives of the ecclesiastics are anything but respectable, and that the profession is in such bad odour that many fathers of families, though good Catholics, will not let a priest enter their houses; but we do not generally find Mexicans deterred by a little bad reputation from occupations where much money and influence are to be had for very little work.

The ill conduct of the Mexican clergy, especially of the monks, is matter of common notoriety, and every writer on Mexico mentions it, from the time of Father Gage—the English friar—who travelled with a number of Spanish monks through Mexico in 1625, and described the clergy and the people as he saw them. He was disgusted with their ways, and, going back to England, turned Protestant, and died Vicar of Deal.

To show what monastic discipline is in Mexico, I will tell one story, and only one. An English acquaintance of mine was coming down the Calle San Francisco late one night, and saw a man who had been stabbed in the street close to the convent-gate. People sent into the convent to fetch a confessor for the dying man, but none was to be had. There was only one monk in the place, and he was bed-ridden. The rest were enjoying themselves in the city, or fast asleep at their lodgings in the bosom of their families.

In condemning the Mexican clergy, some exception must be made. There are many of the country curas who lead most exemplary lives, and do much good. So do the priests of the order of St. Vincent de Paule, and the Sisters of Charity with whom they are associated; but then, few of these, either priests or sisters, are Mexicans.

Among the curious odds and ends which we came upon in Puebla, in the shop of a dealer in old iron and things in general, were two or three very curious old scourges, made of light iron chains with projecting points on the links—terrific instruments, once in very general use. Up to the present time, there are certain nights when penitents assemble in churches, in total darkness, and kneeling on the pavement, scourge themselves, while a monk in the pulpit screams out fierce exhortations to strike harder. The description carries us back at once to the Egyptian origin of this strange custom; and we think of the annual festival of Isis, where the multitudes scourged themselves in memory of the sufferings of Osiris. A story is told of a sceptical individual who got admission to this ceremony by making great professions of devotion, and did terrific execution on the backs of his kneeling fellow-penitents. Before he began, the place was resounding with doleful cries and groans; but he noticed that the cry which arose when he struck was not like these other sounds, but had quite a different accent. The practice of devotional scourging is still kept up in Rome, but in a very mild form, as it appears that the penitents keep their coats on, and only use a kind of miniature cat-o'-nine-tails of thin cord, with a morsel of lead at the end of each tail, and not such bloodthirsty implements as those we found at Puebla.

It seemed to us that the great influence of the priests in Mexico was among the women of all classes, the Indians, and the poorer and less educated half-castes. The men of the higher classes, especially the younger ones, did not appear to have much respect for the priests or for religion, and, indeed, seemed to be sceptical, after the manner of the French school of freethinking. It was quite curious to see the young dandies, dressed in their finest clothes, at the doors of the fashionable churches on Sunday morning. None of them seemed to go to mass, but they simply went to stare at the ladies, who, as they came out, had to run the gauntlet through a double line of these critical young gentlemen. As far as we could see, however, they did not mind being looked at. The poorer mestizos and Indians, on the other hand, are still zealous churchmen, and spend their time and money on masses and religious duties so perseveringly that one wishes they had a religion which was of some use to them. As it is, I cannot ascertain that Christianity has produced any improvement in the Mexican people. They no longer sacrifice and eat their enemies, it is true, but against this we must debit them with a great increase of dishonesty and general immorality, which will pretty well square the account.

Practically, there is not much difference between the old heathenism and the new Christianity. We may put the dogmas out of the question. They hear them and believe in them devoutly, and do not understand them in the least. They had just received the Immaculate Conception, as they had received many mysteries before it; and were not a little delighted to have a new occasion for decorating themselves and their churches with flowers, marching in procession, dancing, beating drums, and letting off rockets by daylight, as their manner is. The real essence of both religions is the same to them. They had gods, to whom they built temples, and in whose honour they gave offerings, maintained priests, danced and walked in processions—much as they do now, that their divinities might be favourable to them, and give them good crops and success in their enterprises. This is pretty much what their present Christianity consists of. As a moral influence, working upon the character of the people, it seems scarcely to have had the slightest effect, except, as I said, in causing them to leave off human sacrifices, which were probably not an original feature of their worship, but were introduced comparatively at a late time, and had already been almost abolished by one king.

The Indians still show the greatest veneration for a priest; and Heller well illustrates this feeling when he tells us how he happened to ride through the country in a long black cloak, and the Indians he met on the road used to fall on their knees as he passed, and ask for his blessing, regardless of the deep mud and their white trousers. However, this was ten years before we were in the country, and I doubt whether the cloak would get so much veneration now. The best measure of the influence of the Church is the fact that when Mexico adopted a republican constitution, in imitation of that of the United States, it was settled that no Church but that of Rome should be tolerated in the country; and this law still remains one of the fundamental principles of the State, in which universal liberty and equality, freedom of the press, and absolute religious intolerance form rather a strange jumble. It is curious to observe that, though the Independence confirmed the authority of the Roman Catholic religion, it considerably reduced the church-revenues, by making the payment of tithes a matter of mere option. The Church—of course—diligently preaches the necessity of paying tithes, putting their obligation in the catechism, between the ten commandments and the seven sacraments, and they still get a good deal in this way.

We sent our horses to the bath at Pueblo. This is usually done once a week in the cities of Mexico. We went once to see the process while we were in the capital, and were very much amused. The horses had been to the place before, and turned in of their own accord through a gateway in a shabby back street; and when they got into the courtyard, began to dance about in such a frantic manner that the *mozos* could hardly hold them in while their saddles and bridles were being taken off. Then they put their heads down, and bolted into a large shed, with a sort of floor of dust several inches deep, in which six or eight other horses were rushing about, kicking, prancing, plunging, and literally screaming with delight. I will not positively assert that I saw an old white horse stand upon his head in a corner and kick with all his four legs at once, but he certainly did something very much like it. Presently the old *mozo* walked into the shed, with his lazo over his arm, and carelessly flung the noose across. Of course it fell over the right horse's neck, when the animal was quiet in a moment, and walked out after the old man in quite a subdued frame of mind. One horse came out after another in the same way, took his swim obediently across a great tank of water, was rubbed down, and went off home in high spirits.

Though slavery has long been abolished in the Republic, there still exists a curious "domestic institution" which is nearly akin to it. It is not peculiar to the plains of Puebla, but flourishes there more than elsewhere. It is called "*peonaje*," and its operation is in this wise. If a debtor owes money and cannot pay it, his creditor is allowed by law to make a slave or _peon _of him until the debt is liquidated. Though the name is Spanish, I believe the origin of the custom is to be found in an Aztec usage which prevailed before the Conquest.

A *peon* means a man on foot, that is, a labourer, journeyman, or foot-soldier. We have the word in English as "*pioneer*" and as the "*pawn*" among chessmen; but I think not with any meaning like that it has come to bear in Mexico.

On the great haciendas in the neighbourhood of Puebla, the Indian labourers are very generally in this condition. They owe money to their masters, and are slaves; nominally till they can work off the sum they owe, but practically for their whole lives. Even should they earn enough to be able to pay their debt, the contract cannot be cancelled so easily. A particular day is fixed for striking a balance, generally, I believe, Easter Monday, just after a season when the custom of centuries has made it incumbent upon the Indians to spend all that they have and all that they can borrow upon church-fees, wax-candles, and rockets, for the religious ceremonies of the season, and the drunken debauches which form an essential part of the festival. The masters, or at least the *administradors*, are accused of mystifying the annual statement of accounts between the labourer and the estate, and it is certain that the Indian's feeble knowledge of arithmetic leaves him quite helpless in the hands of the bookkeeper; but whether this is mere slander or not, we never had any means of ascertaining.

Long servitude has obliterated every feeling of independence from the minds of these Indians. Their fathers were slaves, and they are quite content to be so too. Totally wanting in self-restraint, they cannot resist the slightest temptation to run into debt; and they are not insensible to the miserable advantage which a slave enjoys over a free labourer, that his master, having a pecuniary interest in him, will not let him starve. They have a cat-like attachment to the places they live in; and to be expelled from the estate they were born on, and turned out into the world to get a living, we are told by writers on Mexico, is the greatest punishment that can be inflicted upon them.

There was nothing that we could see in the appearance of these *peons* to distinguish them from ordinary free Indians; and our having travelled hastily through the district where the system prevails does not give us a right to judge of its working. We can but compare the opinions of waiters who have studied it, and who speak of it in terms of the strongest reprobation, as deliberately using the moral weakness of the Indians as a means of reducing them to slavery. Sartorius, however, takes the other side, and throws the whole blame upon the careless improvident character of the brown men, whose masters are obliged to lend them money to supply their pressing wants, and must take the only security they can get. He says, and truly enough, that the system works wretchedly both for masters and labourers. Any one who knows the working of the common English system of allowing workmen to run into debt with the view of retaining them permanently in their master's service may form some faint idea of the way in which this Mexican debt-slavery destroys the energy and self-reliance of the people.

But in one essential particular Sartorius mis-states the case. It is not the money which the masters lend the *peons* to help them in distress and sickness that keeps them in slavery. It is the money spent in wax-candles and rockets, and such like fooleries, for Easter and All Saints; in the reckless profusion of drunken feasts on the days of their patron saints, and on the occasion of births, deaths, and marriages. These feasts are as utterly disproportioned to the means of the givers as the Irish wakes which reduce whole families to beggary. The sums of money spent upon them are provided by the owners of the estates, who know exactly how they are to be spent. If they preferred that their labourers should be free from debt, they could withhold this money; and their not doing so proves that it is their desire to keep the *peons* in a state of slavery, and throws the whole blame of the system upon them.

I have spoken of the *peons* as Indians, and so they are for the most part in the districts we visited; but travellers who have been in Chihuahua and other northern states tell stories of creditors travelling through the country to collect their debts, and, where money was not forthcoming, collecting their debtors instead,—not merely brown Indians, but also nearly white mestizos.

Mexico is one of the countries in which the contrast between great riches and great poverty is most striking. No traveller ever enters the country without making this remark. The mass of the people are hardly even with the world; and there are some few capitalists whose incomes can scarcely be matched in England or Russia. Yet this state of things has not produced a permanent aristocracy.

The general history of great fortunes repeats itself with monotonous regularity. Fortunate miners or clever speculators, who have happened to possess the gift of accumulating in addition to that of getting, often make colossal fortunes. Miners have made the greatest sums, and made them most rapidly. Fortunes of two or three millions sterling are not uncommon now, and we often meet with them in the history of the last century. They never seem to have lasted many years. Before the Independence, the capitalist used to buy a patent of nobility, and leave great sums to his children to maintain the new dignity; but they hardly ever seem to have done anything but squander away their inheritance, and we find the family returning to its original poverty by the third or fourth generation.

Mexico is an easy place to make money in, in spite of the continual disorders that prevail. In the mining-districts most men make money at some time or other. The difficulty lies in keeping it. There seems to be no training better suited for making a capitalist than the life of the retail shopkeeper, especially in the neighbourhood of a mine. A good share of all the money that is won and of all that is lost stops in his till. Whoever makes a lucky hit in a mining-speculation, he has a share of the profits, and when there is a "good thing" going, he is on the spot to profit by it.

When once a man becomes a capitalist, there are many very profitable ways of employing his money. Mines and cotton-factories pay well, so do cattle-haciendas in the north, when honest administradors can be got to manage them; and discounting merchants' bills is a lucrative business. But far better than these ordinary investments are the monopolies, such as the farming of the tobacco-duty, the mints, and those mysterious transactions with the government in which ready cash is exchanged for orders to pass goods at the Custom-house, and the other financial transactions familiar to those who know the shifts and mystifications of that astonishing institution, the Finance-department of Mexico.

We rode from Puebla to Orizaba. Amozoque, the first town on the road, is a famous place for spurs, and we bought some. They are of blue steel inlaid with strips of silver, and the rowel is a sort of cogged wheel, from an inch and a half to three inches in diameter. *(See page 220.)* They look terrific instruments, but really the cogs or points of the rowels are quite blunt, and they keep the horse going less by hurting him than by their incessant jingling, which is increased by bits of steel put on for the purpose. Monstrous as the spurs now used are, they are small in comparison with those of a century or two ago. One reads of spurs, of gold and silver, with rowels in the shape of five-pointed stars six inches in diameter. These have quite gone out now, and seem to have been melted up, for they are hardly ever to be seen; but we bought at the *baratillo* of Mexico spurs of steel quite as large as this.

My companion sent to the Art-exhibition at Manchester a couple of pairs of the ordinary spurs of the country, such as we ourselves and everybody else wore. They were put among the mediæval armour, and excited great admiration in that capacity!

We slept at Nopalucán that night, and rode on next day to San Antonio de Abajo, a little out-of-the-way village at the foot of the mountain of Orizaba. Our principal adventure in the day's ride was that, finding that our road made a détour of a mile or so round a beautiful piece of green turf, we boldly struck across it, and nearly lamed our horses thereby; for the ground was completely undermined by moles, and at every third step the horses' feet went into a deep hole. We had to get off and lead them back to the road.

Orizaba is the great feature in the scenery of this district of Mexico. It is one point in the line of volcanos which stretches across the continent from east to west. It is a conical mountain, like Popocatepetl, and about the same height; measurements vary from twenty feet higher to sixty feet lower. The crater has fallen in on one side, leaving a deep notch clearly visible from below. At present, as we hear from travellers who have ascended it, the crater, like that of Popocatepetl, is in the condition of a *solfatara*, sending out jets of steam and sulphurous acid gas. About three centuries ago its eruptions were frequent; and its Mexican name, *Citlaltepetl*, "Mountain of the Star," carries us back to the time when it showed in the darkness a star-like light from its crater, like that of Stromboli at the present time, when one sees it from a distance.

San Antonio de Abajo is a quaint little village, frequented by muleteers and smugglers. Tobacco, the principal contraband article, is grown in the plains just below; and, once carried up into the paths among the mountains, it is hard for any custom-house officer to catch sight of it.

When there was a government, there used sometimes to be fighting between the revenue-officers and the smugglers; but now, if there is a meeting, a few dollars will settle the disputed question to the satisfaction of both parties, so that the contraband trade, though profitable, is by no means so exciting as it used to be.

On the road towards San Antonio we saw ancient remains in the banks by the road-side, but had no time for a regular examination. We slept on damp mattresses in a room of the inn, where the fowls roosted on the rafters above our heads, and walked over our faces in the early morning in an unpleasant manner. We started before daybreak, and a descent down a winding road, through a forest of pines and oaks, brought us by seven in the morning from the region of pines and barley down to the district where tobacco and the sugar-cane flourish, at the level of 3,000 to 4,000 feet above the sea.

We met a jaunty-looking party in the valley, two women and five or six men, all on good horses, and dressed in the extreme of fashion which the Mexican *ranchero* affects—broad-brimmed hats with costly gold and silver serpents for hat-bands, and clothes and saddles glittering with silver. Martin rode up to us as they passed, and said he knew them well for the boldest highwaymen in Mexico. Had we started an hour or two later we should have met them in the forest, and have had an adventure to tell of. As it was, the descent of three thousand feet had brought us from a land of thieves to a region where highway robbery is never known, unless when a party from the high lands come down on a marauding expedition. It is an unquestionable fact that the Mexican robbers, whose exploits have become a matter of world-wide notoriety, all belong to the cold region of the plateaus, the *tierra fría*. Once down in the *tierra templada*, or the *tierra caliente*, the temperate or the hot regions, you hear no more of them; or at least this is the case in the parts of Mexico we visited. The reason is clear; it is only on the plateaus that the whites, preferring a region where the climate was not unlike that of Castile, settled in large numbers; so that it is there that Creoles and mestizos predominate, and they are the robbers.

We rode over great beds of gravel, cut up in deep trenches by the mountain-streams; then along the banks of the river, among plantations of tobacco, looking like beds of lettuces. As we were riding along the valley, we saw before us a curious dark cloud, hanging over some fields near the river. Our men, who had seen the appearance before, recognized it at once as a flight of locusts, and, turning out of the high-road, we came upon them just as they had settled on a clump of trees in a meadow. They covered the branches and foliage until only the outline of the trees was visible, while the rest of the swarm descended on a green hedge, and on the grass. As for us, we went and knocked them down with our riding-whips, and carried away specimens in our hats; but the survivors took no manner of notice of us, and in about ten minutes they left the trees mere skeletons, leafless and stripped of their bark, and moved across the field in a dense mass towards some fruit-trees a little way off. For days after this, when we met with travellers on the road, or stopped at the door of a cottage to get a light or something to drink, and chatted a few minutes with the inhabitants, we found that our descent of the mountain-pass had brought us into a new set of interests. News of the government and of the revolutionary party excited no curiosity,—talk of robbers still less. At every house the question was, "¿*De donde vienen, Señores?*" "Where are you from, gentlemen?"—and when we told them, "¿*Y estaban allí las langostas?*" "And were the locusts there?" The whole country was being devastated by them; and the large rewards offered for them to the peasants, though they caused dead locusts to be brought by tons, seemed hardly to diminish their numbers. Firing guns had some slight effect in driving off the swarms of locusts; and in some places the reports of muskets were to be heard, at short intervals, all day long. Some idea of the destruction caused by the locusts may be formed from the fact that in six weeks they doubled the price of grain in the district. Fortunately, they only appear in such numbers about once in half a century.

We had ridden a hundred miles over a rough country in the last forty-eight hours, and were glad to get a rest at Orizaba; but on the morning of the third day we were in the saddle again, accompanied by a new friend, the English administrador of the cotton-mill at Orizaba. Until we left the high-road, the country seemed well cultivated, with plantations of tobacco, coffee, and sugar-cane; but as soon as we turned into by-paths and struck across country, we found woods and grassy patches, but little tilled ground, until we arrived at the Indian village which we had gone out of our way to visit, Amatlán, that is to say, "*The place of paper.*"

In its arrangement this village was like the one that I have already described, with its scattered huts of canes and palm-leaf thatch; but the vegetation indicated a more tropical climate. Large fields, the joint property of the community, were cultivated with pine-apples in close rows, now just ripening; and bananas, with broad leaves and heavy clusters of fruit, were growing in the little garden belonging to each hut. The inhabitants stared at us sulkily, and gave short answers to our questions. We went to the cottage of the Indian alcalde, who declared that there was nothing to eat or drink in the village, though we were standing in his doorway and could see the strings of plantains hanging to the roof, and the old women were hard at work cooking. However, when Mr. G. explained who he was, the old man became more placable; and we were soon sitting on mats and benches inside the hut, on the best of terms with the whole village. The life of these people is simple enough, and not unsuited to their beautiful climate. The white men have never interfered much with them; and it has been their pride for centuries to keep as much as possible from associating with Europeans, whom they politely speak of as *coyotes*, jackals. The priest was a *mestizo*, and, as the Alcalde said, he was the only *coyote* in the settlement; but his sacred office neutralized the dislike that his parishioners felt for his race.

These Indian communities always rejoiced in being able to produce for themselves almost everything necessary for their simple wants; but of late years the law of supply and demand has begun to undermine this principle, and the cotton-cloth, spun and woven at home, is yielding to the cheaper material supplied by the factories. Though so averse to receiving Europeans among them, they do not object to go themselves to work for good wages on the plantations. Those who leave their native place, however, bring back with them tastes and wants hitherto unknown, and inconsistent with their primitive way of life.

Another habit of theirs brings them into contact with the "reasonable people," not to their advantage. They are excessively litigious, and their continual law-suits take them to the large towns where the courts of justice are held, and where lawyers' fees swallow up a large proportion of their savings. There is a natural connexion between farming and law-suits; and the taste for writs and hard swearing is as remarkable among this agricultural people as it is among our own small farmers in England.

Theoretically, the Indians in their villages live under the general government, like any other citizens; for, since the establishment of the republic, the civil disabilities which had kept them down for three centuries were all abolished at a sweep, and the brown people have their votes, and are eligible for any office. Practically, these advantages do not come to much at present, for custom, which is stronger than law, keeps them under the government of their own aristocracy, composed of certain families whose nobility dates beyond the Conquest, and was always recognized by the Spaniards. These noble Indians seem to be pretty much as dirty, as ignorant, and as idle as the plebeians—the ordinary field-labourers or "*earth-hands*" (*tlalmaitl*), as they were called in ancient times,—and a stranger cannot recognize their claims to superiority by anything in their houses, dress, language, or bearing; nevertheless, they are the patrician families, and republicanism has not yet deprived them of their power over the other Indians. In early times, when men of white or mixed blood were few in the country, it suited the Spanish government to maintain the authority of these families, who collected the taxes and managed the estates of the little communities. The common people were the sufferers by this arrangement, for the Alcaldes of their own race cheated them without mercy, and were harder upon them than even their white rulers, just as on slave-estates a black driver is much severer than a white one.

Near some of the houses we noticed that curious institution—the *temazcalli*, which corresponds exactly to the Russian vapour-bath. It is a sort of oven, into which the bather creeps on all fours, and lies down, and the stones at one end are heated by a fire outside. Upon these stones the bather sprinkles cold water, which fills the place with suffocating steam. When he feels himself to have been sufficiently sweated, he crawls out again, and has jars of cold water poured over him; whereupon he dresses himself (which is not a long process, as he only wears a shirt and a pair of drawers), and so goes in to supper, feeling much refreshed. If he would take the cold bath only, and keep the hot one for his clothes, which want it sadly, it would be all the better for him, for the constant indulgence in this enervating luxury weakens him very much. One would think the bath would make the Indians cleanly in their persons, but it hardly seems so, for they look rather dirtier after they have been in the *temazcalli* than before, just as the author of *A Journey due North* says of the Russian peasants.

To us the most interesting question about the Mexican Indians of this district was this, *Why are there so few of them?* There are five thousand square leagues in the State of Vera Cruz, and about fifty inhabitants to the square league. Now, let us consider half the State, which is at a low level above the sea, as too hot and unhealthy for men to flourish in, and suppose the whole population concentrated on the other half, which lies upon the rising ground from three thousand to six thousand feet above the sea. This is not very far from the truth, and gives us one hundred inhabitants to the square league— about one-sixth of the population of the plains of Puebla, in a climate which may be compared to that of North Italy, and where the chief products are maize and European grain.

In the district of the lower temperate region, which we are now speaking of, nature would seem to have done everything to encourage the formation of a dense population. In the lower part of this favoured region the banana grows. This plant requires scarcely any labour in its cultivation; and, according to the most moderate estimate, taking an acre of wheat against an acre of bananas, the bananas will support twenty times as many people as the wheat. Though it is a fruit of sweet, rather luscious taste, and only acceptable to us Europeans as one small item of our complicated diet, the Indians who have been brought up in the districts where it flourishes can live almost entirely upon it, just as the inhabitants of North Africa live upon dates.

In the upper portion of this district, where the banana no longer flourishes, nutritious plants produce an immense yield with easy cultivation. The *yucca* which produces cassava, rice, the sweet potato, yams, all flourish here, and maize produces 200 to 300 fold. According to the accepted theory among political economists, where the soil produces with slight labour an abundant nutriment for man, there we ought to find a teeming population, unless other counteracting causes are to be found.

The history of the country, as far as we can get at it, indicates a movement in the opposite direction. Judging from the numerous towns the Spanish invaders found in the district, the numbers of armed men they could raise, and the abundance of provisions, we must reckon the population at that time to have been more dense than at present; and the numerous ruins of Indian settlements that exist in the upper temperate region are unquestionable evidence of the former existence of an agricultural people, perhaps ten times as numerous as at present. The ruins of their fortifications and temples are still to be seen in great numbers, and the soil all over large districts is full of the remains of their pottery and weapons.

How far these settlements were depopulated by wars before the Spanish Conquest, it is not easy to say. During the Conquest itself they did not offer much resistance to the European invaders, and consequently they escaped the wholesale destruction which fell upon the more patriotic inhabitants of the higher regions. Since that time the country has been peaceable enough; and even since the Mexican Independence, the wars and revolutions which have done so much injury to the inhabitants of the plateaus have not been much felt here.

In reasoning upon Mexican statistics we have to go to a great extent upon guess-work. A very slight investigation, however, shows that the calculation made in Mexico, that the population increases between one and two per cent. annually, is incorrect. The present population of the country is reckoned at a little under eight millions; and in 1806, it seems, from the best authorities we can get, to have been a little under six millions. Even this rate of increase, one-third every half-century, is far above the rate of increase since the Conquest; for, at that rate, a population a little over a million and a quarter would have brought up the number to what it is at present, and we cannot at the lowest estimation suppose the inhabitants after the siege of Mexico to have been less than three or four millions. So that, badly as Mexico is now going on with regard to the increase of its population, about ½ per cent. per annum, while England increases over 1-1/2 per cent., and the United States twice as much, we may still discern an improvement upon the times of the Spanish dominion, when it was almost stationary.

Why then has this fertile and beautiful country only a small fraction of the number of inhabitants that formerly lived in it? That it is not caused by the climate being unfavourable to man is clear, for this district is free from the intense heat and the pestilential fevers of the low lands which lie nearer the sea.

It is a noticeable fact that the remains of the old settlements generally lie above the district where the banana grows; and the higher we rise above the sea, the more abundant do we find the signs of ancient population, until we reach the level of 8,000 feet or a little higher. The actual inhabitants at the present day are distributed according to the same rule, increasing in numbers, according to the elevation, from 3,000 to 8,000 feet, after which the severity of the climate causes a rapid decrease.

In making these observations, I leave out of the question the hot unhealthy coast-lands of the *tierra caliente,* and the cold and comparatively sterile plains of the *tierra fría,* and confine myself to that part of the country which lies between the altitudes of 3,000 and 8,000 feet, between which limits the European races flourish under circumstances of climate which also suited the various Mexican races, who probably came from a colder northern country. Now, if we begin to descend from the level of the Mexican plateau—say 8,000 feet above the sea—we find that less and less labour will provide nourishment for the cultivator of the soil, until we reach the limit of the banana, where the inhabitants ought to be crowded together like Chinese on their rice-grounds, or the inhabitants of Egypt in the time of Herodotus. Exactly the opposite rule takes effect; the banana-country is a mere wilderness, and the higher the traveller rises the more abundant become both present population and the remains of ancient settlements.

I suppose the reason of this is to be found in the habits and constitution of the tribes who colonized the country, and preferred to settle in a climate resembling that of their native land, without troubling themselves about the extra labour it would cost them to obtain their food. The European invaders have acted precisely in the same way; and the distribution of the white and partly white inhabitants of the country follows the same rule as that of the Indians.

So far the matter is intelligible, on the principle that the constitution and habits of the races which have successively taken up their residence in the country have been strong enough to prevail over the rule which regulates the supply of men by the abundance of food; but this does not explain the fact of an actual diminution of the inhabitants of the lower temperate districts. They were not mere migratory tribes, staying for a few years before moving forward. They had been settled in the country long enough to be perfectly acclimatized; and yet, under circumstances apparently so favourable to their increase, they have been diminishing for centuries, and are perhaps even doing so now.

The only intelligible solution I can find for this problem is that given by Sartorius, whose work on Mexico is well known in Germany, and has been translated and published in England. This author's remarks on the condition of the Indians are very valuable; and, as he was for years a planter in this very district, he may be taken as an excellent authority on the subject. He considers the evil to lie principally in the diet and habits of the people. The children are not weaned till very late, and then are allowed to feed all day without restriction on boiled maize, or beans, or whatever other vegetable diet may be eaten by the family. The climate does not dispose them to take much exercise; so that this unwholesome cramming with vegetable food has nothing to counteract its evil effects, and the poor little children get miserably pot-bellied and scrofulous,—an observation of which we can confirm the truth. A great proportion of the children die young, and those that grow up have their constitutions impaired. Then they live in close communities, and marry "in-and-in," so that the effect of unhealthy living becomes strengthened into hereditary disease; and habitual intemperance does its work upon their constitutions, though the quantities of raw spirits they consume appear to produce scarcely any immediate effect. Among a race in this bodily condition, the ordinary epidemics of the country—cholera, small-pox, and dysentery—make fearful havoc. Whole villages have often been depopulated in a few days by these diseases; and a deadly fever which used to appear from time to time among the Indians, until the last century, sometimes carried off ten thousand and twenty thousand at once. It seemed to me worth while to make some remarks about this question, with a view of showing that the theory as to the relation between food and population, though partly true, is not wholly so; and that in the region of which we have been speaking it can be clearly shown to fail.

After spending a long morning with the Indians and their *cura*, we took quite an affectionate leave of them. Their last words were an apology for making us pay threepence apiece for the pineapples which we loaded our horses with. In the season, they said, twelve for sixpence is the price, but the fruit was scarce and dear as yet.

Our companion, besides being engaged in the Orizaba cotton-mill, was one of the owners of the sugar-hacienda of the Potrero, below Cordova, and we all rode down there together from the Indian village, and spent the evening in walking about the plantation, and inspecting the new machinery and mills. It was a pleasant sight to see the people coming to the well with their earthen jars, after their work was done, in an unceasing procession, laughing and chattering. They were partly Indian, but with a considerable admixture of negro blood, for many black slaves were brought into the country in old times by the Spanish planters. Now, of course, they and their descendants are free, and the hotter parts of Mexico are the paradise of runaway slaves from Louisiana and Texas; for, so far from their race being despised, the Indian women seek them as husbands, liking their liveliness and good humour better than the quieter ways of their own countrymen. Even Europeans settled in Mexico sometimes take wives of negro blood.

I have never noticed in any country so large a number of mixed races, whose parentage is indicated by their features and complexion. In Europe, the parent races are too nearly alike for the children of such mixed marriages to be strikingly different from either parent. In America and the West Indies we are familiar with the various mixtures of white and negro, mulatto, quadroon, &c.; but in Mexico we have three races, Spanish, pure Mexican, and Negro, which, with their combinations, make a list of twenty-five varieties of the human race, distinguishable from one another, and with regular names, which Mayer gives in his work on Mexico, such as *mulatto, mestizo, zambo, chino*, and so forth. Here all the brown Mexican Indians are taken as one race, and the Red Indians of the frontier-states are not included at all. If we come to dividing out the various tribes which have been or still are existing in the country, we can count over a hundred and fifty, with from fifty to a hundred distinct languages among them.

Out of this immense variety of tribes, we can make one great classification. The men of one race are brown in complexion, and have been for ages cultivators of the land. It is among them only that the Mexican civilization sprang up, and they still remain in the country, having acquiesced in the authority of the Europeans, and to a great extent mingled with them by marriage. This class includes the Aztecs, Acolhuans, Chichemecs, Zapotecs, &c., the old Toltecs, the present Indians of Central America, and, if we may consider them to be the same race, the nations who huilt the now ruined cities of Palenque, Copan, Uxmal, and so forth. The other race is that of the Red Indians who inhabit the prairie-states of North Mexico, such as the Apaches, Comanches, and Navajos. They are hunters, as they always were, and they will never preserve their existence by adopting agriculture as their regular means of subsistence, and settling in peace among the white men. As it has been with their countrymen further north, so it will be with them; a few years more, and the Americans will settle Chihuahua and Sonora, and we shall only know these tribes by specimens of their flint arrow-heads and their pipes in collections of curiosities, and their skulls in ethnological cabinets.

One of the strangest races (or varieties, I cannot say which) are the *Pintos* of the low lands towards the Pacific coast. A short time before we were in the country General Alvarez had quartered a whole regiment of them in the capital; but when we were there they had returned with their commander into the tierra caliente towards Acapulco. They are called *"Pintos"* or painted men, from their faces and bodies being marked with great daubs of deep blue, like our British ancestors; but here the decoration is natural and cannot be effaced.

They have the reputation of being a set of most ferocious savages; and, badly armed as they are with ricketty flint- or match-locks, and sabres of hoop-iron, they are the terror of the other Mexican soldiery, especially when the war has to be carried on in the hot pestilential coast-region, their native country.

CHAPTER XII.
CHALCHICOMULA. JALAPA. VERA CRUZ. CONCLUSION.

The mountain-slopes which descend from the Sierra Madre eastward toward the sea are furrowed by *barrancas*—deep ravines with perpendicular sides, and with streams flowing at the bottom. But here all these *barrancas* run almost due east and west, so that our journey from Vera Cruz to Mexico was made, as far as I can recollect, without crossing one. Now, the case was quite different. We had to go from the Potrero to the city of Jalapa, about fifty miles on the map, nearly northward, and to get over these fifty miles cost us two days and a half of hard riding.

By the road it cannot be much less than eighty miles; but people used to tell us that, during the American war, an Indian went from Orizaba to Jalapa with despatches within the twenty-four hours, probably by mountain-paths which made it a little shorter. He came quite easily into Jalapa at the same shuffling trot which he had kept up almost without intermission for the whole distance. This is the Indian's regular pace when he is on a journey, and I believe that the Red Indians of the north have a similar gait.

We used sometimes to see a village or a house three or four miles off, and count upon reaching it in half an hour. But a few steps further on there would be a barranca, invisible till we came close to it, perhaps not more than a few hundred feet wide, so that it was easy to talk to people on the other bank. But the bottom of the chasm might be five hundred or a thousand feet below us; and the only way to cross was to ride along the bank, often for miles, until we reached a place where it had been possible to make a steep bridle-path zigzagging down to the stream below, and up again on the other side. It is only here and there that even such paths can be made, for the walls of rock are generally too steep even for any vegetation, except grass and climbing plants in the crevices. Our half-hour's ride, as we supposed it would be, would often extend to two or three hours, for on these slopes two or three barrancas—large and small—have sometimes to be crossed within as many miles.

If our journey had been even slower and more difficult, we should not have regretted it; the country through which we were riding was so beautiful. There were but few inhabitants, and the landscape was much as nature had left it. The great volcano of Orizaba came into view now and then with its snowy cone, mountain-streams came rushing along the ravines, and the forests of oaks were covered with innumerable species of orchids and creepers, breaking down the branches with their weight. Many kinds were already in flower, and their great blossoms of white, purple, blue, and yellow, stood out against the dark green of the oak-leaves. Wherever a mountain-stream ran down some shady little valley, there were tree-ferns thirty feet high, with the new fronds forming a tuft at the top of the old scarred trunk. Round the Indian cottages were cactuses with splendid crimson flowers, daturas with brilliant white blossoms, palm- and fruit-trees of fifty kinds. We stopped at one of the cottages, and bought an armadillo that had just been caught in the woods close by, while routing among his favourite ants' nests. He was put into a palm-leaf basket, which held him all but the tip of his long taper tail, which, like the rest of his body, was covered with rings of armour fitting beautifully into one another. One of our men carried him thus in his arms to Jalapa.

The Mexicans call an armadillo "*ayotochtli*," that is, "tortoise-rabbit," a name which will be appreciated by any one who knows the appearance of the little animal.

The villages and towns we passed were dismal places enough, and the population scanty; but that this had not always been the case was evident from the numerous remains of ancient Indian mound-forts or temples which we passed on our road, indicating the existence of large towns at some former period. There is a drawing in Lord Kingsborough's work of a *teocalli* or pyramid at San Andrés Chalchicomula, which we seem to have missed on account of the darkness having come on before we reached the town. We were several times deceived that evening by the fireflies, which we took for lights moving about in some village just ahead of us; and we became so incredulous at last that we would not believe we had reached our journey's end until we could made out the dim outlines of the houses. At the inn at San Andrés we found that we could have no rooms, as all the little windowless dens were occupied by people from the country who had come in for a *fiesta*. There were indeed a good many men loafing about the courtyard, but scarcely any women, and we could hardly understand a fandango happening without them. They thought otherwise, however; and presently, hearing the tinkling of a guitar, we went out and saw two great fellows in broad hats, jackets, and serapes, solemnly dancing opposite to one another; while more men looked on, smoking cigarettes, and an old fellow with a face like a baboon was squatting in one corner and producing the music we had heard. To do them justice, I must say that we found, on further enquiry, they had not come from their respective ranchos merely to make fools of themselves in this way, but that there was to be some horsefair in the neighbourhood next day, and they were going there.

Our not being able to get any supper but eggs and bread, and having to sleep on the supper-table afterwards, confirmed us in the theory we were beginning to adopt, that nature and mankind vary in an inverse ratio; and we were off at daybreak, delighted to get into the forest again. We rode over hill and dale for four or five hours, and then along the edge of a barranca for the rest of the day. This was one of the grandest chasms we had ever seen, even in Mexico. It was four or five miles wide, and two or three thousand feet deep, and its floor was a mass of tropical verdure, with here and there an Indian rancho and a patch of cultivated ground on the bank of the rapid river, whose sound we heard when we approached the edge of the barranca. There were more orchids and epidendrites than ever in the forest. In some places they had killed every third tree, by forming so and close a covering over its branches as to destroy its life; they were flourishing unimpaired on the rotting branches of trees which they had brought down to the ground years before. The rainy season had not yet set in in this part of the country; and, though we could hear the rushing of the torrent below, we looked in vain for water in the forest, until our man Martin showed us the *bromelias* in the forks of the branches, in the inside of whose hollow leaves nature has laid up a supply of water for the thirsty traveller.

We loaded our horses with the bulbs of such orchids as were still in the dry state, and would travel safely to Europe. Sometimes we climbed into the trees for promising specimens, but oftener contented ourselves with tearing them from the branches as we rode below. When saddle-bags and pockets were full, we were for a time at fault, for there seemed no place for new treasures, when suddenly I remembered a pair of old trousers. We tied up the ends of the legs, which we filled with orchids; and the garment travelled to Jalapa sitting in its natural position across my saddle, to the amazement of such Mexican society as we met. The contents of the two pendant legs are now producing splendid flowers in several English hothouses.

By evening we reached the *Junta*, a place where the great ravine was joined by a smaller one, and a long slanting descent brought us to the edge of the river. There was a ferry here, consisting of a raft of logs which the Indian ferryman hauled across along a stout rope. The horses were attached to the raft by their halters, and so swam across. On the point of land between the two rivers the Indians had their huts, and there we spent the night. We chose the fattest *guajalote* of the turkey-pen, and in ten minutes he was simmering in the great earthen pot over the fire, having been cut into many pieces for convenience of cooking, and the women were busy grinding Indian corn to be patted out into tortillas. While supper was getting ready, and Mr. Christy's day's collection of plants was being pressed (the country we had been passing through is so rich that the new specimens gathered that day filled several quires of paper), we had a good deal of talk with the brown people, who could all speak a little Spanish. Some years before, the two old people had settled there, and set up the ferry. Besides this, they made nets and caught much fish in the river, and cultivated the little piece of ground which formed the point of the promontory. While their descendants went no further than grandchildren the colony had done very well; but now great-grandchildren had begun to arrive, and they would soon have to divide, and form a settlement up in the woods across the river, or upon some patch of ground at the bottom of one of the barrancas.

We were interested in studying the home-life of these people, so different from what we are accustomed to among our peasants of Northern Europe, whose hard continuous labour is quite unknown here. For the men, an occasional pull at the *balsas* (the rafts of the ferry), a little fishing, and now and then—when they are in the humour for it— a little digging in the garden-ground with a wooden spade, or dibbling with a pointed stick. The women have a harder life of it, with the eternal grinding and cooking, cotton-spinning, mat-weaving, and tending of the crowds of babies. Still it is an easy lazy life, without much trouble for to-day or care for to-morrow. When the simple occupations of the day are finished, the time does not seem to hang heavy upon their hands. The men lie about, "thinking of nothing at all;" and the women—old and young— gossip by the hour, in obedience to that beneficent law of nature which provides that their talk shall increase inversely in proportion to what they have to talk about. We find this law attaining to its most complete fulfilment when they shut themselves up in nunneries, to escape as much as possible from all sources of worldly interest, and gossip there more industriously than anywhere else, as we are informed on very good authority.

Like all the other Mexican Indians whose houses we visited, the people here showed but little taste in adorning their dwellings, their dresses and their household implements. Beyond a few calabashes scraped smooth and ornamented with coloured devices, and the blue patterns on the women's cotton skirts, there was scarcely anything to be seen in the way of ornament. How great was the skill of the Mexicans in ornamental work at the time of the Conquest, we can tell from the carved work in wood and stone preserved in museums, the graceful designs on the pottery, the tapestry, and the beautiful feather-work; but this taste has almost disappeared in the country. Just in the same way, contact with Europeans has almost destroyed the little decorative arts among most barbarous people, as, for example, the Red Indians and the natives of the Pacific Islands; and what little skill in these things is left among them is employed less for themselves than in making curious trifles for the white people, and even in these we find that European patterns have mixed with the old designs, or totally superseded them.

The Indians lodged us in an empty cane-hut, where they spread mats upon the ground, and we made pillows of our saddles. We were soon tired of looking up at the stars through the chinks in the roof, and slept till long after sunrise. Then the Indians rafted us across the second river; and we rode on to Jalapa, having accomplished our horseback journey of nearly three hundred miles with but one accident, the death of a horse, the four-pound one. He had been rather overworked, but would most likely have got through, had we not stopped the last night at the Indian *ranchos*, where there was no forage but green maize leaves, a food our beasts were not accustomed to. It seems our men gave him too much of this, and then allowed him to drink excessively; and next morning he grew weaker and weaker, and died not long after we reached Jalapa. Our other two horses were rather thin, but otherwise in good condition; and the horse-dealers, after no end of diplomacy on both sides, knocked under to our threat of sending them back to Mexico in charge of Antonio, and gave us within a pound or two of what they had cost us. There, is a good deal of trading in horses done at Jalapa, where travellers coming down from Mexico sell their beasts, which are disposed of at great prices to other travellers coming up from the coast. Between here and Vera Cruz, people prefer travelling in the Diligence, or in some covered carriage, to exposing themselves to the sun in the hot and pestilential region of the coast.

Jalapa is a pleasant city among the hills, in a country of forests, green turf, and running streams. It is the very paradise of botanists; and its products include a wonderful variety of trees and flowers, from the apple- and pear-trees of England to the *mameis* and *zapotes* of tropical America, and the brilliant orchids which are the ornament of our hot-houses. The name of the town itself has a botanical celebrity, for in the neighbouring forests grows the *Purga de Jalapa*, which we have shortened into *jalap*.

A day's journey above it, lies the limit of eternal snow, upon the peak of Orizaba; a day's journey below it is Vera Cruz, the city of the yellow fever, surrounded by burning sands and poisonous exhalations, in a district where, during the hot months now commencing, the thermometer scarcely ever descends below 80°, day or night. Jalapa hardly knows summer or winter, heat or cold. The upper current of hot air from the Gulf of Mexico, highly charged with aqueous vapour, strikes the mountains about this level, and forms the belt of clouds that we have already crossed more than once during our journey. Jalapa is in this cloudy zone, and the sky is seldom clear there. It is hardly hotter in summer than in England, and not even hot enough for the mosquitoes, which are not to be found here though they swarm in the plain below. This warm damp climate changes but little in the course of the year. There are no seasons, in our sense of the word, for spring lasts through the year.

We walked out on the first afternoon of our arrival; and sat on stone seats on a piece of green turf surrounded by trees, that reminded us pleasantly of the village-greens of England. There we talked with the children of an English acquaintance who had been settled for many years in the town, and had married a Mexican lady. They were fine lads; but, as very often happens in such cases, they could only speak the language of the country. Nothing can show more clearly how thoroughly a foreigner yields to the influences around him, when he settles in a country and marries among its people. An Englishman's own character, for instance, may remain to some extent; but his children are scarcely English in language or in feeling, and in the next generation there is nothing foreign about his descendants but the name.

When we reached our hotel it was about sunset, and the heavy dew had wetted us through, as though we had been walking in the rain. This was no exceptional occurrence. All the year round such dews fall morning and evening, as well as almost daily showers of rain. The climate is too warm for this dampness to injure health, as it would in our colder regions. To us, who had just left the bracing air of the high plateaus, it seemed close and relaxing; but the inhabitants are certainly strong and healthy, and one can imagine the enjoyment which the white inhabitants of Vera Cruz must feel, when they can get away from that city of pestilence into the pure air of the mountains.

Our quarters were at the *Veracruzana*, where we occupied a great whitewashed room. A large grated window opened into the garden, where the armadillo was fastened to a tree by a long string, and had soon dug a deep hole with his powerful fore-claws, as the manner of the creature is. The necessity of supplying the "little man in armour" with insects for his daily food gave us some idea of the amazing abundance and variety of the insects of the district. We caught creeping things innumerable in the garden, but narrowly escaped being stung by a small scorpion; and therefore delegated the task to an old Indian, who walked out into the fields with an earthen pot, and returned with it full of insects in about half an hour. We reckoned that there were over fifty species in the pot.

Many of the houses and Indian huts were adorned with collections of insects pinned on the walls in patterns, among which figured scorpions some three inches long; and the centre-ornament was usually a tarantula, said to be one of the most poisonous creatures of the tropics, a monstrous spider, whose dark grey body and legs are covered with hairs. A fine specimen will have a body about as large as a small hen's egg, and, with his legs in their natural position, will just stand in a cheese-plate. The Boots of the hotel went out and caught a fine scorpion for our amusement; he brought it into our room wrapped in a piece of brown paper, and was on the point of letting it out on our table for us to see it run. We protested against this, and had it put into a tumbler and covered it up with a book.

The inner *patio* of the hotel was surrounded with the usual arcade, into which the rooms opened. Close to our door was a long table, with a green cloth, where the Jalapenians were constantly playing *monte*, from nine in the morning till late at night. All classes were represented there, from the muleteer who came to lose his hard-earned dollars, to the rich shopkeepers and planters of the town and neighbourhood.

I went early one afternoon to the house of the principal agent for the Vera Cruz carriers,to arrange for sending down our heavy packages to the coast. There was no one at the office but a girl. I enquired for the master—"*Está jugando*,"—"He is playing," she said. I need not have gone so far to look for him, for he was sitting just outside our bedroom door, and indeed had been there all day. Before he condescended to arrange our business, he waited to see the fate of the dollar he had just put down, and which I was glad to see he lost.

Jalapa was not always the stagnant place it is now. Its pleasant houses and gardens date from a period when it was a town of some importance. In old times the only practicable road from Vera Cruz to Mexico passed this way; and Jalapa was the entrepôt where the merchants had their warehouses, and from whence the trains of mules distributed the European merchandise from the coast to the different markets of the country. By this arrangement, the carrying from the coast was done by a small number of muleteers, who were seasoned to the climate, while the great mass of traders and carriers were not obliged to descend from the healthy region. This was of the more importance, because, though the pure Indians are not liable to the attacks of yellow fever, the disease is as deadly to the other inhabitants of the high lands as to Europeans; and even those of the *mestizos* who have the least admixture of white blood are subject to it. Of late years, this system has been given up, and the carriers from the high lands go down to the coast to fetch their loads, and every year they leave some of their number in the church-yards of the City of the Dead; while many others, though they recover from the fever, never regain their former health and strength. The high-road to Mexico now goes by Orizaba, so that the importance of Jalapa as a trading-place has almost ceased.

Our Mexican journey was now all but finished, and I left my companion here, and took the Diligence to Vera Cruz, to meet the West India Mail-packet. Mr. Christy followed a day or two later, and went to the United States. We dismissed our two servants, Martin and Antonio. Martin invested his wages in a package of tobacco, which he proposed to carry home on his horse, travelling by night along unfrequented mountain-paths, where custom-house officers seldom penetrate. We never heard any more of him; but no doubt he got safe home, for he was perfectly competent to take care of himself, and he probably made a very good thing of his journey. It was quite with regret that we parted from him, for he was a most sensible, useful fellow, with a continual flow of high spirits, and no end of stories of his experiences in smuggling, and hunting wild cattle in the *tierra caliente*, in which two adventurous occupations most of his life had been passed. In his dealings with us, he was honesty itself, notwithstanding his equivocal profession.

We offered Antonio a cheque on Mexico for his wages, as he was going back there, but he said he would rather have hard dollars. We paid his fare to Mexico by the Diligence, and gave him his money, telling him at the same time, that he was a fool for his pains. He started next morning; and we heard, a month or two later, that the coach was stopped the same afternoon in the plains of Perote, and Antonio was robbed not only of his money but even of his jacket and serape, and reached Mexico penniless and half-naked. He was always a silly fellow, and his last exploit was worthy of him.

Mr. Christy sat up till daybreak to see me off, filling up his time by writing letters and pressing plants. When I was gone, he lay down in his bed, in rather a dreamy state of mind, looking up at the ceiling. There was a large beam just above his head, and at one side of it a hole, which struck him as being a suitable place for a scorpion to come out of. This idea had come into his head from the sight of the specimen in the tumbler on the table, who had with great difficulty been drowned in *aguardiente*. Presently something moved in the hole, and the spectator below instantly became wide awake. Then came out a claw and a head, and finally the body and tail of a very fine scorpion, two inches and a half long. It was rather an awkward moment, for it was not safe to move suddenly, for fear of startling the creature, whose footing seemed anything but secure; and if he fell, he would naturally sting whatever he might come in contact with. However, he met with no accident on his way, and getting into another hole, about a yard off, he drew up his tail after him and disappeared. Mr. Christy slipped out of his bed with a sense of considerable relief; and having ascertained that there were no holes in the ceiling above the bed on the other side of the room, he turned in there, and went comfortably to sleep.

My only companion in the Diligence was a German shopman from Vera Cruz, who was sociable, but not of an instructive turn of conversation. When we had descended for a few hours, the heat became intolerable. Scarcely any habitation but a few Indian cane-huts by the way-side, with bananas and palm-trees. We stopped, about three in the afternoon, at a *rancho* in a small village, and did not start again until next morning, a little before day-break. Negroes and people of negro descent began to abound in this congenial climate. I remember especially the waiting-maid at the *rancho*, who was a "white negress," as they are called. Her hair and features showed her African origin; but her hair was like white wool, and her face and hands were as colourless as those of a dead body. This animated corpse was healthy enough, however; and this peculiarity of the skin is, it seems, not very uncommon.

The coast-regions through which I was passing abound in horned cattle, but they are mostly far away from the high-roads. In spite of the intense heat of the climate they thrive as well as in the higher lands. Some are tolerably tame, and are kept within bounds by the *vaqueros*; but the greater proportion, numbering tens of thousands, roam wild about the country. In comparison with these cattle of the *tierra caliente*, the fiercest beasts of the plateaus are safe and quiet creatures. The only way of bringing them into the *corral* is by using tame animals for decoys, just as wild elephants are caught.

Our man Martin, who had once been a *vaquero* on the Vera Cruz coast, used to look upon the bulls of the high lands with great contempt. If you chase them they run away, he said. If you lazo a bull of the hot country, you have to gallop off with all your might, with the *toro* close at your heels; and, if the horse falls, it may cost his life or his rider's.

We thus find the horned cattle flourishing at every elevation, from the sea-level to the mountain-pastures ten thousand feet above it. Horses and sheep show less adaptability to this variety of climates. The horses and mules come mostly from the States of the North, at a level of from 5,000 to 8,000 feet; that remarkable country of which Humboldt's observation gives us the best idea, when he says that, although there are no made roads, wheel-carriages can travel distances of a thousand miles over gently-undulating prairies, without meeting any obstruction on the way.

Numbers of sheep are reared in the mountains, principally for the sake of the tallow, for the consumption of tallow-candles in the mines is enormous. The owners scarcely care at all for the rest of the animal; and popular scandal accuses the sheep-farmers of driving their flocks straight into the melting-coppers, without going through the preliminary ceremony of killing them. People told us that the tallow made in the cold regions loses its consistency when brought down into hotter climates, but we had no means of ascertaining the truth of this.

Artificial lighting by means of tallow was not known to the ancient Mexicans, who could not indeed have procured tallow except from the fat of deer and smaller animals.

Bernal Diaz tells how the Spanish invaders used to dress their wounds with "Indian Ointment." He explains the nature of this preparation in another place. The Spaniards could get no oil in the country, nor anything else to make salve with, so they took some fat Indian who had just been killed in battle, and simply boiled him down.

Our ride next morning was but a few hours, the journey being so divided in order that the passengers may reach Vera Cruz before the heat of the day begins. We passed over a dreary district, generally too dry for anything but cactus and acacias, but now and then, when a little water was to be found, displaying clumps of bamboos with their elegant feathery tufts. Then the railway took us through the dismal downs, with their swamps and sand-hills, and so into Vera Cruz.

The English merchants we had already made acquaintance with were as kind and hospitable as ever, and I found an Englishman, whom we had known before, going as far as Havana by the same packet. The yellow fever was unusually late this year, and, though June had begun, there were but few cases. We heard afterwards that it set in a week or two after our departure, and by its extraordinary severity made ample amends for the lateness of its arrival.

After sunset, the air was alive with mosquitos, and the floors of the hotel swarmed with cockroaches. The armadillo took quite naturally to the latter creatures, and crunched them up as fast as we could catch them for him. I was surprised to find that our word "cockroaches" does not come from the German stock, like most of our names for insects and small creatures, but from the Latin side of the house. The Spanish waiter called them *cucarachas,* and the French ones *coqueraches.* The history of the armadillo ends unfortunately: for some days he seemed to take quite kindly to the diet of bits of meat which we had to put him on, on shipboard, but he fell sick at Havana, and died.

My late companion travelled up into the Northern States, went to the Indian assembly at Manitoulin Island, paid a visit to various tribes of Red Men in the Hudson's Bay Territory—as yet unmissionized, carried away in triumph the big medicine-drum I have already spoken of, and saw and did many other things not to be related here. One sight that he saw, some months later, reminded him of the wild country where we had travelled together. He was in Iowa City, a little town of a year or two's growth, out in the prairie States of the Far West. As he stood one morning in the outskirts, among the plank-houses and half-made roads, there came a solitary horseman riding in. Evidently he had come from the Mexican frontier, a thousand miles and more away across the plains; and no doubt, his waggons and the rest of his party were behind him on the road, beyond the distant horizon of the prairie. By his face he was American, but his costume was the dress of old Mexico, the leather jacket and trousers, the broad white hat and huge jingling spurs. His lazo hung in front of his high-peaked saddle, and his well-worn serape was rolled up behind him like a trooper's cloak. As he approached the town, he spurred his jaded beast, who broke into the old familiar *paso* of the Mexican plains. "It was my last sight of Mexico," said my companion. He saluted the horseman in Spanish, and the well-known words of welcome made the grim man's haggard sunburnt features relax into a smile as he returned the salutation and rode on.

As for myself, my voyage home was short and unadventurous. From Vera Cruz to Havana, most of my companions were Mexican refugees who had been turned out of the country for being mixed up with Haro's revolution or Santa Ana's intrigues. They were showily got-up men, elaborately polite, and with much to say for themselves; but every now and then some casual remark showed what stuff they were made of, and I pitied more than ever the unfortunate countries whose political destinies depend on the intrigues of these adventurers.

In the hot land-locked bay of St. Thomas's we, with the contents of eight or nine more steamers, were shifted into the great steamer bound homeward. I went ashore with an old German gentleman, and walked about the streets. St. Thomas's is a Danish island, and a free port, that is, a smuggling depôt for the rest of the West India islands, much as Gibraltar is for the Mediterranean. It is a stifling place, full of mosquitos and yellow fever, and the confusion of tongues reigns there even more than in Gibraltar, for the blacks in the streets all speak three or four languages, and the shopkeepers six or seven.

We were a strange mixture on board the 'Atrato', over two hundred of us. Peruvians and Chilians from across the isthmus, Spaniards and Cubans, black gentlemen from Hayti, French colonists from Martinique, but English preponderating above all other nationalities. One or two governors of small islands, with their families, maintaining the dignity of Government House, at least as far as Southampton, and unapproachable by common mortals. Army men from West India stations, who appeared to spend their mornings in ordering the wine for dinner, and their evenings in abusing it when they had drunk it. West India planters, who thought it was rather hard that the Anti-slavery Society, after ruining them and their plantations, should moreover insist on their believing themselves to be great gainers by the change. We were all crowded, hot, and uncomfortable, and showed our worst side, but as we neared England better influences got the ascendant again.

It was pleasant to breathe a cooler air, and to feel that I was getting back to my own country and my own people; but with this feeling there was mixed some regret for the beautiful scenes I had left. The evenings of our latitudes seemed poor when we lost the gorgeous sunsets of the tropics, and the sea alive with luminous creatures. When I came on deck one evening and missed the brightest ornament of the sky—the Southern Cross, I felt that I had left the tropics, and that all my efforts to realize the life of the last half-year would produce but a vague and shadowy picture.

Since we left Mexico, I have not cared to follow very accurately even the newspaper intelligence of what has been and still is going on there. It is a pitiable history. Continual wars and revolutions, utter insecurity of life and property, the Indians burning down the haciendas in the South and turning out the white people, the roads on the plains impassable on account of deserters and robbers; sometimes no practical government at all, then two or three at once, who raise armies and fight a little sometimes, but generally confine themselves to plundering the peaceable inhabitants. An army besieges the capital for months, but appears to do nothing but cut the water off from the aqueducts, shoot stragglers, and levy contributions. One leader raises a forced loan among the foreign residents, and imprisons or expels those who do not submit. The leader on the other side does the same in his part of the country, putting the British merchant in prisons where a fortnight would be a fair average life for an European, and threatening him with summary courtmartial and execution if he does not pay.

London newspapers dwell on these details, and tell us that we may learn from the condition of this unfortunate country how useless are democratic forms among a people incapable of liberty, and that very weak governments can commit all sorts of crimes with impunity, from the fact that they have no official existence which foreign powers can recognize; and various other weighty moral lessons, which must be highly edifying to our countrymen in the Republic, who are meanwhile left pretty much to shift for themselves.

All this time the United States are steadily advancing; and the destiny of the country is gradually accomplishing itself. That its total absorption must come, sooner or later, we can hardly doubt. The chief difficulty seems to be that the American constitution will not exactly suit the case. The Republic laid down the right of each citizen to his share in the government of the country as a universal law, founded on indefeasible lights of humanity, fundamental laws of nature, and what not, making, it is true, some slight exceptions with regard to red and black men. The Mexicans, or at least the white and half-caste Mexicans, will be a difficulty. Their claims to citizenship are unquestionable, if Mexico were made a State of the Union; and, as everybody knows, they are totally incapable of governing themselves, which they must be left to do under the constitutional system of the United States; moreover, it is certain that American citizens would never allow even the whitest of the Mexicans to be placed on a footing of equality with themselves. Supposing these difficulties got over by a Protectorate, an armed occupation, or some similar contrivance, Mexico will undergo a great change. There will be roads and even rail-roads, some security for life and property, liberty of opinion, a nourishing commerce, a rapidly increasing population, and a variety of good things. Every intelligent Mexican must wish for an event so greatly to the advantage of his country and of the world in general.

Some of our good friends in Mexico have bought land on the American frontier by the hundred square leagues, and can point out patches upon the map of the world as large as Scotland or Ireland—as their private property. What their gains will be when enterprising western men begin to bring the country under cultivation, it is not an easy matter to realize.

As for ourselves individually, we may be excused for cherishing a lurking kindness for the quaint, picturesque manners and customs of Mexico, as yet un-Americanized; and for rejoicing that it was our fortune to travel there before the coming change, when its most curious peculiarities and its very language must yield before foreign influences.